USING DOCUMENTS IN RESEARCH

When, Where, Why and How

Edited by
Aimee Grant and Helen Kara

I0089936

P

First published in Great Britain in 2026 by

Policy Press, an imprint of
Bristol University Press
University of Bristol
1–9 Old Park Hill
Bristol
BS2 8BB
UK
t: +44 (0)117 374 6645
e: bup-info@bristol.ac.uk

Details of international sales and distribution partners are available at policy.bristoluniversitypress.co.uk

© Bristol University Press 2026

DOI: 10.51952/9781447374947

British Library Cataloguing in Publication Data
A catalogue record for this book is available from the British Library

ISBN 978-1-4473-7492-3 hardcover
ISBN 978-1-4473-7493-0 paperback
ISBN 978-1-4473-7495-4 ePub
ISBN 978-1-4473-7494-7 ePdf

Cover design: Liam Roberts Design
Front cover image: Unsplash/Alexander Grey

Contents

List of figures, tables and boxes

Figures

Tables

Box

Notes on contributors

Helen Abnett is Research Fellow at the Centre for Research in Public Health and Community Care at the University of Hertfordshire, UK. Her research interests centre on improving the quality of public service provision by both understanding and problematising the role of voluntary sector organisations in the provision of these services. Helen earned a PhD in social policy from the University of Kent in 2022, and between 2021 and 2024, she worked with the Third Sector Research Centre at the University of Birmingham. Prior to completing her PhD, Helen spent over 15 years working in a range of roles within the voluntary sector.

Kate Carruthers Thomas is Associate Professor at Birmingham City University, UK, where she conducts transdisciplinary research in gender and critical higher education studies, drawing primarily on educational, sociological and geographical theories and methods. She also works in the field of creative research methodologies, notably innovative research dissemination in the form of illustration, poetry and podcasting. She is a member of the Editorial Advisory Board for the new *Journal of Creative Methods*. Her personal website is at https://thinkthreeways.com.

Anna J. Davis is an expert on foreign policy, international identity and nuclear cooperation in the Eurasia region and the Arctic. She is Director of Sefton Analytics, Fellow of Eurasia Studies at The Jamestown Foundation and regularly teaches courses on qualitative research methods, area studies and international relations of Russia and Eastern Europe at the University of Oxford, where she completed her DPhil (PhD). Additionally, Anna is a Grímsson Fellow with the Ólafur Ragnar Grímsson Centre and the Arctic Circle Secretariat, and a Non-Resident Fellow of the Center for International Trade and Security.

Rosemary Golding is Professor of Music at The Open University, UK, where she has worked since 2009. Rosemary's research focuses on the social and cultural history of music in 19th-century Britain. She has published widely on music education and the music profession. Her work on the history of music, health and well-being has examined the role of music in Victorian 'lunatic asylums' and the use of music as both an entertainment and a cure. Rosemary is co-General Editor of the journal *Nineteenth-Century Music Review* and a Fellow of the Royal Historical Society.

Aimee Grant is Associate Professor and Wellcome Trust Career Development Fellow at Swansea University, UK. Her research uses documents as data and creative research methods, often with the aim of better understanding the lived experiences of underserved groups. Aimee's current research includes an eight-year Wellcome Trust-funded longitudinal qualitative study to understand autistic experiences 'from menstruation to menopause'. She is the author of two documentary analysis texts – *Doing Excellent Social Research with Documents: Practical Examples and Guidance for Qualitative Researchers* (2019) and *Doing Your Research Project with Documents: A Step-by-Step Guide to Take You from Start to Finish* (2022) – and *The Autism Friendly Guide to Pregnancy, Birth and the Fourth Trimester* (2025). She is a Deputy editor for the journal *Autism in Adulthood*, and was added to the Disability Power 100 list in 2023.

Ella Houston is Senior Lecturer in disability studies and a core member of the Centre for Culture and Disability Studies at Liverpool Hope University, UK. Her research focuses on representations of, and audience responses to, disability in advertising. She is the author of *Advertising Disability* (2024).

George Jennings is Senior Lecturer in sport sociology at Cardiff Metropolitan University, UK, where he leads the MA Sport, Ethics and Society course and the MRes pathway in Critical Social Science of Sport, Health and Education. His outputs include *Reinventing Martial Arts in the 21st Century* (2022) and *Martial Arts in Latin Societies* (with Rodríguez and Piedra, 2024). George sits on various editorial and advisory boards, and he is a member of the executive board for the Martial Arts Studies Association. His current projects look at the processes of relearning Wing Chun while co-producing movement inspired by martial arts.

Sarah Johnstone (she/her) is a transdisciplinary designer specialising in design thinking, co-design, design for diversity and qualitative arts-based research. Sarah is currently Postdoctoral Fellow (Design for Health) as part of a two-year collaborative project between QUT Design Lab and Queensland Health's Healthcare Improvement Unit, building on three years of contributions to numerous projects embedding 'design thinking and doing' within healthcare across the state of Queensland, Australia. Beyond healthcare, Sarah has worked on a diverse range of projects across various sectors, including community development, urban development, youth work, aged care, palliative care and the arts.

Helen Kara, Fellow of the Academy of Social Sciences, has been an independent researcher since 1999 and an independent scholar since 2011. She specialises in creative research methods, radical research ethics and creative academic writing, and she teaches doctoral students and staff at higher education institutions worldwide. Her books include *Creative Research Methods: A Practical Guide* (2020), *Research Ethics in the Real World: Euro-Western and Indigenous Perspectives* (2018) and *Qualitative Research for Quantitative Researchers* (2022). Helen founded the International Creative Research Methods Conference, the *Journal of Creative Research Methods* and the Independent Research Ethics Committee.

Evonne Miller is Professor of Design Psychology at Queensland University of Technology (QUT), Australia, and Director of the QUT Design Lab, where contributors reimagine and redesign the future. She is the inaugural Queensland Health Research Chair in Healthcare Design, based at Clinical Excellence Queensland's Healthcare Improvement Unit, where she engages with consumers, clinicians and community to collaboratively co-design creative solutions to improve healthcare. Evonne is a recognised international thought leader in design for health, with expertise in design thinking, participatory co-design, co-production, futures thinking and qualitative arts-based research and knowledge translation.

Órla Meadhbh Murray (she/they) is Assistant Professor of Criminology and Sociology at Northumbria University, UK, and a Fellow of the Institute for Medical Humanities at Durham University, UK. Their research focuses on inequalities in higher education, imposter syndrome and the politics of knowledge production. Their research includes the project 'Gut Feelings', which takes a queer feminist approach to the gut. They are the co-founder of the Institutional Ethnography Network and regularly run institutional ethnography training workshops.

Katarzyna Niziołek is Assistant Professor in the Faculty of Sociology at the University of Białystok, Poland. She holds a PhD in sociology, and her research covers social art, theatre participation and the performative aspects of collective memory. She is author of numerous publications and conference presentations on those topics. She is the initiator and leader of the Social Art Workshop – a collective merging social research with artistic practice and civic engagement. Within that framework, she has curated and produced participatory theatre projects, including: *The Method of National Constellations* (2014–16), *Prayer. A Common Theatre* (2016–17), *Bieżenki* (2018), *Living Torpedoes* (2019) and *The Suitcase* (2021). Her project 'Textile Sociology' explores the use of textiles and textile art in sociological research. She has taught workshops on theatre-based participatory research and practice to students, researchers, educators and arts practitioners.

Victoria Pagan is Senior Lecturer in Strategic Management in the Business School at Newcastle University, UK. Prior to becoming an academic, Victoria spent nearly a decade working in a commercial research and consultancy context with a range of public sector clients. She has published on her exploration of the uses, and impacts of the uses, of non-disclosure agreements in a range of workplace contexts. Her work continues to explore tensions between secrecy and transparency and associated implications for voice, including muting and silencing.

Max Edward Perry is a sociologist and postdoctoral researcher at the University of Edinburgh. He is investigating 'data-driven healthcare' as part of the DARE project, which is funded by the European Research Council and UK Research and Innovation. Max's sociological work has hitherto examined medical records as well as healthcare bureaucracy and databases. He completed his PhD thesis, *A Social Science of Medical Records*, at the University of Bristol in 2024.

José Ragas is Assistant Professor at the Instituto de Historia at Pontificia Universidad Católica de Chile, where he teaches courses related to science and technology studies and global history. José holds a PhD from the University of California, Davis. Prior to his appointment in Chile, he was Mellon Postdoctoral Fellow in the Department of Science and Technology Studies at Cornell University and Lecturer in the history of science and the history of medicine at Yale University. His work has examined the emergence of a techno-social system engineered to capture and store personal data in Peru between 1820 and 1930.

Jen Seevinck is Associate Professor at Queensland University of Technology and a design researcher and practitioner whose work encompasses artistic data visualisations and interactive systems advocating for marginalised issues. Drawing on expertise ranging from machine learning to augmented reality and visual design, she transforms texts, documents and quantitative data into visuals to reveal embedded perspectives. She collaborates with stakeholders from health organisations to government and community organisations, and her outputs include international exhibitions and academic publications. Her arts-based research approach advocates for aged care communities through visual translations of public submissions. Jen co-leads the QUT More-than-Human Futures research group and is a chief investigator at the QUT Design Lab, Australia.

T.J. Thomson is Senior Lecturer at RMIT University, Australia, where he co-leads the News, Technology and Society Network. He is an Australian Research Council DECRA (Discovery Early Career Researcher Award) Fellow. His research is united by its focus on visual communication. A majority of T.J.'s research centres on the visual aspects of news and journalism and the concerns and processes relevant to those who make, edit and present visual news. He has broader interests in digital media, journalism studies and visual culture and often focuses on under-represented identities, attributes and environments in his research.

Abigail Winter (she/her) is a results-driven academic writing well-being coach, mentor and independent researcher, skilled in the analysis of words and data for user needs. She has over 20 years' experience in quality assurance and in change and project management. Her PhD focused on what helps workers in higher education cope with large-scale organisational change, and she was part of the small team that created and developed the concept of academagogy (the scholarly leadership of learning). Her more recent research has focused on professional identity, developing academic writing well-being, mentoring and reflective practice.

1

Introduction

Aimee Grant and Helen Kara

Introduction

Documents offer us an enormous and fascinating source of data for research. Over recent decades, the internet has meant that identifying potential documents can often be done quickly and at limited cost. As a result, documents are more accessible to researchers than ever before. Yet this tremendous resource is woefully under-used, and the ways in which documents are selected and analysed in research studies are rarely discussed in detail. This book aims to plug that lacuna and thus encourage more people to use documents as data.

Critiques of using documents as research data often focus on researchers not being able to know the intended meaning or intent of the authors. However, this concern is grounded in positivist epistemology, and we as researchers can infer a great deal from our knowledge of the context surrounding documents, which is entirely appropriate in interpretivist and constructionist epistemologies (Grant, 2022). A further epistemological reason for turning to documents as data is that documents can tell us things about society that we can't always find out from other sources (Prior, 2003). This can be incredibly powerful, both when documents alone are analysed and when documents are triangulated by conducting research with the authors or consumers, as Max Edward Perry (Chapter 12) and Abigail Winter and colleagues (Chapter 7) highlight.

Also, for ethical reasons, we all need to be using secondary data before we turn to gathering primary data. Research fatigue – that is, the emotional and psychological exhaustion people can feel when asked to take part in *yet another* study – is real (Ashley, 2021). For instance, every time you buy a few groceries in a supermarket or go for a coffee, you get a receipt or an email saying something like 'please go online and give us your feedback', often with an incentive, such as a voucher or a prize you might win. Underserved and other over-researched populations may feel research fatigue even more keenly (Fiorito, 2023).

Research in the Euro-Western paradigm seems almost synonymous with primary data collection. Yet this book shows us, very clearly, that this need not be so. Using documents in research, as Helen Abnett acknowledges in Chapter 8, has an ethical advantage in enabling researchers to answer questions without requiring other people's participation. Of course, in some kinds of research, such as clinical drug trials and opinion polls, primary data collection will always be needed. But many of us could answer our research questions by using secondary data. And many more could reach a partial answer by using secondary sources, thus reducing the amount of primary data we need to gather and analyse.

To be able to do high-quality research and to allow others to learn from and adopt the methods used, it is essential that researchers describe their methods and processes. *Using Documents in Research* provides a series of 12 accessible and practical case studies. These highlight the work of individual researchers or teams from a range of disciplines who are studying different topics and using a range of documents and approaches. To make the case studies as useful as possible for readers, the chapters all contain core information relating to *how* and *why* particular methodological choices were made. This includes information on researcher positionality, ethical issues, challenges experienced by the authors, advantages and limitations of the approach and how to transfer the method to other contexts.

Is this book for me?

We think *Using Documents In Research* in its entirety will be most helpful for people who already have some experience of doing research, such as doctoral students and researchers. (If you have no experience, you might like to start with *Doing Your Research Project with Documents* by Aimee Grant, published by Policy Press in 2022.) This book may be beneficial for social researchers who already have some experience of using documents in research, helping them gain more insights. Equally, it may be useful for social researchers who do not have experience of using documents in research but, for a variety of reasons, are finding it challenging to undertake primary data collection and want to continue their research in another way (and perhaps also publish their work).

Alongside this, individual chapters of the book may be useful for teachers of undergraduates or postgraduates and people supporting students to undertake research projects.

Documents in research

There is no set definition of a 'document', but Aimee has previously suggested that documents are 'content or objects which include written, graphical or pictorial matter, or a combination of these types of content, in order to transmit or store information or meaning' (Grant, 2019, p 11). From this definition, you can see that a very wide range of materials can be considered to be documents – books, posters, bus tickets, certificates, posts and comments on social media, invitations, petitions and many more besides. Moreover, documents are used in research in many disciplines and sectors, such as the humanities, social sciences, geography and health.

Similarly, 'documentary analysis', or 'using documents in research' as we prefer to say these days, does not have a single definition. Hard copy and electronic documents may be collected from a very broad range of sources, such as the internet, archives, organisations, individuals, libraries and governments. Widely varying sample sizes are used, and documents may be analysed with or without an epistemological framework. We lean towards using an established method of data analysis with your documents – for example, discourse analysis, narrative analysis, thematic analysis or content analysis – though, of course, you are free to take a more innovative approach if you wish. *The Handbook of Creative Data Analysis* has a wide variety of options (Kara et al, 2024).

There are some very good reasons for using documents in research. First, a phenomenal number of documents are in existence already, and more are being created all the time. This means that documents are a potentially rich source of data on many topics of interest. Second, using documents as data reduces the 'researcher effect', where researchers inadvertently influence their data during the collection process. This can affect other types of data, such as interview and focus group data, particularly in research on sensitive topics (Law, 2004). Third, if the documents you want to use are freely available online, that makes for a cost-effective and time-saving form of data gathering. Fourth, using documents as data places no burden on humans to generate data for researchers.

We believe that documents are particularly useful for: providing context; researching document-heavy phenomena, such as the media, policy or history; doing case study research; and, in many cases, accessing large samples. However, using documents in research can also present challenges. Some documents are impossible to get hold of, such as most people's personal diaries or commercially sensitive documents from a business. If documents are only available as hard copy, they may be difficult to locate and require travel to access them, and even then they may be misfiled and difficult to find. Some documents are incomplete or poor quality. Comparative research using documents can be problematic if the documents from the entities you want to compare are not themselves easily comparable. If there are a lot of documents relevant to your research question, that can become difficult to manage.

Why we decided to write this book

It is fitting that we first met in around 2017 to discuss 'documentary analysis', as we were referring to it then. We have worked together on a number of other projects while separately using documents in our work.

Aimee first started using documents as data when she was an undergraduate student, to examine how Housing Benefit processes could impact homelessness. Housing Benefit is a UK benefit that pays the rent of people on low income. Aimee used the case files of a housing charity to explore the complex bureaucracy and delays involved. She frequently returned to documents as data throughout her early years as a researcher, working with policy documents, medical and welfare records, meeting minutes, and mainstream and social media, for example. However, at this time, there was only a small amount of literature on using documents as data, so Aimee didn't use documents as fully as she might have. This led to her writing her first book (Grant, 2019), which was based on a series of case studies showing how documents can be used in research projects. This book received a lot of praise for showing what exactly was done and giving practical steps to follow. However, it wasn't as accessible as Aimee had hoped – she had wanted to offer something that would be helpful for undergraduate students doing their research projects. So she wrote another book, published by Policy Press, to help guide people through the process of doing their research with documents and writing it up (Grant, 2022). The relative lack of literature in the area continues to be noted by others (for example, Morgan, 2022), and Aimee felt that this third book of case studies was needed to diversify the literature away from her own and other authors' singular perspectives on doing research with documents.

Helen has used documents as data extensively in evaluation and other commissioned research for over two and a half decades. She has used meeting minutes, annual reports, funding bids, correspondence, leaflets, web pages and many more document types. Helen has also written about using documents in research in several of her books on research methods, and she has included chapters from other researchers who use documents in research in some of her edited and co-edited collections. She has also run workshops on using documents in research at several universities.

How to use this book

We understand that most people won't choose to read a book like this from cover to cover. The good news is that each of the chapters can stand alone.

The book has four themed parts:

Part I: Understanding the past
Part II: Exploring the machinery of governance
Part III: Using official documents
Part IV: Exploring the personal

It was not straightforward to divide up the book into these parts, as chapter authors discuss such a variety of documents, methodological approaches and methods, and some of the chapters could have comfortably fitted into multiple parts. We could have divided the book up in several different ways! As such, you may want to use the contents list, the summaries that follow, or the chapter introductions to search for content related to your document types, analysis methods or areas of interest. That said, we think you will find something fascinating and new in every chapter!

Part I: Understanding the past

We start in Chapter 2 with Katarzyna Niziołek's work on documentary theatre. Documentary theatre can be viewed as both art and research, and it uses personal, literary or official documents as the basis for writing material for theatre. Niziołek introduces the reader to ways documents can be adapted during group discussion or rehearsals. She also outlines ways that the public (or actors) can be involved in re-enactment of past events based on accounts from documents and how to monitor and evaluate this process.

In Chapter 3, Rosemary Golding immerses the reader in Victorian asylum life, focusing particularly on music and accompanying silences. Through her exploration of the available text documents, as opposed to musical scores, Golding uses a reflexive approach to this analysis. The purpose of this research was to better understand these historical mental health institutions. In the chapter, however, she focuses on the 'silences' or gaps in the available accounts.

Chapter 4, the final chapter in Part I, comes from George Jennings, who explores Asian martial arts folklore through a range of books. Jennings uses the theory of martial arts creation (Jennings, 2019) and narrative analysis to explore these documents. In doing so, he tests his theory and provides a clear 12-step method that others can follow. We think the clear description of analysis and theory testing and building will be of interest to a broad readership.

Part II: Exploring the machinery of governance

We start Part II with Victoria Pagan's exploration in Chapter 5 of the use of non-disclosure agreements (NDAs) following instances of discrimination in the workplace. Similar to Golding's analysis (Chapter 3), Pagan notes that silences are poignant throughout. The actual NDA documents were not available to her. Instead, she describes how she selected and used government inquiry documents focused on this topic. Pagan uses a framework of epistemic injustice to guide her abductive analysis, which will be of interest to those using documents to study social justice.

In Chapter 6, José Ragas undertakes a powerful and reflexive exploration of the importance and use of identity documents in the Global South. Ragas' analysis is mostly confined to historical documents that he discovered in archives and flea markets as well as through personal connections. Throughout the chapter, using historical ethnography, Ragas highlights the colonialist leanings of the practice of identity documents and the impacts on those who do not hold such documents.

Following this, in Chapter 7, Abigail Winter and colleagues describe their fascinating use of royal commission documents. Moving away from analysis of the text by academics, Winter et al discuss a transformative frame and arts-based knowledge translation to consider care for older people. This involved members of the public taking part in workshops that were highly emotive for them. Throughout the chapter, Winter et al embed practical guidance for using documents in these less commonly explored arts-based practices.

Part III: Using official documents

In Chapter 8, Helen Abnett discusses the use of charity annual reports and accounts in research. These documents may be analysed in a broad range of ways, but

Abnett discusses the way in which she has worked with colleagues to understand how charities represent themselves and their work in these documents. Through two case studies, Abnett outlines the use of both thematic analysis and qualitative content analysis in exploring charity accounts.

Órla Meadhbh Murray provides an in-depth account of the use of audit documents in Chapter 9. Murray uses Dorothy Smith's institutional ethnography as the research approach, meaning that transcripts of interviews with relevant people formed part of the data alongside other documents. The analysis undertaken by Murray focuses on UK higher education, with the other documents under study being from the National Student Survey. Using a feminist approach, Murray describes the use of institutional ethnography in her study, which can be applied more broadly to other contexts.

The final chapter exploring official documents comes from Anna J. Davis (Chapter 10). While Winter et al bring a new and exciting way of looking at documents related to governance in Chapter 7, Davis focuses on policy documents through the lens of conflict and political turbulence. Davis' documents are associated with nuclear policy in Armenia, Belarus and Ukraine. She offers a gripping account of the challenging process of gaining access to documents during times of conflict and political turbulence and provides guidance for others researching in such contexts. Furthermore, her analysis, using a constructivist approach, showcases the use of critical discourse analysis.

Part IV: Exploring the personal

In Chapter 11, Ella Houston focuses on the ways in which disability is represented in advertisements. Using a cultural disability studies lens, Houston selected relevant advertisements and analysed them with a group of disabled people. Thus, Houston used documents in a similar way to Winter et al in Chapter 7, with the documents serving as a sometimes emotive prompt in semi-structured interviews. Houston also used textual analysis, and she provides a helpful set of considerations for those planning to use co-analysis.

In Chapter 12, the second focusing on the personal, Max Edward Perry uses a science and technology studies framework to understand medical records as social artefacts. Perry's research involved observation in UK outpatient hospital clinics, where he observed clinicians engaging with previously written medical records and creating new records. Using epistemography as a lens for his analysis, he asks why certain questions are present in the templates used to create new medical records and how this shapes doctor–patient interactions.

The final substantive chapter, Chapter 13, comes from Kate Carruthers Thomas, who explains the methods used in the Dear Diary project, which explored women academics' experiences of the COVID-19 lockdown. Powerful data extracts are provided in the chapter. The documents under study were diaries that had been purposefully solicited by Thomas. As in Houston's work (Chapter 11), the research included interviews, although in this case, the interviewees were the diary writers – an approach rarely used by those undertaking research with diaries. Alongside the empirical analysis, Thomas created a digital archive, including diary and interview extracts, allowing further analysis of these documents by a wider audience.

Conclusion

At the end of the book, we include some short concluding thoughts, focusing on ethics and next directions.

We really enjoyed reading the chapters ourselves and hope that you'll enjoy the book. Our aim is for this book to support a broader use of documents in research, thereby growing the field and increasing acceptance and understanding of this approach. If you have any feedback, do feel free to get in touch.

References

Ashley F. (2021) 'Accounting for research fatigue in research ethics', *Bioethics*, 35(3): 270–6.

Fiorito T. (2023) 'Beyond research as a dirty word? Searching for ethical and reflexive ways of doing research with and for migrant communities', *Migration Studies*, art mnad027, advance online publication. doi: 10.1093/migration/mnad027

Grant, A. (2019) *Doing Excellent Social Research with Documents: Practical Examples and Guidance for Qualitative Researchers*, Routledge.

Grant, A. (2022) *Doing Your Research Project with Documents: A Step-by-Step Guide to Take You from Start to Finish*, Policy Press.

Jennings, G. (2019) 'Bruce Lee and the invention of Jeet Kune Do: the theory of martial creation', *Martial Arts Studies*, 8, 60–72.

Kara, H., Mannay, D. and Roy, A. (2024) *The Handbook of Creative Data Analysis*, Policy Press.

Law, J. (2004) *After Method: Mess in Social Science Research*, Routledge.

Morgan, H. (2022) 'Conducting a qualitative document analysis', *The Qualitative Report*, 27(1), 64–77.

Prior, L. (2003) *Using Documents in Social Research*, SAGE.

PART I

Understanding the past

2

Documentary theatre as participatory social research

Katarzyna Niziołek

Summary

- This chapter focuses on using documents – an official investigation report, a non-fiction book, oral history, letters and a play-script – in theatre-based participatory social research.

- Five examples of research into the collective memory of traumatic historical events are given, involving ethnic killings, nuclear disaster, refugeedom, war and the Holocaust.

- A methodological framework is introduced, and ethical issues and the position of researcher-curator are considered.

Introduction

To better understand the complexity of the human condition in the late modern, globalised and turbulent world, a growing number of artists and scientists are turning to performative practices (Domańska, 2007). They are merging the construction of scientific knowledge with the evocative power of artistic expression, often in the form of arts-based research (Leavy, 2009). Underlying these developments is democratisation of culture and art, which brings about the figure of the arts participant – the 'expert of the everyday' (following Habermas, 1981). At the same time, artists and researchers are renouncing their authority and facilitating rather than relaying and recounting the experiential 'material' they collect. In this way, artists, researchers and participants become co-producers of culture and knowledge, which is often seen as plural and polyphonic (multivocal). This co-production is the landmark of a new democratic culture, defined by the potential of the individual to participate not only in the political sphere but also in all other walks of life, including art and science. In the arts, it has been known as the 'social turn' (Bishop, 2006); in social sciences, it is referred to as 'participatory research' (Leavy, 2017).

This is a profound, paradigmatic change, and linked to this are some questions we do not have complete answers to yet. For example, how, in the long run, will this development affect the quality of knowledge or the forms of art we produce as societies? In 1980, cognitive scientists George Lakoff and Mark Johnson introduced the idea of an experiential paradigm that operates through what they call 'imaginative rationality' and 'understanding' (see Lakoff and Johnson, 2003). The latter comes from people's interactions with their surrounding world and between themselves, and their perceptions of those interactions. Hence, it has to be relational, positional and situational. Researchers are part and parcel of those interactions and perceptions, although Lakoff and Johnson did not stress this. Feminist philosopher Donna Haraway (1988) coined the term 'situated knowledges' in relation to the view that objective and disembodied knowledge is impossible and that what we know is not simply subjective but also partial and embodied.

Understanding is actually what qualitative researchers, like me, try to practise every day. We set out to understand social worlds and share that understanding with others. One way to attempt this task is with the use of documents. Social scientists conventionally use pre-existing, 'found' documents created by organisations, institutions and individuals. These can be official reports, press articles or literature, including poetry and play-scripts. We also produce research documents in the form of interview transcripts, field notes, photographs, maps, drawings and so on. When asking research participants to take their own photographs (participatory photography) or to write a diary (personal documents method), we actually elicit document production. The documents used by qualitative researchers are records – be they verbal or visual, analogue or electronic, factual or creative – of people's past experiences.

Based on documents, qualitative researchers usually attempt to 're-enact' research participants' experiences and use them as grounding for theoretical explanations. The concept of 're-enactment' was usefully explained by historian Robert George Collingwood (2018, p 172): 'the events of history are never mere phenomena, never mere spectacles for contemplation, but things which the historian looks, not at, but through, to discern the thought within them'. For Collingwood, re-enactment was an intellectual process that linked past events (the *what happened*) to the intentions of the human agents behind them (the *why they acted that way*). It involved a certain amount of both criticism and imagination, and it was necessarily an insight from a contemporary perspective. Historical documents (records and artefacts) were just the starting point. The historian was to operate as an agent of a historical narration, constructed from the available historical evidence and their own experiences.

In the light of the cultural developments described earlier, a few questions seem particularly valid: How do documents connect with experiences and interactions beyond the textual or visual representations of the past? In what ways are documents performative? What happens when documentary and performative practices meet? Documents, conventionally conceived, draw their status as sources for research from their materiality and relative permanence, while performance is by definition immaterial and temporal. In contrast to this common view, social anthropologist Paul Connerton (2009) pointed out that societies remember mostly in a performative manner. They do so by means of collective rituals and habitualised bodily practices. The ephemerality of performance was also questioned by performance scholars Diana Taylor (2003) and Rebecca Schneider (2011). They argued that embodied practices are carriers of collective memory just as archives are. Taylor called these performative modes of memory transmission 'repertoire'. She saw them as more inclusive than written documents: 'If performance did not transmit knowledge, only the literate and powerful could claim social memory and identity' (Taylor, 2003, p xvii). A look at the practices of documentary theatre used as participatory social research will hopefully help shed some more light on these issues.

For the purpose of this chapter, documentary theatre is defined as a theatre genre that uses personal, literary and official documents as material for theatre writing and performance. In the process, the material is rendered artistically, but it also retains the quality of authenticity or truthfulness connected to a biographical or historical source. A documentary play can be performed either by professional actors or by the very providers of the documentary content as participants and the said 'experts of the everyday' (following Habermas, 1981). Sometimes it can look more like an audience-engaging event or a talking circle than a regular theatre performance. Each of these possibilities can be combined with other forms of social inquiry, such as biographical, narrative, participatory, cooperative, embodied and transformative research.

Writing from the position of researcher-curator

The combination of research, theatre and participation was the focus of my academic and cultural work for nearly a decade. This comprised a series of collaborations with theatre writers and directors, including Michał Stankiewicz, Justyna Zar-Schabowska and Papahema Theatre. First, in *The Method of National Constellations* (2014–16), scripted and guided interactions between the participants made space for embodied remembering of the violent raids by Polish partisans against Belarusian villages in 1946. Second, *Prayer. A Common Theatre* (2016–17) juxtaposed testimonies from *Chernobyl Prayer* by Svetlana Alexievich (2016) with the participants' own experiences, emotions and reflections linked to that deadly nuclear accident. Third, *Bieżenki* (2018) was compiled from the memories of refugees from north-eastern Poland in the First World War, conveyed by their female descendants. Fourth, in *Living Torpedoes* (2019), a group of university students explored their identities in confrontation with letters sent by Polish volunteers for would-be suicidal attacks against Nazi Germans. Finally, *The Suitcase* (2021) was a participatory production of a theatre play of the same title by Małgorzata Sikorska-Miszczuk, inspired by the true story of a French Jew who discovered his late father's suitcase in the Shoah Memorial museum in Paris. Throughout those projects, my research topic was collective memory. More precisely, I looked for ways to reach collective memory with participation and performance – to engage research participants (and participate with them) in a more meaningful, open and power-balanced way and use theatre for that purpose.

My role in those projects can be briefly described as 'researcher as curator', and this provided me with a unique position to conduct theatre-based participatory social research. It is a fluid and demanding role that combines curator and researcher responsibilities and prerogatives. Between Stankiewicz and myself, we defined this as caretaking. I was to manage a theatrical production and take care of the participants while at the same time gathering insights into the dynamics of theatre participation and the collective memory work set off by the practice. Aside from my own experience, in the last decade, arts curatorship has been widely discussed as an occupation that developed from selecting artworks for exhibitions and collections and has expanded to facilitating arts practices and doing research. For example, in 2014, the role of curator in the performing arts was the featured topic in an issue of *Theater* edited by Tom Sellar and Bertie Ferdman, with the focus on 'site-based, transdisciplinary, socially engaged, and participatory performances' where the curator – 'an equal creative and intellectual partner with the artists' – 'establishes the context for such events' (Sellar, 2014, p 1) and conceptualises 'how, where, when, why, and for whom such events are structured and presented' (Ferdman, 2014, p 7). More recently, attention has also been given to researchers looking at themselves as curators when analysing and presenting their work in the social sciences, especially in combination with arts-based research and creative analytic practice (Schmidt and Schultz, 2024).

From documents to theatre: the adaptation of documentary material

The documents used in the five projects were: an official investigation report, a non-fiction book, oral history (familial memories), letters and a play-script. In none of the cases were these used in a conventional manner – that is, as sources to be analysed and interpreted. Instead, they served as incentives for a performative response. They were re-enacted in the sense of taking action rather than narrating history, though the latter could be part of the action. In each of the performances, not only did we use a different documentary material, but we also adapted it accordingly. Overall, we mixed two approaches: citation and intersemiotic translation. For the first, we included text, such as passages from a book, oral history or play-script, in the performances. For the second, we used text to create something different: an embodied experience, a relational structure, a social situation, a space for self-expression, a temporary community. The distinct types of collective memory produced in the projects can be described as: empathetic (*The Method of National Constellations*), emotional (*Prayer. A Common Theatre*), collaged (*Bieżenki*), dialogical (*Living Torpedoes*) and connective (*The Suitcase*).

Empathetic understanding

The Method of National Constellations used an official investigation report into the so-called 'pacifications' of several multi-ethnic villages in north-eastern Poland in winter 1946. 'Pacifications' refers to the massacres of civilians from the Belarusian minority who were believed to be cooperating with the Moscow-installed communist regime. These were carried out by anti-communist partisans operating within the ranks of the National Military Union and under the command of Romuald Rajs, also known as Bury. The investigation by the Institute of National Remembrance Commission for the Prosecution of Crimes against the Polish Nation, concluded in 2005, confirmed that 79 people were killed and many more harmed in the massacres (Instytut Pamięci Narodowej, 2005).

The official report is long and heavy in factual information. It presents the general context of the postwar anti-communist resistance in Poland, follows the course of the investigated events and cites a number of witness testimonies. From that documentary material, the writer-director (Stankiewicz) chose several main topics, including execution by shooting in a forest, saying a prayer in Polish to prove nationality, witnessing one's father being shot to death, trying to escape and save children from a burning house. In a sequence of separate scenes, the historical context and details were minimised and the focus was placed on the social structure of interactions and relations between the historical actors as embodied by the contemporary participants. Roles were given randomly to participants for a particular scene only. These included parents and children, partisans and villagers, Belarusians and Poles, Orthodoxes and Catholics, and commanders and troopers.

Participants were called to the stage in pairs or small groups. There, they followed simple instructions read to them by the narrator (a professional actor), such as: 'Step in field 2'; 'You are a Polish partisan'; 'Take aim'; 'Say: "Daddy, get up!"'; and 'Say it like you mean it'. Their performance was thus a mixture of what they knew and imagined about the past and their own lived experiences and the social roles they fulfilled every day. For example, real-life parents often had a hard time when the scene engaged other participants as children. The majority of participants complied with the instructions, even when they were asked to 'shoot'. The rule was, though, that anyone could leave the performance space at any time. A lot of emotions and involuntary reactions were involved, like laughing in the midst of tragic circumstances. Each performance was followed by a group discussion allowing the participants to decompress, reflect and share.

On the ethical side, we made sure that everyone was informed about the topic of the performance and the way it was to be carried out. The participation type was, by design, directed as opposed to autonomous. Interestingly, a number of participants mentioned in the discussions that in spite of being told what to do, they retained a sense of agency. When taking a role, they felt they could perform it the way they wanted. *The Method of National Constellations* created a framework for people to connect to the past via their immediate embodied experience and interaction with others. The way they used that framework was up to them. Hence, we called the participants Users (in contrast to Observers).

Emotional history

With *Prayer. A Common Theatre*, Stankiewicz and I wanted to exercise a more autonomous and democratic approach. The framework was very simple. First, we asked the participants to read *Chernobyl Prayer* by Svetlana Alexievich (2016). The book belongs to the non-fiction genre. It deals with the disaster that took place in Chernobyl (Ukraine) in 1986, when a reactor in a nuclear power plant exploded, causing both devastating environmental impact and thousands of human casualties. Second, the participants chose the fragments from the book that they felt most affected by. They learned those fragments by heart and later delivered them from memory as part of the performance. To complete their stage appearances, they shared their own reflections, interpretations or recollections, so the performance resembled a book club meeting. By selecting the fragments and sharing their experiences, the participants co-created the performance.

That kind of framework was only possible due to the very specific trait of Alexievich's writing, which is narrative polyphony. Her works typically consist of her heroes' own voices, presented either as monologues (by a firefighter's wife, for example) or as choirs (with local children, for example). In her own words, she writes 'the history of feelings' (Alexievich, 2018, p xix). It is obviously something very different from an official report like the one we worked with before. Sociologist Arlie R. Hochschild calls such an approach 'deep story', by which she means 'narrative *as felt*' (Hochschild, 2016, p ix, emphasis in original). Like Alexievich, she shifts attention from facts or events to feelings. In *Prayer. A Common Theatre*, the participants literally spoke somebody else's words while feeling their own emotions and experiencing their present theatrical moment. That exposed the tensions between the historical past, the documentary material (the record of that past) and the contemporary reading of that material. The theatrical aspect of our relationship to history was perhaps best encapsulated by Alexievich in another of her books, *The Unwomanly Face of War*:

> The narrators are not only witnesses – least of all are they witnesses; they are actors and makers. It is impossible to go right up to reality. Between us and reality are our feelings. I understand that I am dealing with versions, that each person has her version, and it is from them, from their plurality and their intersections, that the image of the time and the people living in it is born. (Alexievich, 2018, p xxi)

Community of remembrance

Whereas *The Method of National Constellations* and *Prayer. A Common Theatre* produced, respectively, empathetic and emotional understandings of the historical past, with *Bieżenki* we wanted to focus more specifically on the notion of post-memory. This concept was introduced by Marianne Hirsch (2012, p 5) to describe 'the relationship that the "generation after" bears to the personal, collective, and cultural trauma of those who came before – to experiences they "remember" only by means of the stories, images, and behaviours among which they grew up'. Thus defined, post-memory is necessarily mediated by imagination and creativity.

The title *Bieżenki* is a vernacular term for 'female refugees'. Again, we started with a non-fiction book – *Bieżeństwo 1915. Zapomniani uchodźcy* (Bieżeństwo 1915. The Forgotten Refugees) by Aneta Prymaka-Oniszk (2016), a Polish writer of Belarusian descent. The book is about a mass wave of refugees who fled from contemporary north-eastern Poland during the First World War. In 1915, the Russians were withdrawing from the advancing German army and burning the countryside over which they passed. The majority of the refugees were peasants and women with children. For the book, Prymaka-Oniszk conducted her own research using documents. She collected pieces of information from libraries, archives and ordinary people to find out what had happened to her grandmother and millions of refugees like her.

Together with Stankiewicz and two literature professors, Katarzyna Sawicka-Mierzyńska and Danuta Zawadzka, we invited several other female descendants of those refugees to share their familial memories of the refugeedom. The scarce memories they had received were mixed with their creative imagination and the intimate recollections of their relationships with their grandmothers or great-grandmothers who survived the refugeedom. Those memories, images and recollections were discussed in workshops and made the content of the performance. The participants also shared keepsakes, photographs, a song and other personal documents. The documentary materials and memorabilia were mixed and matched freely, like a collage. The form of the performance resembled a talking circle. Towards the end, the circle was enlarged by including the audience. Many of them wanted to add to what they heard from the stage. This way, an ephemeral community of remembrance was created. It included not only the actual descendants of the refugees, but also anyone who felt connected to that part of regional history. The video recording of the *Bieżenki* performance is a document in its own right. It carries not only the memory of the refugeedom but also the memory of the performance.

Dialogues with the past

Living Torpedoes was inspired by a letter sent in May 1939, a few months before the outbreak of the Second World War, by three Warsaw residents to a daily newspaper *Ilustrowany Kuryer Codzienny* (Illustrated Daily Courier). It was an appeal to the Polish people 'who urgently wanted to give their life for their Country, not fighting in the army together with the others, but as living torpedoes'. It mobilised hundreds of positive reactions by both men and women, often teenagers or young adults. Those written responses were collected in a history book, *Żywe torpedy 1939* (Living Torpedoes 1939) by Elżbieta Szumiec-Zielińska (2016).

Together with Sawicka-Mierzyńska and two other university colleagues, we teamed with actor and director Justyna Zar-Schabowska, who had participated in *Prayer. A Common Theatre* a couple of years earlier. The participants in the project were undergraduate students in sociology and Polish literature. We used the letters sent by those who volunteered to be living torpedoes as a pretext to explore the contemporary notions of patriotism and heroism and, more broadly, modern changes in social identities, bonds and values. With the performance, we tried to turn the stage into a 'space of appearance', understood as an arena for people acting and speaking and thus revealing their identities to others (see Arendt, 1998). Applied to theatre, this concept entails using the stage as a public space or a forum where participants can present their opinions and beliefs with different theatrical forms and media. In the workshops, group discussions and, eventually, the performance, the historical documents were recontextualised and used in a dialogical manner. The participants read the letters from volunteers, reacted to the appeal published by the newspaper from their contemporary perspective, and shared their own familial memories of the Second World War. With images, props and music, we highlighted the contemporary cultural and media context.

Connective reading

The Suitcase was the most conventional of the documentary theatre projects I curated and used in research. It was a participatory adaptation of a play-script by Polish playwright Małgorzata Sikorska-Miszczuk. The play-script itself is of the documentary genre. It is an artistic rendering of a real event that happened in France and was covered in the press there. A Frenchman named Michel Leleu had, as a child, lost his father Pierre Lévy to the Holocaust. He himself survived the Second World War and years later, in 2005, discovered his father's suitcase exhibited at the Shoah Memorial museum in Paris. The suitcase was on loan from the Auschwitz-Birkenau memorial and museum in Poland – the site of the former German Nazi death camp to which his father had been deported and exterminated. Leleu made a request to the museum that the suitcase remain in Paris, which led to a legal dispute over restitution of the exhibit. Eventually, the suitcase remained in the property of the Auschwitz-Birkenau while being loaned to the Shoah Memorial on a long-term basis. Finding his father's suitcase encouraged Leleu to change his name to Lévy and reclaim his own Holocaust survivor identity.

Sikorska-Miszczuk appropriated that story to look into the personal and collective identity defined by historical trauma, from suppression through to a sense of emptiness, searching for a true self and understanding. The characters included: Narrator, Answering Machine, Jackleen, Franswa Jackoh, Miserable Tour Guide at the Holocaust Museum, Poet (Bruno) and Pantofelnik. In this work, Sikorska-Miszczuk resorts to dark humour and absurdity to convey the feelings of loneliness, living a 'half-life' and need for a connection to the past.

Together with an independent theatre group, Papahema Theatre, we invited sociology graduate students to perform the play in the form of a dramatic reading or reader's theatre. The story of Franswa Jackoh/Michel Leleu was juxtaposed with the students' own experiences of a visit to the POLIN Museum of the History of Polish Jews. For that part of the performance, the students were introduced by their real names, and brief information about what they had found at the museum, metaphorically speaking, was given by a third-person narrator (one of Papahema's actors). The scene directly addressed the question posed by Sikorska-Miszczuk about the role of museums dedicated to the Holocaust in remembering and connecting 'generations after' (Hirsch 2012, p 5) – not limited to the direct descendants of the Holocaust survivors – to the historical past. 'The collapse is still under way – says the Narrator in the play – even though successive generations say: "It was a long time ago" and that "it doesn't concern them". I want to tell people that it does concern them' (Sikorska-Miszczuk and Zapałowski, 2011, p 112).

Theatre and research participation as an ethical choice

In all five performances, documentary theatre was used as participatory social research or, more specifically, theatre-based participatory research. This is something different from more common participatory methods such as participatory action research, community-based participatory research and sociological intervention. Participation is, of course, the shared element. However, in the case of theatre-based participatory research, or participatory theatre for short, participation happens in the theatrical context. That places arts participation at the centre of the practice, which is as much a methodological as an ethical choice, reflecting the broader processes of democratisation in art and science.

Rooted in my own practical experience, as presented earlier, I suggest we should consider types of theatre participation as social roles or models. The basic set of participant roles in theatre would be: Protagonist, User and Co-creator. Each has some more specific variants. For instance, Protagonist can be Source and/or Performer (often using some form of narration), User may become Player or Immerser, and Co-creator can be Co-writer and/or Performer again. There is also Observer, whose role resembles an audience member in conventional theatre. The roles may overlap and intersect, of course.

Typically for my practice, participants were engaged both as Protagonists and Co-creators. They provided arts material based on their life experiences, such as their memories or memorabilia, and they performed on stage and had a say in how they wanted to do that. In *Prayer. A Common Theatre*, *Bieżenki* and *Living Torpedoes*, by taking part in workshops and group discussions, they participated in the production of the performance in an autonomous manner. This can be contrasted with the directed or guided (heteronomous) participation in *The Method of National Constellations* and *The Suitcase*. In the first of these, Users interacted within a predesigned theatrical situation and Observers simply watched them (up to the point of the end discussion when they got together). In the second, Performers were directed like actors in a regular theatre play. I have used some of that terminology already in the earlier sections of this chapter.

There are certain ethical issues connected to the participatory character of theatre-based research. The most specific concerns are about the quality of participation and the cooperation between the participants and the team of artists and researchers, starting with recruitment for a project. My preferred tool is an open call, either for individuals or for groups (in my case, student groups). We have never cast and selected the best participants for the performances. Everyone who wanted to participate could join, no matter their prior theatre-related experiences and competences. As a result, the majority of participants were 'naturals', or non-professionals. I intentionally do not call participants amateurs, as in participatory theatre there is no training for stage acting. Participants may be Performers but they are not amateur actors. They usually do not even take character roles. On stage, they remain themselves. In my experience, when the topic of the performance is relevant to them or the local community, the participants are likely to engage as volunteers.

The relationship between participants and researchers is key to the reliability of any research project. But in the case of theatre-based research, it gets more complicated. Apart from researchers, there are artists involved. We actually cooperate within a positional triangle: artists, researchers and participants. In addition, the researcher may need to divide their attention between doing research and organising theatre. Artist-researcher is, in fact, a rare occurrence in the field of social research. Nevertheless, especially in small-scale projects, some role negotiation and multitasking is usually necessary. Tensions and conflicts may build up along any of the triangle's sides. Artists and researchers may have different visions of the creative process or a different sense of ethics. Participants may feel exploited either for art's sake or for research's sake. They may also find themselves in conflict with each other, be that over character differences, values or positions in the group. Thus, it is important to ensure transparency (state the purpose, explain the method, address expectations), encourage equal cooperation and stay flexible. Ground rules include showing respect, care and open-mindedness.

Last but not least, participants in theatre-based research perform on stage, in front of an audience. To many people, this is potentially a stressful situation. Neither researchers nor artists can deal with that stress for the participants. But we can help them find their way through it with an adequate form of presentation. For example, the formula of the reader's theatre we used in *The Suitcase* was, according to the participants, less stressful than speaking from memory. Calling participants to the stage by their name, like we did in *Prayer. A Common Theatre*, freed them from remembering who comes when. It may also be helpful to allow some spontaneity and improvisation as part of the performance, to suggest that the participants should talk to the audience rather than act in front of them and to introduce imperfection as a natural part of participatory theatre.

Finally, the ethical considerations inherent in participatory theatre using documents to research the workings of collective memory also include sensitivity to the historical content. The documents we employed for the five projects were all connected to some traumatising historical event: ethnic killings, nuclear disaster, refugeedom, war and the Holocaust. Thus, they had to be considered as potentially triggering, especially to people who had experienced something similar in their own lives or whose older relatives had. That risk was transferred to the performances based on those documents and the video documentation created for each of the projects. This should be taken into account when working with historical materials, whether already published or collected directly from the participants. A content notice seems to be a reasonable way to address that risk. When announcing the call for participation, we were always very explicit about what the project was about and how we intended to approach it.

Framework for theatre-based participatory research using documents

Table 2.1 summarises the types of document, document use, participant roles and types of collective memory produced in each of the projects outlined earlier. Drawing from those experiences, as diverse as they were, I have advanced a methodological 'protocol' for theatre-based participatory research. This can be applied and, if need be, freely modified by other researchers in social sciences and humanities. The methodology comprises five general elements:

1. Using a document (for example, a piece of non–fiction literature) as a pretext for engaging participants;
2. Sharing and exploring life histories (memories) in group discussions, workshops and rehearsals;
3. Monitoring the whole process by means of observation and self-observation, including through notes, journals and photographs;
4. Using theatre performance as a form of public expression and wider public (audience) involvement;
5. Following up with group discussions and individual interviews with participants (for example, through a focus group or in–depth interviews).

Conclusion

In the course of my experience with participatory theatre, I have learned that textual documents, theatrical framework and embodied participation jointly facilitate the emergence of what I like to call, following the Deleuzian trope, 'assemblages of memory'. Simply speaking, an assemblage of memory is collective memory seen as constructed of a multitude of objects and materials, be they 'physical, biological, psychic, social, verbal' (Deleuze and Parnet, 1987, p 52), based on connections or conjunctions between them – the 'AND, AND, AND' (Deleuze and Parnet, 1987, p 34). In contrast to the often cited 'social frames of memory' (Halbwachs, 1992), which give things and actions their meaning depending on a particular group's interpretation and interest, it is a more open and inclusive model (metaphor) for collective memory. From that perspective, theatre-based participatory research seems to be instrumental not only in building a more empathetic and embodied understanding of human

Table 2.1: Summary of the projects

Project	Document	Document use	Participants	Memory
The Method of National Constellations	Official investigation report	Relational and interactional structure	Users	Empathetic
Prayer. A Common Theatre	Non-fiction book	Selection of excerpts	Protagonists and Co-creators	Emotional
Bieżenki	Oral history (familial memories)	Workshop and sharing stories, images, objects	Protagonists and Co-creators	Collaged
Living Torpedoes	Letters	Individual reaction	Protagonists and Co-creators	Dialogical
The Suitcase	Play-script	Participatory adaptation	Performers	Connective

experience – especially of our various connections to the historical past – but also in advancing the larger processes of democratisation of knowledge and decolonisation of social science.

Key considerations for using this method

1. Start by considering whether your research topic shows potential for using documents in a performative manner.

2. Think about what documents you can use to spark interest among prospective participants, the relevance of the topic to their lives or their communities, and their 'everyday expertise' or biographical experience that you would like to get closer to.

3. Plan how you will adapt those documents for the stage. Think broadly – it does not have to be a theatre play per se. Decide on the roles the participants will be asked to take in your research in terms of their theatre participation.

4. Get in touch with theatre artists who you would like to collaborate with on your research project. Enlist help from a theatre producer or curator.

5. Organise the creative process. Will group discussions and workshops work for you? Will it be beneficial to combine research using documents with other methods, such as individual interviews?

References

Alexievich, S. (2016) *Chernobyl Prayer: A Chronicle of the Future*, Penguin Books.

Alexievich, S. (2018) *The Unwomanly Face of War*, Penguin Books.

Arendt, H. (1998) *The Human Condition*, The University of Chicago Press.

Bishop, C. (2006) 'The social turn: collaboration and its discontents', *Artforum*, 44(6): 178–83.

Collingwood, R.G. (2018) *The Idea of History*, Lume Books.

Connerton, P. (2009) *How Societies Remember*, Cambridge University Press.

Deleuze, G. and Parnet, C. (1987) *Dialogues*, Columbia University Press.

Domańska, E. (2007) '"Zwrot performatywny" we współczesnej humanistyce' [The performative turn in the humanities], *Teksty Drugie*, 5: 48–61.

Ferdman, B. (2014) 'From content to context: the emergence of the performance curator', *Theater*, 44(2): 5–17.

Habermas, J. (1981) 'Modernity versus postmodernism', *New German Critique*, 22: 3–14.

Halbwachs, M. (1992) *On Collective Memory*, The University of Chicago Press.

Haraway, D. (1988) 'Situated knowledges: the science question in feminism and the privilege of partial perspective', *Feminist Studies*, 14(3): 575–99.

Hirsch, M. (2012) *The Generation of Postmemory: Writing and Visual Culture after the Holocaust*, Columbia University Press.

Hochschild, A. (2016) *Strangers in Their Own Land: Anger and Mourning on the American Right*, The New Press.

Instytut Pamięci Narodowej (2005) 'Informacja o ustaleniach końcowych śledztwa S 28/02/Zi w sprawie pozbawienia życia 79 osób – mieszkańców powiatu Bielsk Podlaski w tym 30 osób tzw. furmanów w lesie koło Puchał Starych, dokonanych w okresie od dnia 29 stycznia 1946r. do dnia 2 lutego 1946', [Information on the final conclusions of the investigation S/28/02/Zi into the case of the killings of 79 persons – residents of Bielsk Podlaski district, including 30 persons known as cart drivers in the forest near Puchały Stare, committed in the period from 29 January 1946 to 2 February 1946]. Available from: https://ipn.gov.pl/pl/dla-med iow/komunikaty/9989,Informacja-o-ustaleniach-koncowych-sledztwa-S-280 2Zi-w-sprawie-pozbawienia-zycia.html

Lakoff, G. and Johnson, M. (2003) *Metaphors We Live By*, The University of Chicago Press.

Leavy, P. (2009) *Method Meets Art: Arts-Based Research Practice*, The Guilford Press.

Leavy, P. (2017) *Research Design: Quantitative, Qualitative, Mixed Methods, Arts-Based, and Community-Based Participatory Research Approaches*, The Guilford Press.

Prymaka-Oniszk, A. (2016) *Bieżeństwo 1915: Zapomniani uchodźcy* [Bieżeństwo 1915. The Forgotten Refugees], Wydawnictwo Czarne.

Schmidt, A. and Schultz, C. (2024) 'Researcher as curator: making room for the politics of emotion in leisure research', *Leisure Studies*, 43(3): 511–21.

Schneider, R. (2011) *Performing Remains: Art and War in Times of Theatrical Reenactment*, Routledge.

Sellar, T. (2014) 'The cure', *Theater*, 44(2): 1–3.

Sikorska-Miszczuk, M. and Zapałowski, A. (2011) 'The suitcase', *PAJ: A Journal of Performance and Art*, 33(1): 93–117.

Szumiec-Zielińska, E. (2016) *Żywe torpedy 1939* [Living Torpedoes 1939], Wydawnictwo Demart.

Taylor, D. (2003) *The Archive and the Repertoire: Performing Cultural Memory in the Americas*, Duke University Press.

3

Music and sound in documents: a case study of music and asylum history

Rosemary Golding

Summary

- This chapter considers the ways in which music and sound can be important for historical research.

- The idea of 'archival silence' is introduced.

- An overview of documents associated with music-historical research in Victorian long-stay mental health institutions is provided.

- Some of the challenges associated with historical documents concerning music are discussed.

Introduction

The study of music has long involved research using documents, from biographical narratives of composers and performers to analysis of notated musical texts, editions and scores. Since the middle of the 20th century, when the study of music's contexts – particularly in social and economic terms – came to the fore, the use of documents has become an essential part of the work of many music researchers. This chapter is focused on text-based documents, rather than musical scores, and aims to explore the ways in which we can generate knowledge about music via the study of such documents. It makes use of my work on music in 19th-century lunatic asylums,[1] an interdisciplinary project based on archival studies of a wide range of asylum institutions. I draw on theories of archival silences and imaginaries, considering the ways in which engaging with questions of music and sound, through careful study of documents, can offer new perspectives on the history of mental health institutions.

Historical method is deeply reflexive, responding to the individual circumstances of each set of documents or materials as well as the specific aims of each project. David Gold (2008, p 18) describes archival research methodology in the following way: 'read absolutely everything and try to make sense of what happened'. Nevertheless, writing history with documents requires engagement far beyond

25

the reconstruction of events and ideas. Traditionally, the historian has been required to deploy critical evaluation of sources and narratives, as well as interpretation. This involves considering alternative ways of understanding the material gathered, identifying bias, analysing which voices and perspectives are present and which are missing, and weighing the evidence for cause and effect. In addition, as we will see, imagination and creativity play a part in historical methodology. The analytical method of archival research using documents requires a critical lens on both the archive itself and its contents (King, 2016). Throughout, historians contend with the fine line between the messiness of reality and the urge to explain and narrate (Gunn and Faire, 2015). This chapter highlights some of the richness of engaging in depth with asylum archives and demonstrates the value of thinking about music and sound when doing so.

Documents are essential for engaging with the music and musical practices of the past. They often tell us the location of musical performance and practice, the people involved and the repertoire performed. Large-scale projects such as the Concert Programmes Database (nd), which draws together historical collections from across Europe, collect sources of this type of information as key data for building up a picture of formal musical life in a particular time and place: what music was performed, when and by whom. They might, in addition, tell us about the qualitative aspects of music: how the music was performed and how it was experienced, received or listened to. Newspaper reports of concerts, for example, in addition to recounting the technical elements of the performance – the repertoire, performers and location – give us a more subjective account of a musical practice, such as information on the size and composition of the audience, the response of the listeners and the critic's own view of both the music performed and the way in which it was performed.

Documents also offer information on how music was thought about and discussed – in particular, the beliefs and ideas about music. This kind of discourse helps us to understand the context for the more immediate elements of music-making, and it may include ideas about music's power to communicate or heal, its relationship with language, its status as an art or a science and its moral function. Like other historical studies, using documents for studying music requires awareness of motivation, authorship, context and bias. Likewise, as with any historical material, even the most comprehensive documents leave gaps in their record. Music is an experiential art form, sounding in time. Evidence and information centred on music often allow us to access different perspectives on musical practice, but at the same time they keep us one step removed from the material of music – its sounding form. The role of the music historian, therefore, is to find different ways of approaching music within its historical context, each of which brings us closer to imagining the experience of music, whether from the perspective of performer, composer or listener.

Studying music and soundworlds of the past has much to offer historians in general, and it may offer new perspectives for studies of contemporary life as well.

Sophia Rosenfeld (2011, p 317), for example, notes the increasing importance of 'auditory history', the challenges of understanding and reconstructing the aural past and the relative lack of evidence, methods and languages for describing and discussing sound, music and listening of the past. She notes the close connection between changing attitudes to sound and listening and changing social attitudes, arguing for the embeddedness of sound experience in social history. However, Rosenfeld was not the first historian to pay attention to sound; Peter Bailey (1996), James H. Johnson (1995), John M. Picker (2003), Mark M. Smith (2004; 2007) and Veit Erlmann (2010), among others, have all used sound and aurality as a focus for historical investigation.

Archival silences and the historical imagination

My research questions the ways in which music has been thought about, studied and used, the connections made between music and other aspects of life, and the day-to-day musical experiences of the people and communities I study. Documents have been central to these endeavours; each of my research projects has focused on a series of archives or documents. Nevertheless, I am constantly drawn to retain as much contact as possible with the material of music, the musical experiences and the soundworld of the period I study.

Gaps in the archival record are not a problem exclusive to music studies. Historians making use of documents inevitably deal with gaps in the information provided by documents, whether it be the details excluded from formal or published reports, the anonymity of people represented by data or the single perspective represented by one half of a set of correspondence. The problem of these kinds of gaps in the documents and archives that we study has come under the scrutiny of historians concerned with the theory and practice of archive studies. In recent years, I have been interested in the concept of 'archival silence' and the ways in which this relates to the study of music. The silences of archive studies refer not to the literal silences that chime directly with studies of music and sound, but to the unfillable gaps in data and narratives that can be drawn from documents and other materials in the archive. What can we *know* from archival documents, and what remains *unknowable*?

The idea of archival silence has been developed by scholars such as Michelle Caswell, whose work has explored spaces between archival data and documents, including the voices and perspectives that are missing. Silences might be deliberate, personal and political, the outcome of structures of power and authority, or the accidental outcome of the ways records are created, stored and catalogued (Caswell et al, 2018). In response to a growing disquiet at the persistence of gaps and silences, scholars have explored new and creative means of addressing them. For example, Caswell and Anne J. Gilliland discuss the role of 'imaginary records', posing potential historiographical solutions to a key gap; they investigate the impact of these records on the narrative as well as the emotions and expectations associated with them (Gilliland and Caswell, 2016).

For music, as noted earlier, even the most complete of records leave silences, offering opportunities for such creative imaginings. Benjamin R. Levy and Laura Emmery's work on archives and music theory notes a shift in ideas about what archives are and what they do as well as changes in archival methods and responses among music scholars, particularly music theorists (see Levy and Emmery, 2021). Levy and Emmery refer to Patricia Hall's work on music from the Auschwitz-Birkenau State Museum archive; Hall outlines the process of working with music manuscripts from the archives, reconstructing the music and the creative 'micro-interventions' necessary for modern performance (see Hall, 2021). In this case, gaps in the archives are filled through creative musical imaginings based on scholarly investigation and experimentation. In doing so, and in bringing music documents to the fore, broader gaps in our understanding of the sonic experience of prisoners and staff at the Auschwitz–Birkenau Nazi concentration camp are identified and addressed. Focusing on one of these silences further helps to surface additional questions around prisoner experience, music and sound, offering new opportunities for enquiry. In the same way, my own research on music and mental health institutions in the 19th century has addressed gaps in understanding and offered new areas for historical focus.

In addition to recognising the silences and problems associated with the production, retention and organisation of archival material (Istvandity, 2021), historians have increasingly been prompted to become aware of, and make explicit, their own positionality in relation to the themes and subjects of their work. This is no less important in music research, with music scholarship having historically prioritised certain modes of enquiry, certain genres and repertoires, and the published musical work and its composer over musical practices and cultures. For example, Debra Hardy states that '[h]istories have always been a way for me to explore and explain the systems we humans find ourselves in', but also notes that it is rare for 'traditional archival histories' to include explicit consideration of researcher positionality (2021, pp 78, 81). My own research on the history of music and mental health reflects my interests and experiences in the widespread impact of music on emotions, its use in therapeutic environments (at the time, not part of my personal experience) and how people think and write about music.

Throughout my work, I have aimed not to position my research as either the prehistory of current music therapy or an overt demonstration of music's potential for therapeutic power. Nevertheless, as my work has garnered public interest and I find myself writing shorter pieces for public engagement, these are the threads which have provoked most interest. I have written previously about the kinds of narrative that result from a musical history of the asylum, which have the potential to hide the more unpleasant aspects of mental health care and its institutions (Golding, 2021). Nevertheless, with the experiences of patients still at the forefront of 'bottom-up' psychiatric history (Smith, 2024), the perspective of music offers new ways to engage with the documents and archives.

Working with materials connected to historical institutions and mental health also introduces questions of ethics for the researcher, particularly when making use of sensitive patient material. All archives maintain the privacy of patients and staff by operating embargoes on material for set periods, but patient records from the 19th century are almost always available to the researcher. Two options are open to the historian, and these are widely used. The first is to anonymise material, using initials to preserve dignity and privacy, so much of which was denied to pauper patients during their lifetime. The second is to use full names of patients in order to share stories and offer patients the 'voice' and individual identity which was also often denied. In many instances, particularly when dealing with materials related to pauper patients, records written by management or medical staff are the only trace of lives otherwise lost to history. My preference is to bring these stories to life as best I can, using full names, dates and details, while avoiding sharing what might be considered private information unrelated to the topic. However, regardless of the manner in which information is presented, sensitivity and care is needed when handling patient data.

Music in the Victorian asylum

My most recent research has focused on music in the Victorian asylum. Here, my research questions are twofold: What music was performed? And how was it connected with the therapeutic work of the institution? The archives of Victorian asylums are particularly rich, especially those of the large, publicly funded pauper asylums, which were required to keep detailed records of day-to-day expenditure, activities and patient treatment as well as data on admissions and outcomes. Asylum history has, unsurprisingly, been an area of enormous growth in tandem with the interest in social history, the medical humanities and *patient-centred* histories (Porter, 1985). Numerous accounts trace the activities of individual institutions, and there is a growing body of published work on lunacy and asylum management, together with work on the establishment of psychiatry as a specialist profession. Asylum histories have also contributed to broader historical narratives and theorisations, with notable contributions from Michel Foucault (1967) and Andrew Scull (1993).

Asylum history in 19th-century Britain captures an important period of upheaval and challenge in both political and social cultures. Prior to the end of the 18th century, there was little provision for people experiencing mental health problems; the poor would be kept at home or in workhouses, with the exception of those in the very few charitable institutions, while the better off would be cared for either at home or in small, private asylums, commonly known as 'madhouses' (Smith, 2020). Towards the end of the 18th century, increasing concern about the treatment of the 'insane' together with a high-profile scandal over the treatment of patients in a very early pauper asylum led to new legislation and oversight. In 1815, counties were given the powers to raise funds to establish an institution for the care of pauper lunatics, and in 1847, this provision was made mandatory and a body of inspectors was created. From the outset, most asylums adopted the principle of 'moral management' in opposition to physical restraint; patients were given strict timetables, pleasant surroundings and a busy schedule of employment and recreation to distract their minds.

While aspects of employment and recreation, medical aspects of diagnosis and treatment, and the structures of management that supported the operation of the 19th-century asylum have been considered by many historians, there has been little study of the musical, aural and sonic elements of the asylum experience. Seeking accounts of music and noise as well as the ways in which they were linked to patient mental health and well-being adds a new dimension to the existing narratives of the Victorian asylum. My research in this area involved searching for accounts of music and noise beyond concerts and formal occasions – including patient accounts of music on the wards and in the corridors – tracking down repertoire and performance spaces and examining published books and pamphlets for ideas about where music fits within theoretical and idealistic accounts of asylum practice.

My approach involved triangulating a wide range of information from written documents to build a detailed narrative of practice as well as a complementary narrative of ideas and perspectives. Documents offer facts, such as quantitative data and information about events; quasi-factual accounts, including records of patient activities and reports of audience behaviour at concerts; and opinions, such as medics' views on the benefits of music for mental health patients. While historical investigation values all forms of evidence, in each case the data available must be treated as a representation of the historical reality, which might be filtered by the perspectives and biases of the writer as well as those of the reader.

Provision for mental health grew from a small number of largely private and charitable asylums at the beginning of the 19th century to over a hundred by 1900. I focused on the archive records of nine English asylums, chosen to represent a range of institutions large and small, older and newer, and catering for paupers, charity patients or the middle classes. I also selected several institutions particularly associated with music (see Table 3.1), such as the pauper asylum at Worcester, which counted the composer Edward Elgar, during his formative years, among its band members.

In each case, I collected existing secondary and primary literature available to me in advance of my archive visit to gain a sense of the overall historical shape of the institution. I noted any indications of musical activity and lists of key names, dates and developments. As my research progressed, it became clear that it was important to know the identities of successive medical superintendents, who had responsibility for the overall management of the asylum, and chaplains, who were often involved in patient recreation and education. I also spent time examining online catalogues to seek out documents and collections that might include musical information and references – I found maps and plans, photographs, patient registers, formal reports and staff wage books and other sources.

The following paragraphs outline how I approached each subset of documents, the kinds of information I gleaned and the ways in which this fed into my understanding of the historical uses of music via a multifaceted approach.

Table 3.1: Summary of asylum archives consulted

Asylum name	Type of institution	Year founded
Bethlem Hospital	Charitable	1377
York Retreat	Charitable (Quaker)	1794
Norfolk County Lunatic Asylum	Pauper (state funded)	1814
West Riding Pauper Lunatic Asylum	Pauper (state funded)	1818
Gloucester Asylum	Initially private, charitable and pauper, then pauper (state funded)	1823
Worcestershire County and City Pauper Lunatic Asylum	Pauper (state funded)	1852
Barnwood House, Gloucester	Private, upper class	1860
Brookwood Asylum, Surrey	Pauper (state funded)	1867
Holloway Sanatorium	Private, middle class	1885

Formal reports

My first port of call within each set of archive documents was the formal reports of each institution, which alerted me to key persons and dates in the history of the asylum, helping me focus my subsequent research. These formal reports were a compulsory part of management practice for state–run institutions from the early 19th century, and formal records became important across all forms of institution as private asylums came within the purview of government oversight and regulatory processes. Printed annual reports contain data on patient admissions, including gender, age and diagnosis, together with summaries of financial accounts and reports from the management. Superintendents' reports from the mid-19th century onwards include sections on recreational activities, and some offer tables of formal activities such as concerts, plays and visits. As asylums grew and the staff teams expanded, the chaplain often took some responsibility for patient well-being and education as well as religion; their provision of classes in singing point to the inclusion of music education, and the chapel choir formed an important part of religious practice in many asylums. In addition to factual information about the forms of music available within each asylum, formal reports often include information about the aims and effects of music.

Data and accounts

The data published in formal records sometimes offer further information about music. Very occasionally, music is recorded as the cause of a patient's illness – for example, a general report notes that a patient was admitted to Bethlem Hospital in 1843 due to 'over study of music' (General Report for the Royal Hospitals of Bridewell and Bethlem, 1843, p 69). Patients' occupations are also recorded, and these include music sellers, instrument makers, performers, music teachers and music students. The earliest published accounts give only an overview of expenditure, but due to the growth in musical activity, later accounts sometimes include summary data on expenses for musical entertainment, musical activities or the asylum band. With the more detailed accounts, I got a much closer sense of how music was funded. Pauper asylum accounts include entries on musical instruments, sheet music and hymn-books for the band and chapel, while accounts related to private asylums show that instruments were bought, repaired and maintained for both patient and staff use. Therefore, the accounts offer information about the material culture of music as well as its use.

Programmes and posters

Some asylum archives have rich collections of programmes and posters from musical events, dating largely from the late 19th century. These often give the fullest account of musical events, including dates, times, venues, performers and repertoire. The West Riding Pauper Lunatic Asylum archive in Wakefield, for example, holds dozens of concert posters from the 1860s to the 1880s, demonstrating that musical life encompassed band, choir and solo performers across patients and staff as well as visiting artists (Scrapbook of Entertainments, 1866–1940). Examining the rich collection of concert programmes held at the Crichton Royal Hospital archives allowed me to identify trends in repertoire, including the balance between solo and ensemble pieces and vocal and instrumental ones, as well as the introduction of patient-led concerts and the regular inclusion of Scottish music (C.R.I. Scrapbook, 1838–1938; Recreation and Printing Scrapbook, 1842–1947). Pristine copies are not always the most historically useful; annotations and additions can add important detail, such as the additions to programmes for concerts and dances at Brookwood Asylum in Surrey that record the numbers of patients and staff attending each event (Register of Entertainments, 1889–1896). The Bethlem Hospital archives include several concert programmes with hand-drawn annotations depicting the performers, offering a rare glimpse of the visual experience of audiences (Volume of Programmes, 1879–1899, 15 February 1897).

Accounts in patient magazines

To begin to understand the aural experience of musical activities, I sought out patient and staff accounts of concerts and dances. Several asylums during the19th century supported the production of patient magazines, which were intended as a form of moral therapy to keep patients occupied and give space for self-expression; at times, these were sold to support the institution financially (see Daskalova, 2022). One example is the Bethlem magazine *Under the Dome*, which provides comments on internal and external concerts and dances. A concert of visiting artists in the chapel in 1896 is described with the reflection: 'many members of our congregation described that as one of the happiest Sunday afternoons they had experienced within or without' (Under the Dome, The Quarterly Magazine of Bethlem Royal Hospital, 1892–1930, 31 June 1896). However, in 1899, an author comments: 'Our band this year is not quite so strong in the number of instruments as in former years, but the Transvaal way has to answer a good deal for this' (Under the Dome, The Quarterly Magazine of Bethlem Royal Hospital, 1892–1930, 31 December 1899).

Case notes

Seeking information about how music was received and experienced on a more individual level is more challenging. Patient case notes often form one of the largest sections of asylum archives. These contain information on patients' conditions, diagnoses and presentation on their arrival as well as at regular points during their residence at the institution. Many patient case notes focus exclusively on the medical details needed to assess their progress. On occasion, however, more detail is included on the patient's day-to-day activities and their responses to these. At the Holloway Sanatorium in Surrey, for example, the mental state of patient Stella Marion James is traced through her responses to music. Her improvement is signalled by dancing, singing and playing the piano, but in contrast a relapse is identified by uncontrolled dancing and night-time singing that disturbs the other patients (Case Book A: Females. Certified patients admitted Aug 1885–Dec 1887, 1885–1907, 27 November 1885). Such detail is particularly interesting when the patient was engaged in musical activity themselves. The case notes of Wullie Thompson at the Royal Crichton Institution in Dumfries, for example, trace his activity as violinist with the institution's band and, in particular, describe his virtuosic performances and the ameliorative effect of music (Crichton Royal Institution Case Book vol 1, p 169).

Published accounts of asylum life and ephemera

Beyond the formal institutional archives, there exists a wide range of additional documents, both published and unpublished, which add extra layers to our understanding of the ways music was included and experienced in 19th-century asylums. Many specialist medics published books, pamphlets or collections of lectures that give further detail on their practices and ideas; these often include information about the medics' views on music, its inclusion in management plans and anecdotes about its effect on patients. For example, in his 1838 *Treatise*, Medical Superintendent William Ellis (1780–1839) recommends the provision of music rooms, patient concerts and visiting performers, allowing for interaction between patients and recollection of performances and moral and intellectual pleasures (Ellis, 1838). Published patient accounts are less common, but several give clear information about day-to-day life in the asylum, including examples of music being played in both formal and informal contexts. In one case, John Perceval (1838) narrates the noisy circumstances of his stay in the Ticehurst private asylum, which include singing and piano playing by fellow patients. Asylum archives also include unpublished documents from patients such as poetry, prose, requests for discharge and letters, though these rarely contain concrete information on recreational activities.

Together, these documents begin to fill out some of the silences surrounding music, sound and patient experience in 19th-century asylums. Bringing them together offers the opportunity to construct a narrative that considers the ways in which music was used and experienced, the perspectives on its value and the tensions between music as good or ill, cause or cure.

Remaining silences

Despite the rich archives associated with Victorian asylums, silences remain around the uses of music and the soundworlds of the patients. While we have a good deal of information about formal musical offerings in many cases, there is little evidence regarding the way in which music was experienced and few details of performance style or competence. We have almost no information about the instruments in use, the vocal timbre of singers, their performance abilities, the behaviour of the audiences, the contexts surrounding formal performances or even, in many cases, the spaces in which performances were held. Some performance spaces survive, and photos from the end of the 19th century often show these with sofas, tables, plants and pictures – a far cry from the modern concert-going experience.

There is even less evidence of informal music-making, sound and noise. The accounts we have suggest that asylums were full of music, from pianos on wards and in rooms to uncontrolled noise and singing. As patient notes, accounts and diagnoses suggest, music could be an indication of well-being or of mental distress.

Putting together the information we can glean from documents gives us only a partial account of the experiences of music. But research based on documents also benefits from wider contextualisation. Music – and the rest of asylum life – existed within a specific built and natural environment; asylums were typically placed outside a town, often on a hillside, with access to plenty of fresh air and clean water, but away from the local population. Many asylums were arranged symmetrically, with equal accommodation for men and women at each end and shared areas, such as offices and the dining hall, in the centre. Often, recreation and religious spaces were claimed from these areas on a temporary basis or spaces were shared on a permanent basis – dining halls often had multiple uses – though sometimes new structures were built for these purposes. The provision of music and patients' and staff members' experience of it were closely connected to physical spaces, and where extant, these can give us further indications of the ways in which music was present. In addition, and common to many aspects of music history, we usually lack historical contexts, such as the instruments used, the acoustics of venues once furniture and audiences are taken into account, the bustle of background noise and, perhaps most crucially, the 'historical ear' of listeners past.

Music history and beyond

What might musical documents add to other disciplines? Sound and listening are a key part of history and modern culture. Investigating historical and contemporary phenomena from the perspective of music and sound offers opportunities for capturing different narratives about the contexts in which people work and live as well as the roles and practices of music and sound. Sound studies emerged as a discipline in the late 20th century, and sound and music are increasingly recognised as key elements within interdisciplinary study, appearing in conjunction with disciplines such as literature, geography and environmental studies, psychology and health (Leyshon et al, 1998; Gouk et al, 2018; da Sousa Correa, 2020).

Seeking details about music and sound in archives also introduces new perspectives, broadening the historical narrative and leading the historian to search for a different set of documents, with new questions and aims. For example, examining the data around concert attendance tells us about ways in which patients were segregated into those able to benefit from recreational activities and those kept away; ways in which senior managers were integrated into the regular activities of the institution; and numbers and ratios of patients and attendants. Tracing the performances of visiting artists places the asylum in a broader commercial network of travelling performers, some of whom must have based a considerable proportion of their career on such events. The ability to travel in this way speaks to developments in music business and management as well as in transport and communication.

Plotting musical performances and performers also informs our understanding of the role and relationship of asylum institutions to their nearby towns or cities. At the same time as asylums sought to become self-sufficient communities with their own farms, hospitals and entertainments, they were deeply connected with local urban areas through both commerce and philanthropy. Asylum music was supported by local amateur and professional performers, and in turn, in some cases, asylums offered premises and opportunities to the nearby community. This negotiation of space and relationships, often via musical events, forms a key element in the changing positioning of the asylum throughout the 19th century.

Since the mid-20th century, many historians have sought to investigate history from the 'ground up', examining the lives and experiences of ordinary people in order to rebalance historical priorities and narratives. The implications for research using documents have been immense: previously, formal documents, which are more readily available, were at the heart of histories based around politics, institutions or military campaigns; however, the new approach requires researchers to dig more deeply into the archives in search of new voices, and this often requires additional interpretation and imagination too. Thinking about aural experiences of music and sound as part of this requires even further triangulation of evidence together with imaginary leaps. We can never fully put ourselves in the shoes of those who came before, but by collecting and sifting information from documents and beyond, we can begin to engage closely with those experiences as part of a broader understanding of historical actors and contexts.

Conclusion

My own work is centred on the use of documents to investigate all aspects of musical life, performance and experience, as well as other elements of sound and aurality and their conceptualisation and cultural role. Bringing together information from a range of documents can help to build a rich picture of the ways in which music was performed, listened to and thought about in previous times.

What challenges remain for music studies and the use of documents? The fleeting nature of aurality and the difficulty of capturing aural experience mean that sound and music are frequently absent from both historical and contemporary research. Capturing the experience of music via written documents, together with other sources – such as archival ephemera, instruments, buildings and, for more recent histories, sound recordings – requires careful reading in the fullest sense.

Documents also have great potential for creative engagement with history. Imaginative and artistic responses to the documents of music offer new developments; where written narratives end, the imaginary can help us to empathise with historical experiences and to conceive of a more personal response on the part of the creative artist. It is the very challenges of engaging with music and sound via documents, then, that add to the rich potential of their use for new perspectives and opportunities in our understanding of history, of past experiences and perspectives, and of the human condition.

Key considerations for using this method

- Searching for information about music and sounds in documents requires a multifaceted approach.

- Using a variety of qualitative and quantitative methods, and working with the wide range of documents available, is necessary to build a rounded picture of life and experience, whether in the past or the present day.

- Considering aspects of music and sound can offer valuable new perspectives for other disciplines.

- Thinking creatively about the gaps or 'silences' that exist in the evidence gained from documents is important for developing new questions and approaches.

Note

[1] Throughout the chapter, I make use of historical terms and concepts which are anathema to today's understanding of mental health and its treatment. These terms are retained for historical

accuracy, but are not intended to condone the approaches and ideas which characterised the long-stay institutions of Victorian Britain.

References

Bailey, P. (1996) 'Breaking the sound barrier: a historian listens to noise', *Body and Society*, 2(2): 49–66.

Case Book A: Females. Certified patients admitted Aug 1885-Dec 1887 (1885–1907). Part of Holloway Sanatorium Hospital for the Insane (Wellcome Closed stores WMS 2 Shelfmark: MS 8159). Available from: https://wellcomelibrary.org/item/b19129932

Caswell, M., Cole, H. and Griffith, Z. (2018) 'Images, silences, and the archival record: an interview with Michelle Caswell', *disClosure: A Journal of Social Theory*, 27: 21–7.

Concert Programmes Database (nd). Available from: www.concertprogrammes.org.uk

C.R.I. Scrapbook (1838–1938) Part of Records of Crichton Royal Hospital, Dumfries and Galloway Archives DGH1/6/17/1. Available from: https://wellcomecollection.org/works/qbqnpe4v

Daskalova, M. (2022) *Printing and Periodical Culture in the Nineteenth-Century Asylum*, unpublished PhD thesis, University of Strathclyde.

da Sousa Correa, D. (ed) (2020) *The Edinburgh Companion to Literature and Music* (Edinburgh Companions to Literature and the Humanities), Edinburgh University Press.

Ellis, W. (1838) *A Treatise on the Nature, Symptoms, Causes, and Treatment of Insanity*, Samuel Holdsworth.

Erlmann, V. (2010) *Reason and Resonance: A History of Modern Aurality*, Zone.

Foucault, M. (1967) *Madness and Civilization: A History of Insanity in the Age of Reason* (trans R. Howard), Tavistock.

General Report for the Royal Hospitals of Bridewell and Bethlem, and of the House of Occupations: for the year ending 31st December, 1843 (1844), Part of Bridewell Royal Hospital, Bethlem Royal Hospital Archive BAR-03. Available at: https://wellcomecollection.org/works/xp259a42

Gilliland, A. and Caswell, M. (2016) 'Records and their imaginaries: imagining the impossible, making possible the imagined', *Archival Science*, 16: 53–75.

Gold, D. (2008) 'The accidental archivist: embracing chance and confusion in historical scholarship', in G. Kirsch and L. Rohan (eds) *Beyond the Archives: Research as a Lived Process*, Southern Illinois University Press, pp 13–19.

Golding, R. (2021) *Music and Moral Management in the Nineteenth-Century English Lunatic Asylum*, Palgrave Macmillan.

Gouk, P., Kennaway, J., Prins, J. and Thormahlen, W. (eds) (2018) *The Routledge Companion to Music, Mind, and Well-Being*, Routledge.

Gunn, S. and Faire, L. (eds) (2015) *Research Methods for History*, Routledge.

Hall, P. (2021) 'Giving voice to a foxtrot from Auschwitz-Birkenau', *Music Theory Online*, 27(3). Available from: https://mtosmt.org/issues/mto.21.27.3/mto.21.27.3.hall.pdf

Hardy, D. (2021) 'Using positionality and theory in historical research: a personal journey', *Journal of Cultural Research in Art Education*, 38: 78–94.

Istvandity, L. (2021) 'How does music heritage get lost? Examining cultural heritage loss in community and authorised music archives', *International Journal of Heritage Studies*, 27(4): 331–43.

Johnson, J. (1995) *Listening in Paris: A Cultural History*, University of California Press.

King, M. (2016) 'Working with/in the archives', in S. Gunn and L. Faire (eds) *Research Methods for History*, Routledge, pp 15–30.

Levy, B. and Emmery, L. (2021) 'Archival research in music: new materials, methods, and arguments', *Music Theory Online*, 27(3). Available from: https://mtosmt.org/issues/mto.21.27.3/mto.21.27.3.levyemmery.pdf

Leyshon, A., Matless, D. and Revill, G. (eds) (1998) *The Place of Music*, Routledge.

Perceval, J. (1838) *A Narrative of the Treatment Experienced by a Gentleman, during a State of Mental Derangement; Designed to Explain the Causes and the Nature of Insanity*, Effingham Wilson.

Picker, J.M. (2003) *Victorian Soundscapes*, Oxford University Press.

Porter, R. (1985) 'The patient's view: doing medical history from below', *Theory and Society*, 14(2): 175–98.

Recreation and Printing Scrapbook (1842–1947) Part of Records of Crichton Royal Hospital, Dumfries and Galloway Archives DGH1/6/17/2. Available from: https://wellcomecollection.org/works/vruyy366

Register of Entertainments (1889–1896) Brookwood Asylum archives, Surrey History Centre 3043/1/11/2/2.

Rosenfeld, S. (2011) 'On being heard: a case for paying attention to the historical ear', *American Historical Review*, 116(2): 316–34.

Scrapbook of Entertainments (1866–1940) West Riding Pauper Lunatic Asylum archives, West Yorkshire Archive Service, Wakefield C85/1382.

Scull, A. (1993) *The Most Solitary of Afflictions: Madness and Society in Britain, 1700–1900*, Yale University Press.

Smith, L. (2020) *Private Madhouses in England, 1640–1815: Commercialised Care for the Insane*, Palgrave Macmillan.

Smith, M. (2024) 'Asylum history from the bottom up', *Psychology Today*, 19 May. Available from: www.psychologytoday.com/gb/blog/a-short-history-of-mental-health/202405/asylum-history-from-the-bottom-up

Smith, M.M. (ed) (2004) *Hearing History: A Reader*, University of Georgia Press.

Smith, M.M. (2007) *Sensing the Past: Seeing, Hearing, Smelling, Tasting, and Touching in History*, University of California Press.

Under the Dome, The Quarterly Magazine of Bethlem Royal Hospital (1892–1930) Bethlem Royal Hospital Archive UTD-01 to UTD-09.

Volume of Programmes (1879–1899) Bethlem Royal Hospital Archive BEN-01.

4

Folklore in Asian martial arts: using documents to test the theory of martial creation

George Jennings

Summary

- Martial arts studies is a relatively young field that has its own emerging theories based on different data sources and research designs.

- This chapter tests and expands the theory of martial creation by using documents in the form of introductory books written for and by martial arts practitioners.

- The narrative analysis of three notable case studies in Asian martial arts folklore confirms a working hypothesis that migration and isolation are key contributors to moments of inspiration to create a new martial art system.

- The chapter concludes with a guide to how the method for testing and potentially enhancing theories can be used in other fields.

Introduction

Each academic field has its unique theories built off the back of empirical research using a variety of research designs and data sources. This chapter outlines, tests and expands a specific theory in the nascent field of martial arts studies: the theory of martial creation (Jennings, 2019). Moreover, this contribution presents three exemplars of a widespread creation myth concerned with pragmatic issues of combat, pedagogy and personal survival during a time of social and political upheaval: the wandering monk Bodhidharma (also known as Damo), who was the inventor of Shaolin Kung Fu; the Daoist sage Zhang Sanfeng, who was the founder of Taijiquan; and the Shaolin nun Ng Mui and her protégé Yim Wing Chun, who were the matriarchs of Wing Chun. Taking an initial sample from my personal collection of martial arts books intended for beginners and practitioners of specific and various styles, I expand my analysis to a wider set of such texts by a broad set of authors from different martial arts lineages, schools and countries. After reading into sufficiently detailed (and peopled) foundation myths, I demonstrate how the theory of martial creation can be used not just for its original purpose of understanding the inspiration and actions of more contemporary and verifiable real-life founders, but also to understand mythic figures. This analysis is accompanied by a consideration of how researchers working in other fields might use this method to test a theory using documents as data.

Asian martial arts are rich in folklore, from tales of supernatural power in unusual bodily regions to the daring deeds of undefeated feudal swordsmen (Lewis, 1998; Roe, 2023). Martial folklore also contains treasured tales of how many of those seemingly ancient fighting systems were founded by specific individuals. Anthropologist Thomas A. Green (2003) notes commonalities in the inspiration for the creation of specific martial arts, including the founders observing animals locked in combat, which are indicative of the Chinese respect for the order of the cosmos.

Historians have taken a critical view on martial arts foundation myths as more recent creations reflective of new, nationalistic styles created out of rudimentary schools (Lorge, 2016). Sixt Weztler (2014) categorises foundation myths, considering them from the perspective of religious studies, while cultural theorist Paul Bowman (2016) points to the potential of these stories to illuminate the beliefs and wishes of modern martial artists buying into their narratives, such as notions of a slight, female progenitor. Faith in these stories is certainly an important factor in the power of their core narrative, which has characters overcoming seemingly insurmountable obstacles. Belief in these stories might be due to key components of the narrative structure – such as mobility (travel) and isolation (for reflection) – that make them plausible to modern-day audiences.

The studies mentioned were carried out in fields such as cultural studies and history, where methods are not routinely delved into (and are sometimes not referred to at all), with authors offering some insightful ideas through original, gripping essays. My background in the sociology of sport requires a more explicit position on methods. With such a readership in mind, this chapter aims to add to methodological knowledge on how we might study textual data on martial arts mythology. It also extends and applies the theory of martial creation (Jennings, 2019), a thesis on how and why a person might create a new martial art system under specific social, political and economic circumstances. The original theory was based on three case studies of martial arts developed in the 20th century, albeit in different contexts (Victorian and Edwardian Britain, 1960s California and 1990s Mexico).

This chapter, in contrast, delves into one specific culture (China) across time periods. Popular texts (such as Lewis, 1998) and encyclopaedias (such as Crudelli, 2008) as well as a more recent contribution from Roe (2023) illustrate the rich collection of folklore on the Chinese martial arts within wider Asian traditions. Moreover, Chinese foundation myths are prevalent in many systems and in practitioner-oriented books. In my practice of the systems and through my ethnographies on them since 1998, I have often witnessed practitioners buying and borrowing books containing details of these myths – which are often found within introductory chapters. Such books are typically hybrid in content, mixing historical, philosophical and technical material, which frequently adds to their appeal among beginners and experienced learners alike.

Theoretical framework

The theory of martial creation (Jennings, 2019) is based on six core assumptions united by a concern for the personal and the social. The biographies of founders are considered in terms of their wider social history, following Mills' (1959) notion of the sociological imagination. This is coupled with the merging of habit, crisis and creativity, taken from Shilling's (2008) re-reading of pragmatism vis-à-vis embodiment. The habits of the practitioners are interrupted by an intersection of personal troubles and social issues, resulting eventually in creative moments in which a martial art (or combination of styles) is modified to suit the new personal (internal) and social (external) reality.

The six stages deemed necessary for such martial creation are as follows:

1. Founders must have a background as *practitioners* in one or more martial art(s).
2. They must achieve a level of *competence, confidence* and *charisma* in order to gather a following.
3. Yet, they will *not* be the top students, official gatekeepers, or lineage holders of their original system.
4. They must identify a *problem* or face a personal, political or social *crisis* that aggrieves them.
5. They will then devise a *solution* through a revised fighting, human development and training system.
6. Their passing (whether expected or unexpected) can create added *chaos*, thus fuelling the cycle of *creativity* among future generations of practitioners. (Jennings, 2019, p 65, emphasis in original)

The theory of martial creation was based on three real-life 20th-century founders: Edward Barton-Wright (Bartitsu), Bruce Lee (Jeet Kune Do) and Marisela Ugalde (Xilam). My analysis in 2019 drew on my ethnography of Xilam, which included a life history of its living founder, Marisela Ugalde, alongside wider academic research on the other two martial arts. However, Bruce Lee remained my main case study, and my article (Jennings, 2019) was part of a special issue on his martial arts legacies.

Hitherto, the theory has been scrutinised and applied to a hybrid Italian yoga style by Di Placido (2020). He added elements of the work of Bourdieu and Foucault to enrich the theory. Perhaps the theory of martial creation could be critiqued on the grounds of the different sources of data and existing knowledge on the three arts of Bartitsu, Jeet Kune Do and Xilam, with the examples of

Bartitsu and Xilam and their less documented creators contrasting with the better-known Jeet Kune Do. Another criticism could be that the three arts stem from different cultures.

Although the theory of martial creation was originally envisaged as applying to genuine historical and contemporary figures, Sara Delamont suggests it 'could also be applied to the mythical founders of martial arts systems' (personal communication, 10 November 2020). After musing on the model with the famous mystical creators of older martial arts in mind, I pondered on adding mobility and isolation to the theory. In this sphere, the stories of supposed founders Bodhidharma, Ng Mui and Zhang Sanfeng portray them as having been forced to migrate across China and eventually seeking refuge and settling in remote areas where they were able to reflect, draw on natural forms of inspiration (animals fighting) and create new martial art systems for personal and sociopolitical reasons. They used their prior martial arts knowledge as well as new insights to tackle recently imagined issues (such as Shaolin monks falling asleep during meditation or a young woman needing to learn an effective self-defence system within a year).

In the next section, I break down my methods in a step-by-step fashion.

Methods

Paradigms and positionality

I hail from a sport and exercise sciences background, which tends to follow a positivist approach to knowledge production. I later specialised in interpretivist social science, which often explores alternative individual and cultural realities (relativist ontology) that are shaped as knowledge in different societies (social constructivist epistemology). In recent years, I have been attracted to the pragmatist paradigm (as in Shook, 2023), which influenced Shilling's (2008) writings, which in turn stimulated my writing on the theory of martial creation. It is important to acknowledge these indirect academic influences and lineages of thought, just as it is important to study the family trees of martial arts schools, which contain knowledge that is transmitted and built across generations. Like Markula and Silk (2011), I see paradigms as linked to the initial purposes of research rather than as fixed world-views.

Research question and hypothesis

After reviewing the academic literature for previous research and scholarship on martial arts invention and founders, I posed the question: How can the theory of martial creation be used for examining the stories behind the mythical Asian founders? Later, I refined this to focus on the Chinese martial arts styles. As an interpretivist qualitative researcher, I do not normally develop hypotheses, so I conducted periods of reflection, imagining the stories I had heard and read. All of the stories seemed to involve some kind of travelling hero or heroine who was forced to relocate (the element of *migration*) and seek refuge in solitude (the element of *isolation*) where they could contemplate a modified form of combat. This is akin to the notion of the knight-errant, key to the depiction of Chinese philosophies on screen (Teo, 2021).

Based on these reflections, my expanded theory of martial creation comprises eight steps; the two new elements are reflected in steps 5 and 6:

1. Founders must have a background as *practitioners* in one or more martial art(s).
2. They must achieve a level of *competence*, *confidence* and *charisma* in order to gather a following.
3. Yet, they will *not* be the top students, official gatekeepers or lineage holders of their original system.
4. They must identify a *problem* or face a personal, political or social *crisis* that aggrieves them.
5. This problem will cause them to *move away* from the source of their original martial training and community.
6. Within a more peaceful, *secluded* environment, the martial artist will be inspired by their immediate social and natural surroundings.
7. They will then devise a *solution* through a revised fighting, human development and training system.
8. Their passing (whether expected or unexpected) can create added *chaos*, thus fuelling the cycle of *creativity* among future generations of practitioners.

Sampling and sources

From my ethnographic projects (from 2004 onward), I have found that many long-term martial artists, over the years, proudly curate their own personal libraries of books on this subject, often lending texts to trusted classmates or giving them away during times of transition, such as when moving home. (Incidentally, as I was writing this chapter, one of my Taijiquan classmates shared photos of his old books on our school's WhatsApp group, offering them for free to anyone in the group.) The sample of texts analysed for this study represents a range of such books – non-academic publications written primarily by influential martial artists (as opposed to qualified historians). These include rare finds only available within a specific Wing Chun lineage (Fong, 1982), more commercially established texts on Wing Chun (Tse and Ip, 1998; Gee, Meng and Loewenhagen, 2004); a generic book on martial arts (Goodman, 2000), a coffee table encyclopaedia on global fighting systems (Crudelli, 2008), a second-hand book on Wing Chun passed on by my Taijiquan teacher (Kernsprecht, 1997) and books on Taijiquan that I bought when I first started to learn the art in my twenties (Wong, 1996; Frantzis, 2003). While most of these books were already in my possession, I extended the sample with two more purchases: one older book on martial arts myths and legends (Lewis, 1998), which I had previously borrowed from one of my Wing Chun seniors; and a more recent book that I came across in a commercial bookstore (Roe, 2023). The sample is, therefore, representative of the kinds of texts I have bought, borrowed and perused since beginning in the martial arts as a teenager in the late 1990s. The more recent books appear to be more critical of the myths.

The number three has an attractive and memorable rhythm, used commonly to structure sentences (Moran, 2018), and I have followed a tripartite structure (see Jennings, 2019) of assessing three distinct yet related case studies: Bodhidharma, the patriarch of Shaolin Kung Fu; Zhang Sanfeng, the alleged inventor of Taijiquan; and Ng Mui and Yim Wing Chun, the female co-founders of Wing Chun Kung Fu. These cases are united by their supposed roots going back to the legendary Shaolin Temple. The trio are also well-known through stories available in a wide variety of commercial written and audio-visual sources, although I have deliberately avoided analysing films, documentaries and media such as comics in order to focus on martial arts books, a specific kind of document circulated within martial arts pedagogies, which is academically overlooked.

Data handling

The martial arts books were kept at my home along with other research items (unlike teaching materials, which I store at my university office). This minimised the need to carry the texts around, in which case they could have been damaged. I handled the books carefully and avoided annotating them directly (wishing to preserve their long-standing quality and value). Many of the texts were heavy, even somewhat cumbersome, illustrated editions that require care and attention, and some of them were out of print. Some were signed by a renowned author, meaning they were valuable. Therefore, I kept them in a safe place and avoided eating and drinking while working with them.

First, I searched for any entries on the foundation myths. Many of the books did not have an index, so I scoured the content cover to cover to look for relevant sections. Pages with relevant material were flagged using small sticky notes, making it easy for me to reopen the page when required. I selected my long dining table as the area where I opened the books and transcribed text on my laptop. Handedness is especially apparent in martial arts practice (Jennings, 2022). As a left-hander, I kept the books on my left side, turning to the text and then returning to my computer ahead of me. This required intense concentration, so while I normally try to work standing up, in this case I decided to sit so that I could give all my attention to the transcription and analysis. I transcribed key extracts related to the stories in a Word document and checked for accuracy. At this stage, each source was kept separate.

Analysis

Initial reading and data sorting drove the first stage of analysis. After dwelling on the highlights I had identified from each document, I copied quotes from their original position within my transcripts to combine similar extracts in three new documents, one for each case study. I considered the data as storied data, as in conventional narrative research where the spoken word is transcribed, and I looked for patterns in plot, structure, characters and action (Smith and Sparkes, 2009). I noted such patterns in a separate research journal, where I could also draw theoretical diagrams by hand. After scanning the data and spotting details on migration and isolation, I highlighted the relevant passages in bold, which helped with later identification.

There is little doubt that the storied data on martial arts founders offers us glimpses into narrative. Narrative inquiry is concerned with the collection, analysis and representation of storied data. It is normally underpinned by the interpretivist paradigm, which acknowledges different ways of perceiving the world (relativist ontology), and an interrelated form of knowledge driven by the social milieu of the storyteller and analysis (social constructivist epistemology; Smith, 2016). Accordingly, as the person collecting, analysing and editing stories informed by theoretical ideas, I was crucial to the knowledge production. The interpretivist paradigm considers physical things such as forces applied to the body via techniques as being real, while social constructs such as myths of the martial arts are considered as personal interpretations redeveloped with each telling, read or listen. Indeed, Jones (2004) reminds us that authors of martial arts books are actively involved in interpretation and retelling through their imagination.

I broke the three documents on Shaolin Kung Fu, Taijiquan and Wing Chun down into components: (1) the sociopolitical context; (2) the supposed founder's biography; (3) the crisis point that they faced; (4) the moment of inspiration; and (5) the creative development and spread of the martial art. These points of focus were based on the first five elements of the original theory of martial creation. This analysis was abductive, enabling me to test the theory of martial creation while extending it with two new elements: the mobilities of the founders in the guise of their travels and their periods of relative isolation. This created an eight-stage theoretical model. I argue that the added elements provide readers with a sense of belief in the story, and this led me to consider the notion of plausibility structures (see Berger, 1990).

Ethical considerations

Islas Contreras and Jennings (2023) note that many of the scholar-practitioners investigating the Brazilian martial art Capoeira are of White European origin, and this is also the case with Asian styles. It is important to acknowledge my position as a White British scholar relatively removed from Chinese culture and language.

Although the veracity of the foundation myths is debatable, I regard these stories as forms of intangible cultural heritage that are worthy of care and respect, despite their potentially fictional and politically motivated nature. As a social scientist with limited historical and linguistic training, I strive to be cautious and sensitive to Chinese cultural norms and their potential connection to alternative world-views,

Eastern philosophies and religions. My intention is not to discredit the quality of non-academic martial arts writers' storytelling, or their scholarly credentials, but to present the key elements of their narratives through the model of the theory of martial creation. This is to avoid taking a gatekeeper perspective on the 'truth' behind a given narrative, martial creation or biography – a position that comes with issues of power. Finally, I strive to avoid editing the names of the historical figures, places and arts, opting instead to display their original rendering in the authors' own manners. The presentation of Chinese terms therefore varies in the analysis of the three examples from Chinese martial arts in the following section.

Analysis

The personal and the social

The three foundation myths all contain details on the personal biographies of the founders alongside the challenging social times they lived in, as outlined in Table 4.1.

Migration and isolation as fuel for inspiration

Although the stories vary – and the accounts of each story differ in terms of length and the actual dates and details – they all tend to mention moments of forced travel from the founders' original homelands or martial arts communities, leading to secluded areas in which the founders were inspired during a period of relative isolation away from peers. Table 4.2 provides details from each of the three stories.

Table 4.1: The personal and social dimensions of the founders' lives

	Bodhidharma	Zhang Sanfeng	Ng Mui and Yim Wing Chun
Personal	Bodhidharma had schooling in various martial arts in India as well as the Buddhist scripture and meditation.	Zhang Sanfeng had trained in martial arts and Daoist healing practices since childhood due to poor health. He experienced a personal crisis in terms of his contribution to humanity and his spiritual knowledge.	Shaolin nun Ng Mui was skilled in Shaolin martial arts and healing practices. Yim Wing Chun was a slightly built teenage girl who was being harassed by a local bandit, Leung. She had no fighting skills.
Social	The Shaolin Temple was prone to attacks from bandits, so the monks needed a form of self-defence and physical development.	Little is known about Zhang Sanfeng's social and political origins. He is often depicted as a wandering sage without any kinship ties or dynastical duties.	The Southern Shaolin Temple had been ransacked, leading Ng Mui to flee. Violence against women and poor law enforcement led to females learning to fight.

Applying this method in other fields

To use this method in other disciplines, the researcher (or researchers) first needs to identify an established theory of interest to them. This theory would ordinarily not be originally conceived from a documents-based research project, meaning the use of documents as data offers a fresh source of information. In other words, theories created from research designs such as ethnography, life history, action research and questionnaire surveys are examined through a different set of ingredients. The theory is used as a template to analyse the dataset in question, which may vary from books to magazine and newspaper articles – as seen in the diverse datasets examined elsewhere in this edited collection. For the sake of consistency, a specific type of document should be selected. This of course depends on the complexity and scope of the study. A full PhD thesis might have a chapter dedicated to the analysis of pamphlets, another chapter on syllabi, and a further chapter on technical literature. The method described here is based on a small, discrete study stemming from a previous theoretical article. Such a congruent sample would allow for the collection of data from similar contexts in order to focus on key characteristics of such a cultural setting. The aim is to make sense of the data through the established theory, but these need to be relevant to one another – the establishment of a sensible fit between the theory and the sample is a priority for the researcher.

After the relationship between the theory and textual data is confirmed, the scholar turns to wider reading on the topic that could lead them to think outside the confines of the selected theoretical framework. For example, might there be elements missing from the theory that could help unpack the complexity of the cases presented in the data? Coinciding with this reading, the researchers draw on their prior experience, knowledge and understanding, which may also contribute to a form of working hypothesis or addition to the theory. These ideas could be mapped or charted using physical and digital tools so that the theory can be visualised in a fresh manner.

The next steps involve collecting and becoming immersed in the fresh dataset. The documents are read and re-read in full, and the elements of the documents are identified. When reading, comfort and correct posture should be considered, as the health of the researcher is paramount. The most relevant parts of the documents are transcribed or copied in full in word-processing documents, using separate files for each source, and this is checked for any typos or other errors. Handedness should be taken into account as the researcher switches from manual reading to typing across one or more screens. Spacing and layout of the transcripts should be considered to ensure these are easy to read. The researcher also begins to identify crucial parts of the textual data and select any key case studies and examples. These key elements of stories are ordered according to the structure of the narrative, mixing quotes and extracts from different sources as appropriate. The researcher can add notes and memos against certain extracts. Over time, tables can be used to represent elements of the theory or narrative, such as key characters, elements of the plot and messages from the story. The individual cases are then analysed on

Table 4.2: Migration, isolation and inspiration of the founders

	Bodhidharma	Zhang Sanfeng	Ng Mui
Migration	Bodhidharma was from India (or Persia) and migrated to the Chinese court. Having been refused by the Emperor, Bodhidharma sought refuge in the Shaolin Temple.	Zhang Sanfeng wandered from the Shaolin Temple to Wudang Mountain.	Shaolin nun Ng Mui was forced to flee the Southern Shaolin Temple due to it being attacked and burned down.
Isolation	After being rejected by the temple as well, Bodhidharma entered a state of deep meditation in a cave.	Zhang walked aimlessly, feeling sad about not making any real contribution to humanity.	She fled to an isolated mountainous region, where she was able to help people in the local community.
Inspiration	Bodhidharma witnessed the fatigue of monks, who were falling asleep during extended periods of meditation and scripture recital, and he knew that martial arts could help them have a better balance between study and physical practice.	He spotted animals in combat and had an epiphany to create a soft, yielding art reflective of the Dao (the proper Way).	Ng Mui witnessed a snake and a crane locked in combat. After encountering Yim Wing Chun, who was being harassed, Ng Mui devised a simplified form of Kung Fu that could be learned quickly.

their own before making direct comparison between them. Then, the theory and its potential additions or revisions can be tested against the dataset.

When writing about the theory testing, depending on the space available in the research output – as in a book chapter or a journal article, which are limited in terms of space, or a monograph, which may have room for one case per chapter – the researcher might opt to present one, two, three or more case studies. The quotations from the original documents should retain the authors' style, though notes, sensitivity warnings or corrections may be required. The researcher should practise reflexivity and be open about their power and position in being able to collect, edit and comment on a set of documents written by others who may have less privileged positions or hail from different time periods and cultures, so as not to fall into the traps of presentism, colonialist academic attitudes and cultural appropriation.

Conclusion

Asian martial arts possess an array of rich stories, including foundation myths about how and why fighting systems were created. Among the Asian cultures, the Chinese martial arts stand as a notable case of powerful folklore worthy of continued analysis. Meanwhile, although martial arts studies is now a flourishing field with many empirical exemplars, there is a gap in knowledge in terms of how scholar-practitioners can go about their research using systematic methods. Just as those involved in martial arts studies need to know about theories, definitions, taxonomies and so on in, it is important that they discuss methods. In this chapter, I selected my theory on how and why a martial art is founded (the theory of martial creation) and tested it using documents-based data. I expanded the original six-point theory with two important elements central to the process of creation: the migration and isolation of the supposed founding figure. These elements are common in many important cultural stories, such as religious tales showing moments of divine inspiration. This may be a key reason why some practitioners find foundation myths believable, as these elements might establish the plausibility of foundation myths – why their structure, characters and plot all seem quite reasonable to us.

This chapter is intended for social scientists and those working in the humanities who wish to be more explicit in terms of reporting and reflecting on their methods when using documents in research. It offers a methodological blueprint for how one might go about using documents for research on martial arts. It provides an example of how to test and expand a theory using a structured method. Readers may want to trial the 12-step method outlined next in their own disciplines, fields and vocations.

Key considerations for using this method

Step 1: Identify a theory of interest.

Step 2: Consider how the theory might be applied to textual data.

Step 3: Read relevant literature on the topic.

Step 4: Develop initial ideas from your prior experience.

Step 5: Use tools for mapping your ideas.

Step 6: If relevant, handle documents/other sources to find a representative set of sources across time periods, country of origin, and so on.

Step 7: Handle the documents in a suitable space that fits with your mode of embodiment.

Step 8: Transcribe all the relevant text from each source. Do not be concerned with repeated details or varied reporting.

Step 9: Combine sources to create distinct cases. Analyse each case separately using a clear and consistent technique.

Step 10: Compare the cases, again using a clear and consistent technique. Tables can be used to identify areas of congruence.

Step 11: Represent data in their original form.

Step 12: Treat the data in a dignified fashion, especially if they pertain to cultures different from you as the story analysis and story (re)teller.

References

Berger, P.L. (1990) *The Sacred Canopy: Elements of a Sociological Theory of Religion*, Knopf.

Bowman, P. (2016) 'Making martial arts history matter', *International Journal of the History of Sport*, 33(9): 915–33.

Contreras Islas, D. and Jennings, G. (2023) 'A typology of martial art scholar-practitioners: types, transitions, and tensions in Capoeira', *Societies*, 13(10): art 214. doi: 10.18452/27543

Crudelli, C. (2008) *The Way of the Warrior: Martial Arts and Fighting Skills from around the World*, Dorling Kindersley.

Di Placido, M. (2020) 'Blending martial arts and yoga for health: from the Last Samurai to the first Odaka Yoga warrior', *Frontiers in Sociology*, 5: art 597845. doi: 10.3389/fsoc.2020.597845

Fong, A. (1982) *Fong's Wing Chun* (Vol 1), Fong's Wing Chun Federation Headquarters.

Frantzis, B. (2003) *The Big Book of Tai Chi*, Thorsons.

Gee, G., Meng, B. and Loewenhagen, R. (2004) *Mastering Kung Fu: Featuring Shaolin Wing Chun*, Human Kinetics.

Goodman, F. (2000) *Practical Handbook: Kung Fu*, Dorling Kindersley.

Green, T.A. (2003) 'Sense in nonsense: the role of folk history in the martial arts', in T.A. Green and J. Svinth (eds) *Martial Arts in the Modern World*, Praeger, pp 1–12.

Jennings, G. (2019) 'Bruce Lee and the invention of Jeet Kune Do: the theory of martial creation', *Martial Arts Studies*, 8: 60–72.

Jennings, G. (2022) '"Filthy lefties!": The humorous stigmatization of left-handers in historical European martial arts', *STAPS*, 136(2): 17–36.

Jones, S. (2004) *The Intelligent Warrior: Command Personal Power with Martial Arts Strategies*, Thorsons.

Kernsprecht, K. (1997) *On Single Combat* (2nd edn), Wu Shu Verlag Kenrsprecht.

Lewis, P. (1998) *Myths and Legends of the Martial Arts*, Prion.

Lorge, P. (2016) 'Practising martial arts versus studying martial arts', *International Journal of the History of Sport*, 33(9): 904–14.

Markula, P. and Silk, M. (2011) *Qualitative Research for Physical Culture*, Palgrave Macmillan.

Mills, C.-W. (1959) *The Sociological Imagination*, Oxford University Press.

Moran, J. (2018) *First You Write a Sentence: The Elements of Reading, Writing…and Life*, Penguin.

Roe, A.J. (2023) *Legendary Masters of the Martial Arts: Unraveling Fact from Fiction*, YMAA.

Shilling, C. (2008) *Changing Bodies: Habit, Crisis, Creativity*, SAGE.

Shook, J. (2023) *Pragmatism*, The MIT Press.

Smith, B. (2016) 'Narrative analysis in sport and exercise: how can it be done?', in B. Smith and A.C. Sparkes (eds) *Routledge Handbook of Qualitative Research in Sport and Exercise*, Routledge, pp 260–73.

Smith, B. and Sparkes, A.C. (2009) 'Narrative inquiry in sport and exercise psychology: what can it mean, and why might we do it?', *Psychology of Sport and Exercise*, 10(1): 1–11.

Teo, S. (2021) *Chinese Martial Arts Film and the Philosophy of Action*, Routledge.

Tse, M. and Ip, C. (1998) *Wing Chun: Traditional Chinese Kung Fu for Self-Defence and Health*, Piatkus.

Weztler, S. (2014) 'Myths of the martial arts', *JOMEC Journal*, 5: 1–12.

Wong, K.-K. (1996) *The Complete Book of Tai Chi Chuan*, Vermillion.

PART II

Exploring the machinery of governance

5

Using government inquiry documents in research to raise voices suppressed by non-disclosure agreements

Victoria Pagan

Summary

- This chapter describes qualitative research using abductive analysis of naturally occurring, publicly available government inquiry documents.

- The research was inspired by high-profile cases in the media covering workplace abuses perpetrated by powerful people, which were hidden by legal mechanisms that are colloquially referred to as non-disclosure agreements.

- I explain my ontological and epistemological position as a critical management researcher before describing the documents and my analysis.

- This approach can help to reveal secrets and stories that may have been deliberately hidden and marginalised.

Introduction

When bad things happen to us in our workplaces, the incidents may be hidden through silencing practices. But sometimes there are glimpses of careful resistance through crafted accounts documented in the public domain, and these can reveal secrets. This chapter is an account of the qualitative research I have been undertaking using abductive analysis of documentary material submitted as evidence to the UK parliamentary inquiry into the use of non-disclosure agreements (NDAs) in discrimination cases (Women and Equalities Committee, 2019). The chapter is structured as follows: First, I offer some context about me as a researcher and the development of this research project. Then, I outline a case study of how the research was done, why it was done and the ethical considerations. I then discuss applicability to other research topics and contexts, and conclude with a summary of key points.

Research process

Researcher positionality, ontology and epistemology

Before I get into the substance of the research in this chapter, it is perhaps helpful to situate myself as an author and researcher. My ontological position is aligned with constructionism, as I believe that reality is never singular or static, but in a state of perpetual manufacture by all participating social actors. The researcher is a key part of this. As Cunliffe (2003, p 993) writes: 'researchers actively constitute reality as they study it'. As such, I do not believe there is any objective social reality external to me that I can study. Rather, I believe there are social situations and interactions where I am not present but with which I am familiar in my own world (Pina-Cabral, 2014) and that these can be explored by engaging with the talk and texts of those who are or were present. Ontologically, I am within the social world: 'social realities and ourselves are intimately interwoven as each shapes and is shaped by the other in everyday interactions' (Cunliffe, 2008, p 124). I am not positioned outside looking into social worlds; I am part of them and they are part of me. Therefore, my work is influenced by my becoming (Cunliffe, 2004; Pagan, 2019) – that is, my choices and decisions in relation to research areas, topics and materials are not made in a vacuum, nor are they static. They are influenced temporally and socially by where I have been, what I have done, where I am now, where I may go and my interactions with others. Specifically, at present, I work in a UK business school within a subject area that involves teaching and research on management and organisations, leadership and work from a critical perspective (see, for example, Pullen et al, 2017). I had a commercial career in economic development consultancy before my academic career, and the two dovetail, with the lingering influence of my earlier career experiences from a range of workplace settings carrying through to my academic research.

Epistemologically, therefore, I follow more subjectivist approaches to understanding the creation of social reality, with knowledge from within, through research that is embedded within social contexts. My work is also characterised by reflexivity, emerging from an initial definition by Pollner (1991, p 370) as an 'unsettling'. This denotes insecurity regarding the basic assumptions, discourse and practices used in describing reality, adopting Cunliffe's understanding that the researcher accounts for their own interference in the context that 'we are inventors not representers of realities' (2003, p 988; see also Cunliffe, 2002; 2004). The researched, researcher access and research agendas are interrelated, and there is no singular point of control; methods and accounts are multiple (Hibbert et al, 2014). I take account of my theoretical and substantive interests, emotional investment and experiences throughout the entire research process (Dickson-Swift et al, 2009; Candiotto, 2019). In relation to the research explored in this chapter, my gender and work lives are examples of interests and experiences that both unsettle and are unsettled through the research process.

Researching management and organisation from a critical perspective – specifically in those streams of studies related to ethics, responsibility and social justice – frequently includes engaging with unethical and unjust management, leadership and organisational practices across a range of settings. These practices are often reported to be knowingly undertaken by organisational actors in extremely powerful roles, with practices including lies, physical and/or emotional violations, exploitation and abuse of position, all of which result in myriad harms (Pagan, 2022). It is certainly possible to undertake primary research on such topics – through ethnographic methods, for example (Ybema et al, 2009). But where access is more difficult to negotiate, using documents can be another way to gain insights.

As Coffey (2014, p 367) writes, 'most qualitative research takes place in settings that are "documented" in various ways'. The documents include organisational and state records, notes, memos, emails, diaries, letters, maps, photos, newspaper and media reports, advertising materials, websites and social media (Coffey, 2014). These materials can be considered forms of naturally occurring data (Potter, 2002), as the researcher plays no direct part in their production and the original purpose of the material is not to provide data for research. Prior (2008, p 821) proposes understanding documents as 'active agents', and they can be used in research to understand their creation, development and use in terms of their content holding knowledge/information (Rapley and Rees, 2018). In my research, documents both represent and describe actions, interactions and conversations that have taken place without my direction as a researcher (Corti, 2018).

Theoretical context and empirical setting

The theoretical area I write about in this chapter is situated within the literatures on epistemic injustice and silencing. Fricker has created a foundational framework, theorising epistemic injustice as 'distributive unfairness in respect of epistemic goods such as information or education' (2007, p 1), which results in individuals being harmed as knowers. Epistemic injustice may be executed through practices of silencing (Kinouani, 2020), which can include 'when an audience fails to identify a speaker as a knower' and 'the truncating of one's own testimony in order to ensure that the testimony contains only content for which one's audience demonstrates testimonial competence' (Dotson, 2011, pp 242, 244). Thapar-Björkert et al also analyse the reproduction of injustices through the everyday, 'removing the victim's agency and voice' (2016, p 144). Gayatri Chakravorty Spivak (1988) first emphasises the severity of epistemic injustice by defining 'epistemic violence', specifically in relation to coloniality and imperialism that not only silences but obliterates any value of others. Those who are othered by intersections of race (for example, Liu, 2022; Muzanenhamo, 2022), by gender (for example, Thapar-Björkert et al, 2016), by neurodiversity (for example, Catala et al, 2021) and by sexuality (for example, Halliwell, 2019) will find it harder to evidence epistemic injustice than those with more privilege. In this respect, epistemic injustice and violence can be related to decolonial concepts such as epistemicide (for example, Santamaria, 2023) and epistemic destitution (for example, Mignolo and Walsh, 2018).

When I began this research, there were some high-profile cases in the media related to abuses perpetrated by powerful people in a range of organisational settings that had been hidden, suppressed or silenced by legal mechanisms. These included actions of named individuals, such as Harvey Weinstein (Garrahan, 2017; Keltner, 2017) and Philip Green (Gardner, 2019; Syal, 2019), as well as hidden behaviours in academia (Croxford, 2019; Stokel-Walker, 2019). People in power were finding ways to silence victims of misconduct, including sexual harassment, in their workplaces. NDAs are part of this. Such agreements are documents, and I was interested to explore the relationship between these silencing practices and injustice – for example, their taking away the ability of the victim to speak about their experiences (Thapar-Björkert et al, 2016) and their use of sexist prejudice, affecting the credibility of victims (Fricker, 2007).

Confidentiality on the part of both employer and employees in relation to their work and organisation is implied in standard employment contracts (Chartered Institute of Personnel and Development, 2021), but when employment relationships are ending, additional written agreements may be made between organisational actors. These might include specific wording for the protection of commercially and/or reputationally sensitive information through contractually preventing its sharing and distribution (The Law Society, 2019). This use of NDAs can be interpreted as legitimate (Acas, 2013); however, there are instances where potentially illegitimate use has become more apparent, specifically where there have been experiences of misconduct on the grounds of sex, race, disability and other protected characteristics (for example, Addley and Sabbagh, 2018). NDAs in these instances may focus on knowledge of an experience involving at least two organisational actors where the effects of the experience are unequal, with a promise made in writing not to share this knowledge, which is framed as legally binding and having detrimental consequences for any breach. While it is recognised that both women and men are implicated in the signing of NDAs in relation to workplace misconduct, research undertaken by Speak Out Revolution (2023) showed that 79 per cent of experiences of misconduct are reported by women. In these reports, 62 per cent of perpetrators of workplace harassment are men, and 26 per cent of the reported experiences include the signing of NDAs. Research in a range of workplace contexts continues to find that women are subject to certain forms of workplace misconduct more often than men – these forms of misconduct include verbal abuse and humiliating behaviour (Eurofound, 2017; Brown et al, 2021), incivility (Braddy et al, 2020; Smith et al, 2021) and sexual harassment (Trades Union Congress, 2016; Equality and Human Rights Commission, 2018; Raj et al, 2020).

The empirical context for this work is the UK parliamentary inquiry into the use of NDAs in discrimination cases (Women and Equalities Committee, 2019). This inquiry was selected because it represents a coherent piece of work in the public domain exploring issues that would ordinarily be difficult to access in live organisations. In more standard organisational research, managers would not want to reveal any wrongdoing within their organisation, and indeed they may be legally prevented from revealing this even if they wanted to. Similarly, employees, even if not subject to NDAs, could be reluctant to share any knowledge of events within their organisations because of the confidentiality implied in their employment contracts.

Using documents to help foreground suppressed stories

Generating the documents: the inquiry

In the UK, elements of government activity are considered through a set of parliamentary committees. These include policy review, legislative processes, operational practices and spending (UK Parliament, nd). A particular type of parliamentary committee, the House select committee, comprises elected Members of Parliament, who serve in the House of Commons, to investigate particularly prominent policy issues. The Women and Equalities Committee is one such committee. The Women and Equalities Committee began an inquiry into the use of NDAs in discrimination cases in November 2018 (Women and Equalities Committee, 2018a). This built on a range of prior work examining sexual harassment, including a specific inquiry focusing on sexual harassment in the workplace, through which it was found that NDAs were being potentially misused to cover up episodes of misconduct (Women and Equalities Committee, 2018b). The subsequent inquiry, which is the focus of the research reported here, aimed to examine the use of NDAs across all cases of harassment and discrimination, including on the basis of sex and other protected characteristics such as race, disability, and pregnancy and maternity. The Women and Equalities Committee invited the submission of evidence guided by questions on the use of NDAs, harassment, discrimination, access to legal advice and potential safeguards. The last evidence was published in June 2019.

The documents

Anybody can submit written evidence to public inquiries. In this case, evidence was submitted through a form on the inquiry website, which was open from 13 November 2018 to 31 January 2019. Sixty-eight pieces of written evidence were collected from members of the public, academics, representatives of legal organisations, of private sector organisations and of public sector organisations, and representatives of trades unions and other employee support organisations. There were ten oral evidence sessions, at which witnesses gave their evidence in person in response to questions from the members of the committee. These sessions were transcribed, allowing them to be used as documentary evidence. The final set of documents comprises eight pieces of correspondence between the committee and other government departments, regulatory bodies and selected individuals as part of their request for information. All these documents are publicly available from the UK Parliament website (see Women and Equalities Committee, nd).

The NDA documents themselves were not available during the research. There are restrictions on who can view them, based on what has been negotiated between the signatories. There are other sets of documents available that I did not analyse in any depth. The first is the associated web pages. The web pages did not offer any stories of NDA use and effect, so they were used only to help me understand the context of the inquiry. The second set of documents I did not analyse are the interim and final reports produced by the committee. There are pieces of work that have undertaken analysis of these types of document as research materials in their own right – as, for example, sense-making narratives (Brown, 2004) and mechanisms for change (Brown et al, 2012). In my work, I was concerned with focusing on the accounts given to the inquiry, and I did not want my own analysis to be influenced by the interpretations, conclusions and recommendations drawn by the committee in such reports. A third set of documents I set aside are reports in the media and posts on social media. While news stories were certainly part of my inspiration for the research, I was less interested in how the inquiry was being reported and commented on, and more interested in the experiential stories revealed through the inquiry itself.

Research questions and analysis

Ashcraft and Muhr (2018, p 206) describe encountering 'empirical provocations' in their work, and I used this conceptualisation for my own encounters with specific pieces of the data. While I did not begin with precise research questions, my interest was in understanding the experiences of signing NDAs in workplace situations where misconduct, discrimination and other negative behaviours had taken place. I was interested in the impact and effects of signing NDAs, particularly in relation to the theoretical framing of silencing and epistemic injustice. The provocations emerged from the language used in the documents. To embed myself in the material, I began by printing out all the documents because, for me, reading on screen is uncomfortable and I value the opportunity to scribble thoughts, draw shapes and diagrams, and colour and highlight elements as I go. My interaction with the printed documents was later complemented by the use of NVivo software for data management.

I read all the documents to familiarise myself with their shape, style and content. I put them into four categories according to the voice of the author: accounts of people who had signed NDAs, employer perspectives, legal perspectives, and everything else. There were sometimes crossovers between these categories – for example, where someone had put in a written submission but this was also included in a transcript from an oral evidence session. I used coloured sticky notes to mark these for easy cross-referencing.

The analysis followed abductive theorising (Earl Rinehart, 2021; Thompson, 2022; Vila-Henninger et al, 2022), a process that involves situating the data in iterative consideration with existing literature. Abduction enables researchers to explore the data in ways that are non-linear and reflexive, allowing for 'a scholarship of possibilities' (Cunliffe, 2018, p 1429). I followed Earl Rinehart's (2021) approach of moving between deep embedded reading of the material and spending time away from it to allow for both immediate response and rumination. Following the initial, functional reading described earlier, I re-read the documents to make observations in terms of the provocations experienced (see Reissner, 2019, for a further example of the application of abductive theorising).

My observations were influenced by my interest in the impact and effects of signing the NDAs. These enabled me to notice and be provoked by particular words and phrases, and I recorded those moments that stood out as being impactful expressions of the experiences written about in the documents. I highlighted and starred them, drew arrows and generally annotated them by hand. Earl Rinehart (2021, p 303) describes 'immersion in and deliberate turning or moving away from the task of scrutinising evidence to be open to possibilities', with researchers (1) taking time with the empirical material, (2) noticing, recognising and responding to the material they are engaging with and (3) moving back and forth between and within literature and empirical material so as to resist linearity.

Raising voices and ethical considerations

The dataset must be considered incomplete because of the restrictions experienced by those subject to NDAs. However, following Mattingly (2019, p 417), my research has involved 'close consideration of interlocutors' experience of suffering', and the accounts given to the inquiry include descriptions of some horrific workplace experiences that could have had limited attention otherwise. Given the amount and content of material, I have been on several analytic journeys. For example, one analytic journey identified provocations in the language of violence (including references to 'abuse', 'victim', 'perpetrator', 'hurt', 'fear' and 'pain') as well as the reclaiming of agency to resist (including references to 'fight', 'anger', 'hearing voice', 'standing up' and 'winning'; Pagan, 2021). Another was provoked by a victim's use of the term 'gagging', which prompted a mental picture of an object being forced by one body into the mouth of another and led me towards concepts of restraint and control (Pagan, 2023). This emotional labour has been identified previously in research based on documents (Grant, 2018). Despite the relative privilege of all the organisational actors involved, in these instances, the privilege and epistemic authority of the victim is always inferior to that of the perpetrator (Keltner, 2017; Prasad, 2018) and the costs to the victim are frequently higher than those to the perpetrator (Pagan, 2021; 2023). In particular, 'recovery of the self after a traumatic event requires … the ability to authoritatively tell one's story, to testify about what one has experienced. It also requires a recognitive response to that testimony' (Jackson, 2018, p 5). So the use of something like an NDA to prevent such storytelling and hearing is potentially very detrimental.

My research was approved by my institutional ethics approval framework, which considered the work to be low risk in terms of potential harms to participants and researcher. Beyond this statutory framework, I reflected on other ethical implications. There are indicators in the accounts that reveal the contributors' degrees of privilege, such as mentions of particular professions and references to job status through seniority and locations of work, including head offices. These are the submissions of those whose privilege and resources were such that they both knew about and were able to respond to the inquiry. This raises valid questions about the value of this research, given that the scale of epistemic violence and injustice is significantly more severe for those who have fewer resources for resistance, including marginalised and minoritised people (Thapar-Björkert et al, 2016; Halliwell, 2019).

In justifying the place and contribution of this research, I propose that amplifying the voices of oppressed actors draws attention to the structural oppression that enables abuse and violence, which, if attended to, could be addressed to the benefit of many others. Some documents, like NDAs, silence people, while others, such as the inquiry contributions, allow some people's voices to come through. It is important to acknowledge that it was not possible to take into account marginalisation by gender, race, ethnicity, sexuality and other protected characteristics given that these characteristics were not explicitly identified by those submitting evidence. Regretfully, therefore, I have been unable to take a fully intersectional approach to the analysis. However, using documents in this way can help to amplify some voices that, arguably, some powerful people would prefer to be silenced. While far from ideal, as those hurt by bad workplace practices have no direct control of the full content of the narrative and may only offer general, ambiguous and imprecise accounts, this use of documents does show that power is incomplete and may be resisted. Some of the accounts given to the inquiry describe violence and trauma that provoked an emotional response from me, and I drew on advice and guidance from colleagues who have experience of working with this sort of material (see, for example, Grant, 2018; Silverio et al, 2022).

Overall, the advantages of using documents in this research include their free availability and access to a full coherent set of documents for a particular inquiry (Scott, 1990). The topic area is sensitive, and it would be very difficult to undertake in-depth qualitative research using methods such as interviews or focus groups, so documents offer a way to gain some knowledge and understanding. The documents included in this inquiry offer different perspectives on the topic, so an ongoing element of this research is to switch my focus from the victims to other stakeholders, including those representing employers. What do they say about their use of NDAs? What are the impacts and affects from their perspective? In terms of challenges, one is the volume of material, with many pages to give consideration to. Another challenge could be a counter to this – only a relatively small number of people shared their stories, so the documents can only ever offer a glimpse of particular experiences based on the few accounts provided. However, as characterises qualitative research, depth is what is of value, and no claims of generalisability are made. Malterud et al (2016, p 7) also speak of 'information power' to guide qualitative research in relation to 'the contribution of new knowledge from the analysis'. Additionally, the inquiry and its documents ripple into other activities around this topic, such as the important activist work of organisations like Can't Buy My Silence and Speak Out Revolution,[1] such that new or expanded areas of research may be identified.

Conclusion

It is possible to access documents relating to UK parliamentary business stretching back over the decades via The National Archives[2] as well as documents that are 'live' on the website, covering daily parliamentary business. Given the range of responsibilities of political governance, it would be possible to undertake research using such documents from a variety of disciplinary and contextual positions. This could include history, in social, economic and governance terms, politics, economics, sociology and social policy, to name but a few. The accessibility of such documents means that the data available may be of value for projects with short deadlines, including student projects. The method could be further developed from a more quantitative perspective – for example, in analysing financial, economic and accounting documents to understand decision making and policy. In other contexts where silenced voices can be amplified through documentary analysis, there is important work being undertaken using archival documents to draw attention to racism in healthcare (Smith, 2020; 2021) and to foreground other historical absences by race, ethnicity, class, sexuality, gender and political position (Caswell and Cifor, 2016; 2021; Caswell et al, 2017). Overall, when treated with care, documents of these kinds are powerful as they can reveal secrets and stories that have been deliberately hidden.

Key considerations for using this method

- Think about the purpose of the document as originally produced and any implications for its use in your research.

- Aim for clarity on the position of documents – for example, oral transcripts are from 'live', in-the-moment conversations that may be less curated and more 'natural' than written submissions, which are generally more crafted.

- Look for absences, in terms of authorship, as well as presences, such as who is 'speaking', considering their importance and what the implications may be.

- Reflect on the theoretical perspective that frames your work and its impact on your analysis.

- Be transparent about any decisions to include/exclude documents that may be within the bounds of your research, and recognise when documents may be important but inaccessible (in this case, NDAs).

Notes

1   See: www.cantbuymysilence.com; www.speakoutrevolution.co.uk.
2   See the UK Government Web Archive at: www.nationalarchives.gov.uk/webarchive.

References

Acas (2013) 'Code of Practice 4: Settlement Agreements (under section 111A of the Employment Rights Act 1996)', *Acas*, 29 July. Available from: www.acas.org.uk/acas-code-of-practice-settlement-agreements

Addley, E. and Sabbagh, D. (2018) 'British #MeToo scandal puts non disclosure agreements in spotlight', *The Guardian*, 24 October. Available from: www.theguardian.com/world/2018/oct/24/british-metoo-scandal-puts-non-disclosure-agreements-in-spotlight

Ashcraft, K.L. and Muhr, S.L. (2018) 'Coding military command as a promiscuous practice? Unsettling the gender binaries of leadership metaphors', *Human Relations*, 71(2): 206–28.

Braddy, P.W., Sturm, R.E., Atwater, L., Taylor, S.N. and McKee, R.A. (2020) 'Gender bias still plagues the workplace: looking at derailment risk and performance with self–other ratings', *Group and Organization Management*, 45(3): 315–50.

Brown, A., Bonneville, G. and Glaze, S. (2021) 'Nevertheless, they persisted: how women experience gender-based discrimination during postgraduate surgical training', *Journal of Surgical Education*, 78(1): 17–34.

Brown, A.D. (2004) 'Authoritative sensemaking in a public inquiry report', *Organization Studies*, 25(1): 95–112.

Brown, A.D., Ainsworth, S. and Grant, D. (2012) 'The rhetoric of institutional change', *Organization Studies*, 33(3): 297–321.

Candiotto, L. (2019) 'From philosophy of emotion to epistemology: some questions about the epistemic relevance of emotions', in L. Candiotto (ed) *The Value of Emotions for Knowledge*, Springer, pp 3–24.

Caswell, M. and Cifor, M. (2016) 'From human rights to feminist ethics: radical empathy in the archives', *Archivaria*, 81: 23–43.

Caswell, M. and Cifor, M. (2021) 'Revisiting a feminist ethics of care in archives', *Journal of Critical Library and Information Studies*, 3(2): 1–6.

Caswell, M., Migoni, A.A., Geraci, N. and Cifor, M. (2017) '"To be able to imagine otherwise": community archives and the importance of representation', *Archives and Records*, 38(1): 5–26.

Catala, A., Faucher, L. and Poirier, P. (2021) 'Autism, epistemic injustice, and epistemic disablement: a relational account of epistemic agency', *Synthese*, 199(3–4): 9013–39.

Chartered Institute of Personnel and Development (2021) 'Contracts of employment', *CIPD*. Available from: www.cipd.org/uk/knowledge/factsheets/terms-conditions-contracts-factsheet

Coffey, A. (2014) 'Analysing documents', in U. Flick (ed) *The SAGE Handbook of Qualitative Data Analysis*, SAGE, pp 367–79.

Corti, L. (2018) 'Data collection in secondary analysis', in U. Flick (ed) *The SAGE Handbook of Qualitative Data Collection*, SAGE, pp 164–81.

Croxford, R. (2019) 'UK universities face "gagging order" criticism', *BBC*, 17 April. Available from: www.bbc.co.uk/news/education-47936662

Cunliffe, A.L. (2002) 'Reflexive dialogical practice in management learning', *Management Learning*, 33(1): 35–61.

Cunliffe, A.L. (2003) 'Reflexive inquiry in organizational research: questions and possibilities', *Human Relations*, 56(8): 983–1003.

Cunliffe, A.L. (2004) 'On becoming a critically reflexive practitioner', *Journal of Management Education*, 28(4): 407–26.

Cunliffe, A.L. (2008) 'Orientations to social constructionism: relationally responsive social constructionism and its implications for knowledge and learning', *Management Learning*, 39(2): 123–39.

Cunliffe, A.L. (2018) 'Wayfaring: a scholarship of possibilities or let's not get drunk on abstraction', *M@n@gement*, 21(4): 1429–39.

Dickson-Swift, V., James, E.L., Kippen, S. and Liamputtong, P. (2009) 'Researching sensitive topics: qualitative research as emotion work', *Qualitative Research*, 9(1): 61–79.

Dotson, K. (2011) 'Tracking epistemic violence, tracking practices of silencing', *Hypatia*, 26(2): 236–57.

Earl Rinehart, K. (2021) 'Abductive analysis in qualitative inquiry', *Qualitative Inquiry*, 27(2): 303–11.

Equality and Human Rights Commission (2018) *Turning the Tables: Ending Sexual Harassment at Work*, Equality and Human Rights Commission. Available from: www.equalityhumanrights.com/turning-tables-ending-sexual-harassment-work

Eurofound (2017) *6th European Working Conditions Survey: 2017 Update*, Publications Office of the European Union.

Fricker, M. (2007) *Epistemic Injustice: Power and the Ethics of Knowing*, Oxford University Press.

Gardner, B. (2019) 'Sir Philip Green scandal shows that the law on NDAs must change, Lord Hain says', *The Telegraph*, 8 February. Available from: www.telegraph.co.uk/news/2019/02/08/sir-philip-green-scandal-shows-law-ndas-must-change-lord-hain

Garrahan, M. (2017) 'Harvey Weinstein: how lawyers kept a lid on sexual harassment claims', *Financial Times*, 23 October. Available from: www.ft.com/content/1dc8a8ae-b7e0-11e7-8c12-5661783e5589

Grant, A. (2018) 'Shock and offence online: the role of emotion in participant absent research', in T. Loughran and D. Mannay (eds) *Emotion and the Researcher: Sites, Subjectivities, and Relationships* (Studies in Qualitative Methodology, Vol 16), Emerald Publishing, pp 143–58.

Halliwell, P. (2019) 'The psychological & emotional effects of discrimination within the LGBTQ, transgender, & non-binary communities', *Thomas Jefferson Law Review*, 41(2): 222–37.

Hibbert, P., Sillince, J., Diefenbach, T. and Cunliffe, A. (2014) 'Relationally reflexive practice: a generative approach to theory development in qualitative research', *Organizational Research Methods*, 17(3): 278–98.

Jackson, D.L. (2018) '"Me too": epistemic injustice and the struggle for recognition', *Feminist Philosophy Quarterly*, 4(4): 1–19.

Keltner, D. (2017) 'Sex, power, and the systems that enable men like Harvey Weinstein', *Harvard Business Review*, 13 October. Available from: https://hbr.org/2017/10/sex-power-and-the-systems-that-enable-men-like-harvey-weinstein

Kinouani, G. (2020) 'Silencing, power and racial trauma in groups', *Group Analysis*, 53(2): 145–61.

Liu, H. (2022) 'How we learn whiteness: disciplining and resisting management knowledge', *Management Learning*, 53(5): 776–96.

Malterud, K., Siersma, V.D. and Guassora, A.D. (2016) 'Sample size in qualitative interview studies: guided by information power', *Qualitative Health Research*, 26(13): 1753–60.

Mattingly, C. (2019) 'Defrosting concepts, destabilizing doxa: critical phenomenology and the perplexing particular', *Anthropological Theory*, 19(4): 415–39.

Mignolo, W.D. and Walsh, C.E. (2018) *On Decoloniality: Concepts, Analytics, Praxis*, Duke University Press.

Muzanenhamo, P. (2022) 'Black scholarship: autoethnographies and epistemic (in) justice', *Discourses on Culture*, 18(1): 79–87.

Pagan, V. (2019) 'Being and becoming a "good" qualitative researcher? Liminality and the risk of limbo', *Qualitative Research in Organizations and Management: An International Journal*, 14(1): 75–90.

Pagan, V. (2021) 'The murder of knowledge and the ghosts that remain: non-disclosure agreements and their effects', *Culture and Organization*, 27(4): 302–17.

Pagan, V. (2022) 'Fantasy to (evade) order: vicarious schadenfreude', *Ephemera: Theory & Politics in Organization*, 22(1): 173–88.

Pagan, V. (2023) '21st century bridling: non-disclosure agreements in cases of organizational misconduct', *Human Relations*, 76(11): 1827–51.

Pina-Cabral, J. (2014) 'World: an anthropological examination (part 1)', *Journal of Ethnographic Theory*, 4(1): 49–73.

Pollner, M. (1991) 'Left of ethnomethodology: the rise and decline of radical reflexivity', *American Sociological Review*, 56(3): 370–80.

Potter, J. (2002) 'Two kinds of natural', *Discourse Studies*, 4(4): 539–42.

Prasad, V. (2018) 'If anyone is listening, #MeToo: breaking the culture of silence around sexual abuse through regulating non-disclosure agreements and secret settlements', *Boston College Law Review*, 59(7): 2507–49.

Prior, L. (2008) 'Repositioning documents in social research', *Sociology*, 42(5): 821–36.

Pullen, A., Harding, N. and Phillips, M. (2017) 'Introduction: feminist and queer politics in critical management studies', in A. Pullen, N. Harding and M. Phillips (eds) *Feminists and Queer Theorists Debate the Future of Critical Management Studies* (Dialogues in Critical Management Studies, Vol 3), Emerald, pp 1–11.

Raj, A., Johns, N.E. and Jose, R. (2020) 'Gender parity at work and its association with workplace sexual harassment', *Workplace Health and Safety*, 68(6): 279–92.

Rapley, T. and Rees, G. (2018) 'Collecting documents as data', in U. Flick (ed) *The SAGE Handbook of Qualitative Data Collection*, SAGE, pp 378–91.

Reissner, S.C. (2019) '"We are this hybrid": members' search for organizational identity in an institutionalized public–private partnership', *Public Administration*, 97(1): 48–63.

Santamaría, D.R.L. (2023) 'From epistemic injustice to epistemicide: a comparative analysis of the two concepts', *Electronic Notebooks of Philosophy of Law*, 48: 314–45.

Scott, J. (1990) *A Matter of Record: Documentary Sources in Social Research*, Polity Press.

Silverio, S.A., Sheen, K.S., Bramante, A., Knighting, K., Koops, T.U., Montgomery, E. et al (2022) 'Sensitive, challenging, and difficult topics: experiences and practical considerations for qualitative researchers', *International Journal of Qualitative Methods*, 21. doi: 10.1177/1609406922112

Smith, A.E., Hassan, S., Hatmaker, D.M., DeHart-Davis, L. and Humphrey, N. (2021) 'Gender, race, and experiences of workplace incivility in public organizations', *Review of Public Personnel Administration*, 41(4): 674–99.

Smith, K.M. (2020) 'Facing history for the future of nursing', *Journal of Clinical Nursing*, 29(9–10): 1429–31.

Smith, K.M. (2021) 'No medical justification: segregation and civil rights in Alabama's psychiatric hospitals, 1952–1972', *Journal of Southern History*, 87(4): 645–72.

Speak Out Revolution (2023) 'Speak Out Dashboard', *Speak Out Revolution*. Available from: www.speakoutrevolution.co.uk/dashboard

Spivak, G.C. (1988) 'Can the subaltern speak?', in C. Nelson and L. Grossberg (eds) *Marxism and the Interpretation of Culture*, Macmillan, pp 271–313.

Stokel-Walker, C. (2019) 'UK universities issue 11K non-disclosure agreements in five years', *Times Higher Education*, 11 April. Available from: www.timeshighereducation.com/news/uk-universities-issue-11k-non-disclosure-agreements-five-years

Syal, R. (2019) 'I was told of hundreds of grievance cases against Philip Green, says peer', *The Guardian*, 23 May. Available from: www.theguardian.com/business/2019/may/23/philip-green-peter-hain-says-told-of-hundreds-of-grievance-cases-peer

Thapar-Björkert, S., Samelius, L. and Sanghera, G.S. (2016) 'Exploring symbolic violence in the everyday: misrecognition, condescension, consent and complicity', *Feminist Review*, 112(1): 144–62.

The Law Society (2019) 'Practice note: non-disclosure agreements and confidentiality clauses in an employment law context', *The Law Society*, 12 December. Available from: www.lawsociety.org.uk/topics/employment/non-disclosure-agreements-and-confidentiality-clauses-in-an-employment-law-context

Thompson, J. (2022) 'A guide to abductive thematic analysis', *The Qualitative Report*, 27(5): 1410–21.

Trades Union Congress (2016) *Still Just a Bit of Banter? Sexual Harassment in the Workplace in 2016*, Trades Union Congress. Available from: www.tuc.org.uk/research-analysis/reports/still-just-bit-banter

UK Parliament (nd) 'Committees', *UK Parliament*. Available from: www.parliament.uk/business/committees

Vila-Henninger, L., Dupuy, C., Van Ingelgom, V., Caprioli, M., Teuber, F., Pennetreau, D. et al (2022) 'Abductive coding: theory building and qualitative (re) analysis', *Sociological Methods and Research*, 53(2): 968–1001.

Women and Equalities Committee (2018a) 'Non-disclosure agreements: committee to examine wider issues', *UK Parliament*, 13 November. Available from: www.parliament.uk/business/committees/committees-a-z/commons-select/women-and-equalities-committee/news-parliament-2017/nda-launch-17-19

Women and Equalities Committee (2018b) 'Sexual harassment in the workplace inquiry', *UK Parliament*, 25 July. Available from: https://publications.parliament.uk/pa/cm201719/cmselect/cmwomeq/725/72502.htm

Women and Equalities Committee (2019) 'The use of non-disclosure agreements in discrimination cases inquiry', *Parliament.UK*, 11 June. Available from: https://publications.parliament.uk/pa/cm201719/cmselect/cmwomeq/1720/172002.htm

Women and Equalities Committee (nd) 'The use of non-disclosure agreements in discrimination cases inquiry | Publications', *UK Parliament*. Available from: https://committees.parliament.uk/work/6022/the-use-of-nondisclosure-agreements-in-discrimination-cases-inquiry/publications

Ybema, S., Yanow, D., Wels, H. and Kamsteeg, F.H. (2009) 'Studying everyday organizational life', in S. Ybema, D. Yanow, H. Wels and F.H. Kamsteeg (eds) *Organizational Ethnography: Studying the Complexities of Everyday Life*, SAGE, pp 1–20.

6

Investigating identity documents through historical ethnography

José Ragas

Summary

- This chapter is an invitation to consider identity cards as key historical sources in analysis.

- Drawing on mixed methods from historical ethnography and science and technology studies, it discusses how to take advantage of this particular type of artefact and considers its long-term implications.

- Given that identity documents exist worldwide, insights are provided on how to frame broader questions from local settings.

Introduction

Identity documents have existed for nearly two centuries – long before we started carrying around debit and credit cards and portable devices such as smartphones and even iPods or Walkmans. Whether it be passports, driving licences, national ID cards, visas or just a piece of paper or plastic validated by some authority, identity documents have become part of us, shaping who we are and who we claim to be. Many of these documents are easy to find in everyday life as we pull them out casually from our pockets or wallets several times a day. Others are less visible, like those identity documents that emerge from the archives and which scholars treat as rare gems. Their sudden appearance elicits mixed feelings among researchers, depending on what kind of identity papers they find or the period when the papers were produced. Although they share many common features (such as size and material), each one tells a particular history of hope, disarray, despair, anxiety or even violence, especially in some regions of the Global South, where having an identity document or not having one could mean the difference between life and death.

This chapter approaches the fascinating yet complex nature of identity documents as artifacts housed in archives and historical collections. Identity documents are capable of conjuring contradictory emotions and memories. For researchers, they offer the possibility of connecting the owners' personal dimensions to the techno-social developments that take place at global scale (Caplan and Torpey, 2001; About et al, 2013). Over the past two centuries, ordinary individuals have embraced identity documents to navigate through daily life but also to overcome surveillance, inequality and mobility restrictions as well as racial and gender barriers imposed by those who envision territories comprised by homogenous and heteronormative citizens. Drawing from my own experience with identity documents as a (non-)citizen and immigrant as well as my experience with the archives as a historian of technology, I reflect on how we can approach these artifacts to restore the personal and social narratives of those who have manufactured, authenticated, forged and carried them.

Before we move forward, perhaps it is a good time to set out what an identity paper is. Despite their variety of formats and their evolving nature from print to digital, an identity paper can be defined as an artifact used by individuals to authenticate their identity through personal information previously registered by an authority (Lyon, 2009). For the purposes of this chapter, I examine only those identity documents generated by national or local authorities, looking also at the tension that emerged between policy makers and citizens who were granted (or not granted) such documents. Importantly, I distinguish these specific artifacts from those circulating over the past centuries that were used for personal or private purposes. This working definition also helpfully situates a particular group of documents as analytical instruments in the exploration of broader issues connected to citizenship, statelessness, human rights and other current pressing issues (Piazza, 2004; Mehmood, 2008).

As I explain in the following pages, while such artifacts may appear mundane, they offer exciting possibilities to expand our methodological skills and to explore wide-ranging aspects of society. As with any other artifacts from our daily life, before we navigate archives and digital collections, it is important to acknowledge what these objects mean nowadays and what they represented to our ancestors not long ago. It is also important to recognise how fortunate we are to have one of these pieces of paper or plastic with us. Not having an identity paper (or even not having the proper one) can impede us from accomplishing daily in-person activities that we often take for granted, such as entering a facility, withdrawing money at a bank or attending a meeting. In other scenarios, lacking an identity paper opens the possibility of being denied entry into a country, being denied asylum or being arrested for not providing valid proof of identity. In the past, identity cards were granted only to specific groups of people. Women were not able to possess one in certain regions, since they were not able to vote. The same was true for other groups excluded on the basis of race, class, religion or other social criteria (Ragas, 2020a; Da Escóssia, 2021). The ubiquitous presence of identity documents today is part of the history that scholars are unearthing by using them as privileged instruments of analysis.

Positionality

As a scholar, I have been working with identity documents for a decade and a half. However, my personal experience with them goes back much longer to my childhood and adolescence in Lima, Peru, and continues today as I am an immigrant settled in Chile and applying for permanent resident status. As a non-White individual from the Global South, my numerous identity cards have shaped how I can move, my ethnicity, my social and professional status, and how authorities project onto me their postcolonial policies in a context shaped by high global spatial mobility and radical far Right discourses. Very often in the archives, I have found evidence of individuals experiencing challenges similar to those I have gone through abroad and when I return home. Consequently, my personal experience has helped me to critically inform my professional work with these artifacts and the way I approach them when I investigate their genealogy. One of the most important lessons I have learned during my research is that we need to restore the social and personal dimension to identity documents if we want to comprehend their extraordinary capacity to prompt global responses from organisations and states as well as emotional responses from their bearers.

Whether you have already decided to use identity papers in your research or you just happen to find these during your archival work, this chapter is for you. Since these are sensitive artefacts, it is important to remember that we are not dealing with just another historical object. Ultimately, we are dealing with artifacts intimately connected with people: people approved the provision of a specific identity card, people manufactured them, and some people were granted them and some were not. In what follows, I guide you through examples, methods and recommendations on how to do research with these objects while treating them with care and respect. Thus, the next time you use your own identity card in your daily life, you will be aware of the profound and long-term implications involved in such a small, rectangular piece of plastic.

Explaining my research

As happens with many research topics, I came to study identity cards by chance. My original PhD project was about something totally different. After an exploratory field trip to search for sources for my initial topic, I realised that the project was not feasible. A conversation with my advisor during a trip to Cusco was crucial in reorienting my efforts. 'Why don't you take a look at that research on migration that you talked to me about a while ago?', he asked. He was referring to when I was studying rural migrants as part of my master's degree in Lima – as I was going through my notes and sources, I came across a peculiar incident that took place in Peru in the early 1950s: a senator sought to enforce the use of 'internal passports' for gypsies and rural migrants to prevent them from entering the capital city (Pardo-Figueroa, 2000). Immediately, I recalled having seen one of those internal passports, though it was from an earlier period; it had been issued in the early years of the Republic of Peru in the 1820s (Ragas, 2021). I asked myself: Why has this specific document persisted? Why did it resurface a century later and target Indigenous migrants and gypsies?

To solve these queries, my PhD examined how identity documents have shaped the development of citizenship in modern Peru for over a century (Ragas, 2015). Coincidentally, this field was taking off at the time (Peacock et al, 2023). The 9/11 attack had occurred just a few years earlier, and the growing concern on global security and surveillance was being responded to by scholars with a focus on how societies created security apparatuses in the past. Scholars were also examining the emergence of a surveillance society and the attacks on civil liberties and personal privacy. Journals such as *Surveillance & Society* (founded in 2002) facilitated the discussion and hosted theoretical debates in the context of the changing global landscape of the 'war on terror' (Marx, 2002; Lyon, 2009). Historians joined the collective efforts, since some of them had been working on identification and police surveillance long before 9/11 (Caplan and Torpey, 2001; About et al, 2013).

Thus, identification and surveillance had become an expansive field by the time I was writing my thesis. However, despite the new perspectives being proposed by colleagues in various fields, there were just a few works that approached the subject of identity cards, and these were limited mostly to the previous decade (Bennett and Lyon, 2008). My fieldwork took me not only to state and municipal archives, but also to private collections. It also placed me in unexpected sites, such as the occasion when I was in front of a high-ranking police officer who was suspicious about my interest in the history of the Peruvian police and its identification practices. Back in California, I ended up writing the thesis from a conventional historical perspective. The committee and my advisor were pleased with the dissertation, but I was not entirely satisfied. If I wanted to take full advantage of the universe around identity documents, I needed to learn new methods and perspectives. So, I applied to be a postdoctoral fellow at Cornell University in a completely different area – the Department of Science and Technology Studies became my home for two years.

Historians, technology and archives

Both faculty and graduate students at Cornell introduced me to novel forms of thinking and new approaches to my subject, with an approach that paid attention to identity documents as technological objects while emphasising their continuous social interactions. I felt like I had been given access to a large toolbox instead of the hammer and screwdriver I had been using up to then. I also learned that *the* method – the one and only that applies to your specific research project – does not exist. What I had to do was 'build' my own 'method' from other methods and experiences shared by researchers in various fields. This is particularly true when you work with unusual sources (for me, identity documents) and in contexts where previous scholarship does not necessarily fit. My postdoctoral tenure and the advice from my mentors at Cornell were crucial in my learning how to build a methodological strategy and frame the problem from a case study embedded within a global scale.

As a scholar originally trained in historical methods, I decided to use historical ethnography to examine the long-term interaction between humans and identity documents. Also known as ethnohistory or archival ethnography (Douglas and Di Rosa, 2020), historical ethnography is defined by Stephanie Decker and Alan McKinlay (2020, p 26) as an 'ethnographic fieldwork in the past', while Nir Rotem (2024) understands it as 'the agile journey of ethnographers who traverse history'. The Annales school (Le Roy Ladurie, 1966) and E.P. Thompson (1993) embraced this perspective very early on as part of an effort to circumvent the restrictions imposed by the written records in pre-industrial societies and a restrictive notion of the 'archive'. By defying these disciplinary notions and actively experimenting with new sources (or revisiting the conventional ones with new lenses) and new spatial frameworks (including microhistory and regional history), practitioners of historical ethnography delivered a rich constellation of works. In doing so, they introduced new actors (such as peasants, Indigenous communities, people who were enslaved, urban poor, women, people who were illiterate) and practices (from popular culture to local resistance) coexisting and operating in complex environments within a broader temporal arc.

Consequently, rather than being a rigid field, historical ethnography turned into an expansive yet malleable arena where past and present merges; the ethnographic gaze was used in an ambitious effort to gain a better understanding of the social world in which various agents operated (Atwood, 2021; Nemer, 2022; Yates-Doerr and Labuski, 2023). With this, in tandem with the social construction of technology approach, I could emphasise the social and political role of agents (or 'users') that interacted with technological artifacts. As the proponents of this approach state, users are constantly creating new ways to appropriate certain devices (here, identity documents), generating an endless cycle that extends the original purpose of the artifacts (Lindsay, 2003; Oudshoorn and Pinch, 2003). I took advantage of both perspectives to explore both the material and subjective dimensions of the way identity documents have been inscribed over the past two centuries.

The historical ethnography methodology has proven to be valuable in Peru and other countries in the Global South (Lund, 2001; Gordillo, 2006). With most of Peru's population only recognised as citizens in the late 1970s due to the high rate of illiteracy in the country, it was obvious that examining documented people alone over time might lead to misinterpretations of how Peruvians transitioned from colonial subjects to modern citizens. Therefore, I focused also on undocumented individuals, who comprised nearly 90 per cent or more of the population in the time frame I was looking at. I called them 'techno-invisibles' since they remained non-existent to a state that deliberately refused to grant them official recognition through identity cards, conjuring segregationist motivations based on illiteracy and racism (Ragas, 2020a). The lack of documents did not necessarily mean that these groups lacked autonomous mechanisms to identify themselves at local and communal levels. By studying the expansion of identity documents as the tension between documented and undocumented populations (rather than just considering these documents in relation to the former group), I was able to complicate the understanding of citizenship in rural and urban areas as well as in subaltern groups (Indigenous people, Afro-descendants, Asians) in the Andes region and elsewhere (Ragas, 2020b).

Exploring internal passports in Latin America

From the universe of historical identity documents I chose to work with in my PhD project, internal passports were the most intriguing and challenging. For starters, there was no book, paper or scholarly study dedicated to this artifact in Latin America, despite some vestiges of their presence across the hemisphere. Archives and collections were not necessarily more generous than academic databases in providing tangible evidence of these early documents. When conventional archives do not provide a solution, it is necessary to expand the repertoire of places to consult. I did find some internal passports in the archives, but I found others in flea markets. Friends and colleagues from other countries and regions in Peru kindly shared their own documents and findings when they learned through conversations and social media that I was looking for these elusive objects for my project. In the end, I was able to collect a few of them while continuing my search for indirect information about how they were used between 1820 and the mid-1850s in the nascent Peruvian Republic.

It may seem quite obvious, but it is important to consider case studies within a broad geographic framework, preferably a global or transnational one. While the literature in a field may focus overwhelmingly on the Global North, it is important to incorporate examples from regions such as Africa, Asia, the Middle East and Latin America and the Caribbean whenever possible (Barnes, 1997). In my research, I found several examples from the former Soviet Union, South Africa and – of course – European countries (Breckenridge, 2008). Considering the colonial and subsequent postcolonial trajectory of my case study, I found it more interesting to establish connections with South Africa, India and the Global South. Nonetheless, it is important not to dismiss the influence of the Global North given that this region often provided role models for the local elites in the Global South.

Analysing internal passports

When approaching internal passports through the historical ethnography perspective explained earlier, I focused on four research questions: What was the materiality of these artifacts? What kind of early personal data did they contain? What was their purpose? How did these artifacts interact with human bodies?

Materiality

Given that internal passports were issued by the new Republic in a moment of turmoil and scarcity, when paper became a commodity, the passports served as ammunition for both the royalists and the patriots (Gitelman, 2014; Ragas, 2021). On one side, the new authorities managed to obtain a supply of paper necessary to secure the proper functioning of the nascent autonomous administration, which included issuing internal passports to monitor spatial movement between the capital city and the rest of the country. Ink and stamps were also among the range of instruments employed to authenticate such documents. Occasionally, these were difficult to find outside the capital and authorities had to substitute by drawing the national seal or recycling papers to print the internal passports. On the other side, during the height of the war, the patriot army confiscated portable printers that could be used to print newspapers and political pamphlets, also halting the creation of any other administrative procedure or document.

Personal data

In the first portable identity document, personal data were used to register and exhibit physical features, mainly from the face. Usually, the document began with a formulaic introduction that described the bearer of the passport. But the core information was on the left side of the document, which was often called *filiación* (identity affiliation). The number of physical markers varied, but in one document, authorities demanded to know the 'status' of the traveller, along with their 'age', 'colour', 'face', 'hair', 'eyes', 'nose', 'mouth' and 'height'. With this information, inspectors had to build a mental picture of the bearer, which they relied on to grant them permission (or not) to continue their journey. What is fascinating about this is that it shows that long before the massification of the photograph, there was a need to register biometric information. Such an endeavour had its difficulties. For instance, inspectors did not receive any particular training to register such features. This meant that the terms and keywords used to code an applicant's features varied from place to place and even from inspector to inspector.

Purpose

Another aspect to consider is that internal passports were issued to grant safe passage in certain areas during times of conflict and political instability. Travellers had to carry them and show them once they arrived at the next military post. During the journey, they had to be careful not to lose the document or expose it to any damage that could risk the revision of the document. Over time, including when the internal conflict was over, Peruvian authorities extended the use of internal passports for surveillance purposes. This was especially the case after 1839, when an authoritarian constitution was approved, paving the way for a new cycle of political violence with warlords and further instability in the country. The internal passports were Peruvians' first experience of carrying a portable identity card. They were used for three and a half decades before being revoked by an incoming liberal regime. Up to then, the only other personal document people could use was the birth certificate, which was not issued very easily. These remained stored in local parishes and were not officially recognised by the state.

Embodiment

Internal passports created an intimate relationship with people's bodies. They represented specific bodies and were attached to those same bodies to authenticate the information recorded in sheets of paper and validated by signatures and stamps. Despite the expendable nature of the passports (they were discarded once the individuals arrived at their destinations), the documents were not just another object. Given that the passports contained sensitive information and their possession could determine the possibility of moving from one place to another, they were intercepted by some people. Manipulation of the passports involved technical knowledge of how to reproduce an official document or change information contained in it. Sometimes, the falsification of internal passports was successful, and individuals could pass inspection and move to another destination. Sometimes this strategy did not work, and offenders were fined or arrested. In fact, unauthorised changes to personal papers became more frequent in the decades following the use of internal passports, prompting authorities to respond with new mechanisms to secure the authenticity of personal papers.

Advantages and disadvantages of using identity documents as data

Identity documents can illuminate angles and problems sometimes overlooked when examining other sources. One major advantage of working with identity documents is their heterogeneity. The forces that prompted the implementation of such artifacts (including migration, liberal democracy, surveillance, political rights) have emerged in most parts of the world over the past two centuries. But they did not emerge at the same pace everywhere. Every nation/region had to embrace identity documents to confront certain developments and challenges, and they did so on their own terms. Consequently, no two national documents are exactly the same, even if they are of the same type. Only in the past few years have there been efforts to homogenise the manufacturing of identity cards, based on international regulations and security measures. This is particularly true for passports and national identity cards. The variety of materials used in their production as well as the information contained in them are important attributes of how societies in the past responded to global challenges.

Another reason why identity documents are excellent sources is their inherent capacity to connect personal experiences with broader phenomena. We can learn a lot about a particular period or a social group by examining how they gained access to or why they were denied certain documents. Women, for instance, have been granted voting cards at different moments in the past century, while some communities have been denied voting cards due to the racial or religious prejudices of authorities. The presence of objects like these in the archives reflects only part of the history; investigating how individuals used their identities in multiple settings or how they avoided being discovered as undocumented is one of the most challenging (yet the most exciting) parts of working with these sources. Memoirs (when they are available), testimonies and interviews may contribute a more personal approach to understanding administrative procedures such as the approval or rejection of an official document (Garton Ash, 1997).

Working with sources like identity documents also brings challenges. Perhaps the most common problem is where to find them. Long before the creation of the unified national identity card, documents used to authenticate people's personal information relied on numerous institutions – such as the police, the church, the civil registry or other state branches – and certain kinds of identity document are easier to find than others. For instance, there is a better chance of gaining access to birth certificates than there is of accessing national identity cards. Passports have usually been stored in special sections of official records and are well preserved. Some entities made copies of these documents, giving one to the applicant and keeping another in their archives, to our benefit. Identity cards, on the other hand, were issued singly and delivered to individuals, making it difficult to find physical traces of them in public repositories.

One way to overcome this inconvenience is to search in repositories such as social media, where people sometimes post photos of their ancestors' or living relatives' old identity documents accompanied with a story about them. Collectors and enthusiasts also share their findings and possessions on the internet. Occasionally, I have found documents at a flea market. In all these cases, of course, there are ethical guidelines for their use, which involve protecting the privacy of the former bearer and citing the location the artifact came from. Still, the scarcity of documents in the archives should be considered a critical piece of information in the analysis, not just an impediment to further exploration. The sudden or prolonged absence of a specific kind of document in a certain period may be due to structural changes in a country or an unexpected transition from a democracy to an authoritarian regime (and back to a democracy again). These situations require a different strategy, and my recommendation is to incorporate oral histories or supplementary collections whenever possible.

Conclusion

Over the past few years, scholars have reported on the many challenges experienced by documented citizenship and the role identity documents have played in this process. On the one hand, in the past two decades, more individuals than ever have been registered and granted an identity card for the first time. A combination of factors, including the rise of progressive governments (as in the Latin American 'pink tide'), the commodities export boom, the prolonged periods of political stability and the aggressive implementation of social programmes, have led to massive identification campaigns in the first decades of the new century (Hunter and Brill, 2016). The outcome has been impressive, and these efforts have certainly contributed to reducing the historical gap between documented and undocumented populations, especially in the Global South. For example, since the 2010s, India has been able to document nearly one billion individuals using a highly developed system called Aadhaar, which provides new citizens with a 12-digit unique identification number (Zelezny, 2012). In Peru, the share of undocumented people in the population reached an unprecedented low of 1 per cent in the mid-2010s (Vega Bendezú, 2013, p 52).

This accomplishment, however, has faced major setbacks. The rise of the radical Right, the mass migration from the Mediterranean Sea, Venezuela and the Middle East, and the COVID-19 pandemic with its lockdowns have tested the limits of nationhood, inclusion and citizenship around the world. Early optimism about incorporating new citizens and delivering proper documents such as identity cards, birth certificates and death certificates has been weakened, with narratives of anger and animosity against newcomers and visa applicants sometimes present. The COVID-19 virus, on the other hand, pushed health infrastructures to the limit, making it difficult to verify deaths and, subsequently, issue death certificates. The pandemic also prompted the emergence (or return) of documents such as vaccination cards and mobility passes to, respectively, manage the advancement of immunisation programmes and avoid spreading the virus by limiting the access of populations to public spaces.

Given this complex and grim scenario, it is important to study how people have interacted with new cards and personal papers while navigating adverse circumstances. The historical ethnography approach can help to reconstruct the efforts of governments and policy makers in the recent (and distant) past to incorporate individuals into citizenship while also observing the strategies of subaltern groups to negotiate the formation of their identity through bureaucracy and instead preserve their own identity and personal data. It is also important to defy the state–individual relationship in our analysis and recognise the existence of multiple mediators that speed up bureaucratic procedures or circumvent official approval through forged documents.

Examining current issues through a methodology that focuses on sociocultural aspects of technological systems and devices within a long-term framework enables us to establish why they are not necessarily 'new'. Conversely, many issues related to the distribution of identity documents should be studied as part of historical legacies of colonialism and exclusion based on gender, class and race factors. As stated earlier, it is more appropriate to focus on specific human groups to better understand how identification has interacted over time with them and what policies can be applied based on this interaction. Most of these groups are vulnerable, and their social existence has been either neglected or deliberately repressed through identity cards. Not surprisingly, policy makers have weaponised identity documents against these groups for decades (even centuries), arguing that they do not fit into certain notions of citizenship managed by local elites and a privileged part of the population.

In my opinion, three social groups are relevant to explore today: Indigenous groups, historically relegated by nation-states and denied citizen status in contrast to their urban or White counterparts; the urban poor, whose number has abruptly grown in certain countries due to mass migration, neoliberal policies and the pandemic; and the LGBTQ+ community, who are subjected to humiliating procedures and treatments in order to obtain official documents that represent their new identity. Each one of these groups have encountered – and continue to encounter – numerous obstacles in obtaining respect and social benefits from the often-narrow horizons of nationhood and citizenship projected by identity documents. They have also developed important (and original) strategies to show their discontent – whether through mobilisations or artistic protests. All of these aspects should be considered for a more comprehensive understanding. Native American groups, for example, have issued their own passports, defying the authority of national institutions and Western documents. In a similar manner, the LGBTQ+ communities have exposed the hypocrisy of rigid categories contained in identity documents, leading to debates on gender and fluid identities. The urban poor and immigrants are struggling to obtain identity cards and gain access to public services and other benefits (Da Escóssia, 2021).

Of course, in our complicated world, there are many other groups and issues that deserve close and urgent examination by scholars and policy makers. The cases suggested here – as well as others – should be examined from an in-depth and long-term perspective, collecting their voices and experiences and proposing further steps on how curb exclusion. Doing so would allow us to repair a set of injustices that we as historians and scholars find in the archives and which are still present today as we write or read these stories.

Key considerations for using this method

- Identity documents constitute one of the most ubiquitous (yet elusive) technologies nowadays. In our current moment of high mobility and rising animosity against minorities, it is necessary to investigate the genealogy of these artifacts and how they have granted rights and prompted social and political rights for our ancestors.

- By examining their dual nature as both social and technological devices, we gain a better understanding of how identification technology shapes our identities and the multiple ways we can intervene with such artifacts to align them with our expectations.

- Socio-technical analysis of these devices offers a window onto themes and issues often overlooked (citizenship, spatial mobility, inclusion, development and so on) in the present and over the past two centuries.

- The historical ethnography method offers the possibility of reinserting identity documents into the complex interaction of agents, practices and infrastructures in the past by reading the historical evidence in a different way.

- Identity documents are not like any other source: they are sensitive artifacts that hold sensitive information. This information should be treated with respect, following ethical guidelines, even where the bearers passed away a long time ago.

- Identity documents have proved to be extraordinary malleable devices over time, and we should consider this in order to explain how we can take advantage of them to reduce inequality and lack of documentation.

References

About, I., Brown, J. and Lonergan, G. (eds) (2013) *Identification and Registration Practices in Transnational Perspective: People, Papers and Practices*, Oxford University Press.

Atwood, B. (2021) *Underground: The Secret Lives of Videocassettes in Iran*, MIT Press.

Barnes, T. (1997) 'Am I a man? Gender and the pass laws in urban colonial Zimbabwe, 1930–1980', *African Studies Review*, 40(1): 59–81.

Bennett, C.J. and Lyon, D. (eds) (2008) *Playing the Identity Card: Surveillance, Security and Identification in Global Perspective*, Routledge.

Breckenridge, K. (2008) 'The elusive panopticon: the HANIS project and the politics of standard in South Africa', in C.J. Bennett and D. Lyon (eds) *Playing the Identity Card: Surveillance, Security and Identification in Global Perspective*, Routledge, pp 39–56.

Caplan, J. and Torpey, J. (eds) (2001) *Documenting Individual Identity: The Development of State Practices in the Modern World*, Princeton University Press.

Da Escóssia, F. (2021) *Invisíveis. Uma etnografia sobre brasileiros sem documento*, FGV Editora.

Decker, S. and McKinley, A. (2020) 'Archival ethnography', in R. Mir and A.-L. Fayard (eds) *The Routledge Companion to Anthropology and Business*, Routledge, pp 17–33.

Douglas, B. and Di Rosa, D. (2020) 'Ethnohistory and historical ethnography', in *Oxford Bibliographies*, Oxford University Press.

Garton Ash, T. (1997) *The File: A Personal History*, Vintage Books.

Gitelman, L. (2014) *Paper Knowledge: Toward a Media History of Documents*, Duke University Press.

Gordillo, G. (2006) 'The crucible of citizenship: ID-paper fetishism in the Argentinean Chaco', *American Ethnologist*, 33(2): 162–76.

Hunter, W. and Brill, R. (2016) '"Documents, please": advances in social protection and birth certification in the developing world', *World Politics*, 68(2): 191–228.

Le Roy Ladurie, E. (1966) *Les paysans de Languedoc*, Bibliothèque Génerale de l'École des Hautes Études.

Lindsay, C. (2003) 'From the shadows: users as designers, producers, marketers, distributors, and technical support', in N. Oudshoorn and T. Pinch (eds) *How Users Matter: The Co-Construction of Users and Technology*, The MIT Press, pp 29–50.

Lund, S. (2001) 'Bequeathing and quest. Processing personal identification papers in bureaucratic spaces (Cuzco, Peru)', *Social Anthropology*, 9(1): 3–24.

Lyon, D. (2009) *Identifying Citizens: ID Cards as Surveillance*, Polity Press.

Marx, G.T. (2002) 'What's new about the 'new surveillance'? Classifying for change and continuity', *Surveillance & Society*, 1(9): 9–29.

Mehmood, T. (2008) 'India's new ID card: fuzzy logics, double meanings and ethnic ambiguities', in C.J. Bennett and D. Lyon (eds) *Playing the Identity Card: Surveillance, Security and Identification in Global Perspective*, Routledge, pp 112–27.

Nemer, D. (2022) *Technology of the Oppressed: Inequity and the Digital Mundane in Favelas of Brazil*, The MIT Press.

Oudshoorn, N. and Pinch, T. (eds) (2003) *How Users Matter: The Co-Construction of Users and Technology*, The MIT Press.

Pardo-Figueroa, C. (2000) 'Los gitanos y el proyecto de control migratorio de 1952', *Boletín del Instituto Riva-Agüero*, 27: 309–55.

Peacock, V., Bruun, M.K., Dungey, C.E. and Shapiro, M. (2023) 'Surveillance', in H. Nieber (ed) *The Open Encyclopedia of Anthropology*. Available from: www.anthroencyclopedia.com

Piazza, P. (2004) *Histoire de la carte nationale d'identité*, Odile Jacob.

Ragas, J. (2015) *Documenting Hierarchies: State Building, Identification, and Citizenship in Modern Peru*, PhD thesis, Department of History, University of California, Davis.

Ragas, J. (2020a) 'Forgotten faces, missing bodies: understanding techno-invisible populations and political violence in Peru', in A. Sims Bartel and D. Castillo (eds) *The Scholar as Human: Research and Teaching for Public Impact*, Cornell University Press, pp 93–107.

Ragas, J. (2020b) 'The official making of undocumented citizens in Peru, 1880–1930', in B. Fallaw and D. Nugent (eds) *State Formation in the Liberal Era: Capitalisms and Claims of Citizenship in Mexico and Peru*, University of Arizona Press, pp 107–26.

Ragas, J. (2021) 'Internal passports, forgery, and subversive practices in early republican Peru', *Journal of Social History*, 55(1): 27–45.

Rotem, N. (2024) 'Historical ethnography: key characteristics and the journey before, during, and after the archival field', *Forum: Qualitative Social Research*, 25(2). doi: 10.17169/fqs-25.2.4106

Thompson, E.P. (1993) *Customs in Common: Studies in Traditional Popular Culture*, The New Press.

Vega-Bendezú, K. (2013) 'Relación entre el Estado y las poblaciones vulnerables a través del acceso a los documentos de documentación e identificación', *Nombre*, 1(1): 38–78.

Yates-Doerr, E. and Labuski, C. (eds) (2023) *The Ethnographic Case* (2nd edn), Mattering Press.

Zelazny, F. (2012) *The Evolution of India's UID Program: Lessons Learned and Implications for Other Developing Countries* (CGD Policy paper 008). Center for Global Development.

7

From public document to engaging experiences: arts-based research and knowledge translation

Abigail Winter, Sarah Johnstone, Jen Seevinck,
T.J. Thomson and Evonne Miller

Summary

- Arts-based outcomes can lead to transformative learning experiences for participants.

- This chapter discusses the use of public documents for arts-based research outcomes.

- In the research discussed, documents were transformed into co-respondence letters.

- In addition, machine learning was used to create an artwork.

Introduction

Formal written organisational and institutional documents can serve as intriguing and informative research data. These documents, ranging from official reports, position papers and training manuals to meeting minutes and emails, offer unique contextual insights that researchers can analyse to identify patterns, trends and issues. Despite the potential, however, document-based research remains an underused research method (Grant, 2019; Dalglish et al, 2020). Our research explored how a unique set of public documents – public submissions (letters) to a royal commission – could provide a source for arts-based research and knowledge translation that might engage the public differently with aged care.

This chapter describes the methodological way that we used public submissions to Australia's 2019–21 Royal Commission into Aged Care Quality and Safety as data to create multiple arts-based research outputs, extending and amplifying the voices of those who had taken the time to write a submission. We detail two of the ways these submission documents have been used to answer the research question: How can we translate texts into engaging and accessible arts-based outputs that foster authentic engagement and transformative learning experiences?

The public source documents: submissions to a royal commission

Royal commissions are formal public inquiries established by some governments to investigate and report on specific issues of significant public concern. Their findings and recommendations often lead to legislative changes, policy reforms and heightened public awareness. They aim to gather a wide range of perspectives and experiences, inviting public submissions which capture individual stories and experiences while also highlighting systemic issues and areas needing reform.

As such, royal commissions provide a unique source of data. This is certainly true of the 2019–21 Royal Commission into Aged Care Quality and Safety in Australia, which was launched after investigative journalism exposed substandard and abusive care in Australian residential aged care. Over the period from 8 October 2018 to 1 March 2021, there were 23 public hearings (involving 641 witnesses) and a total of 10,574 public submissions. Comparative media monitoring reveals that, unfortunately, on the dates of the respective interim reports, the aged care royal commission received 300 per cent less media coverage than a concurrent royal commission on banking (Connolly, 2019). Given that the general public's awareness of and engagement with the aged care royal commission's findings were minimal, creative arts-based methods offered an evocative and provocative way to ensure that these stories were encountered and remembered, and to engage people in critical conversations about aged care now and in the future.

The potential of arts-based research and arts-based knowledge translation

The aged care royal commission highlighted the isolation and powerlessness felt by residents in a 'hidden-from-view system' (Royal Commission into Aged Care Quality and Safety, 2019, Vol 1, p 1). In our project, we intentionally deployed arts-based research and arts-based knowledge translation activities to help bring the difficult and often confronting stories from the royal commission to key audiences, including policy makers, peak bodies (non-governmental organisations representing groups of people, such as the International Disability Alliance), providers and the general community. As Prince (2022, p 95) argues, it is important to create space for people's 'stories to be heard, witnessed and interconnected across time, space, and place, to one another, and connected to vital information buried in official government reports and archives'. This is what arts-based research and arts-based knowledge translation are designed to do.

Documents submitted to public calls, such as those provided for a royal commission, generally have only a single life as the submission itself. Submissions are read by those involved, but often not by anyone else. This leaves them in a liminal space, with potential for transformation and change, but often no further action taken. But within these liminal texts is a wealth of data that could serve as inspiration and source documents for arts-based approaches. As Thomas (2001, p 274) explains, art has a unique ability to 'evoke, inspire, to spark the emotions, to awaken visions and imaginings, and to transport others to new worlds'. The arts can articulate and could instigate change on issues that are often ignored or considered taboo. They can also foster empathy and imaginative engagement with the lives of others.

For researchers, arts-based research integrates diverse creative arts into any part of the research process, from data collection to analysis and dissemination (Leavy, 2015). Art can be visual art, such as photography, drawing and painting, performances of dance, drama and music, and literary activities such as creative writing and poetry. More specifically, in arts-based knowledge translation (see Kukkonen and Cooper, 2019), art is used to communicate and disseminate research knowledge in different ways to diverse audiences.

Selecting the documents

Our research team for the projects described in this chapter was made up of five researchers from a mixed humanities/social science faculty: Creative Industries, Education and Social Justice. Our team included three designers, a former journalist and a writing coach. One of the designers was a professor of design psychology, one was a practising artist, and one was a recent PhD graduate and the research coordinator for the broader project. The research coordinator selected and downloaded submissions from the royal commission. She then categorised them according to their source (concerned citizen; person with a link to aged care – for example, a child of someone in residential aged care; employee; residential aged care business owner). Then we spent time immersing ourselves in the documents, reading and re-reading them to ensure we were all familiar with the contents.

We did not approach the analysis of the documents using any standardised or systematic process, for three main reasons: First, a thorough analysis process had already been conducted by the commissioners and their team. Every single submission had been recorded, reviewed and used to inform the royal commission inquiry. Second, we did not have the resources to conduct a thorough analysis of such a large dataset. It included (but was not limited to) 1,205 separate files from public hearings, 132 post-hearing submissions, 484 witness statements and over 10,000 public submissions. Third, each of the 10,000 submissions were difficult to access, with each document heavily nested in the royal commission's online archive.[1] In addition, many submissions were uploaded as scanned document images (rather than editable PDFs). This made text analysis difficult without the use of speciality software. Also, the scans were not always high quality and, indeed, some were too blurry to read at all – what John Scott (1990, p 28) calls a 'problem of literal understanding'.

In terms of challenges at this stage, there were two main ones. The first was that the process for reading these documents was not user-friendly for a team of researchers, let alone members of the general public who would be included in our research. We solved this by downloading documents to use and working with hard copies rather than electronic ones in our workshops and activities. The second challenge was to do with the content of the submissions themselves, which is always going to be an issue when working with public documents. Some were written in a very dry, unemotional style, which we felt might be difficult for people to engage with in our amplification efforts. Others were at the other extreme of the spectrum – full of emotion and vivid, sometimes horrific, details. This broad range of submissions meant that we had to read many of them (some of which were heartbreaking) to find ones that we felt told a strong story but were not too traumatic for our engagement purposes, something also noted by Katarzyna Nizołek in Chapter 2.

Transforming the documents

Conceptually, we frame this work as transformation, following Mezirow (2003, p 58), who describes transformative learning as being able to change perspectives and mindsets in order to be 'more inclusive, discriminating, open, reflective, and emotionally able to change'. This would later be described as increasing peoples' ability to understand different perspectives (Mezirow, 2009; Baumgartner, 2012). Later developments of the theory emphasise the criticality of reflection, emotion and intuition (Mezirow, 2009), which are the building blocks of the arts-based knowledge translation that we practise. Arts-based knowledge translation uses creative arts techniques (visual, literary, performative and more) to transform data (usually a lived experience of the researcher-artist or another) into an experience that is shareable with others (Parsons and Boydell, 2012; Miller, 2024). These arts-based knowledge translation methods (reformatting the documents into different forms; machine learning) were deployed at a public exhibition called Time to Listen.

The first unusual arts-based knowledge translation method we used with the royal commission documents involved selecting three submissions and reformatting them as letters. We called this a *co-respondence letter writing* activity. Our second use of documents as a source at the exhibition involved the development of a *machine learning artwork* that used the words 'not', 'be' and 'heard' from one submission (one of the three used for the co-respondence letter writing activity). Unsupervised machine learning is the training of computers to adapt their outputs based on the use of algorithms or statistical models and without explicit instruction. In many ways, the process is a precursor to generative artificial intelligence image generation such as Midjourney or DALL·E.

Our third use of documents as a source for the exhibition – not discussed further in this chapter – involved two found poetry provocations: viewing of some researcher-created found poems on digital screens; and a found poetry drop-in workshop. Found poetry is poetry that is created from existing text (see, for example, Patrick, 2016; Amos, 2019). Outside the exhibition – also not further discussed here – found poetry was used as a separate activity in four public workshops to introduce the public to research poetry. We also ran workshops for academics and researchers on poetry as a research method, using the royal commission submissions as the dataset. Using the same three submissions from the co-respondence letter writing activity, we invited participants to work through

Table 7.1: Engagement methods

Method	Engagement
Exhibition – co-respondence	10 responses
Exhibition – machine learning artwork	Around 50 people
Exhibition – found poetry	Around 50 people
Found poetry	Around 30 people
Found poetry research workshops	Around 40 people
Advocate card game playtesting	Around 40 people

different ways of creating research poetry using documents as text. Finally, and completely separately, we developed a card game called Advocate to help promote empathy and increase understanding and advocacy skills for workers in aged care, which we playtested four times with different audiences.

All of the engagement for these arts–based knowledge translation methods is summarised in Table 7.1.

Ethical considerations

Full university ethical clearance was obtained for all of the data collected at the workshops (Queensland University of Technology Ethics Approval 4618). The research was conducted with members of the public attending the Time to Listen exhibition – which was widely advertised on social media (and had about 50 attendees) – as well as academics and research students. This meant that in addition to the usual information sheets and signed consent forms, we were careful to explain the research in plain language and to answer any questions potential participants had. As already noted, we took care to select example documents for the public-facing purposes that, while representative of the submissions, were not the most harrowing descriptions of experiences in aged care that we had collected for the broader project. Our ethical consent documents also included contact information for support agencies, such as Lifeline, in case participants were distressed. In addition, the entrances to the exhibition space had signage warning people that there were possibly distressing images and stories on show. These notices also served to warn members of the public that they were entering a research space. Finally, the space itself was selected because it was away from the public thoroughfares through the university. These all combined to ensure that those attending the exhibition intended to be there.

Engaging with document data differently

Case 1: Co-respondence letter writing

In our first arts–based knowledge transfer method, we invited visitors to the exhibition to read a submission and write a letter in response to the author. We thought this would provide a clear purpose for their reading of the submissions (Britt et al, 2017). Also, because the purpose of the funding was to amplify the voices from the royal commission submissions, we hoped that writing a letter would enable active engagement and perhaps provoke deeper reflections on the content of the submissions. By asking the visitors to respond with a letter, they would have to think about not only what was in the submission but also how it related to their own life and experiences.

The biggest challenge we faced with this use of documentation was in choosing the submissions to use for the co-respondence activity. We wanted to be sure that chosen submissions were relatively short, because we did not know how long visitors to the exhibition would be willing to engage with the activity. We also wanted to make sure that the three submissions were different in terms of story in case anyone wanted to read/respond to more than one.

Because of her in-depth knowledge of the submissions, the research coordinator chose three of the less personal and emotive submissions for this activity, ensuring that these were submissions with either a name or a pseudonym, as many of the submissions were submitted anonymously or had their identity redacted. We printed them on different coloured paper – Heather's submission was on yellow paper (Figure 7.1), Rose's was on pink (Figure 7.2) Maria's was on green (Figure 7.3). The colours themselves were not meaningful – they were simply the colours of the A4 paper that we already had available. We created co-respondence letter templates for the responses from the exhibition attendees. These began with 'Dear <name of the person who wrote the submission – Heather, Maria, or Rose>'. The rest of the page had lines all the way down for the participants to write on. These were printed on coloured paper to match the paper used for the submissions.

The co-respondence activity was set up at a table to the side of the exhibition space, with seats for visitors, and the printed submissions and letter response templates on the table. There were also information sheets explaining the research purpose of the activity as well as ethical consent forms for visitors to sign. Because of the timing of the exhibition (in the aftermath of the 2020–21 COVID-19 lockdowns), we put many pens on the table and placed disinfectant wipes in clear sight so that visitors could be confident that the pens were cleaned between uses. Finally, at the end of the table were three letter boxes, painted dark green. Once participants had read a submission and written a letter in response, they were invited to 'post' their letter into a letter box.

The transformative learning goal of this activity was to encourage people to engage with the material on a personal level, through their sense of discomfort with and empathy towards the content of the document's text. Ten response letters were received from members of the public and the academic community who attended the exhibition over one day. They ranged in length from a couple of sentences to full-page letters (see Figure 7.4).

The exhibition space was a modern, double-height, open-plan area with sparsely placed furniture, a large, elongated digital wall and a large spherical

Figure 7.1: Heather's submission

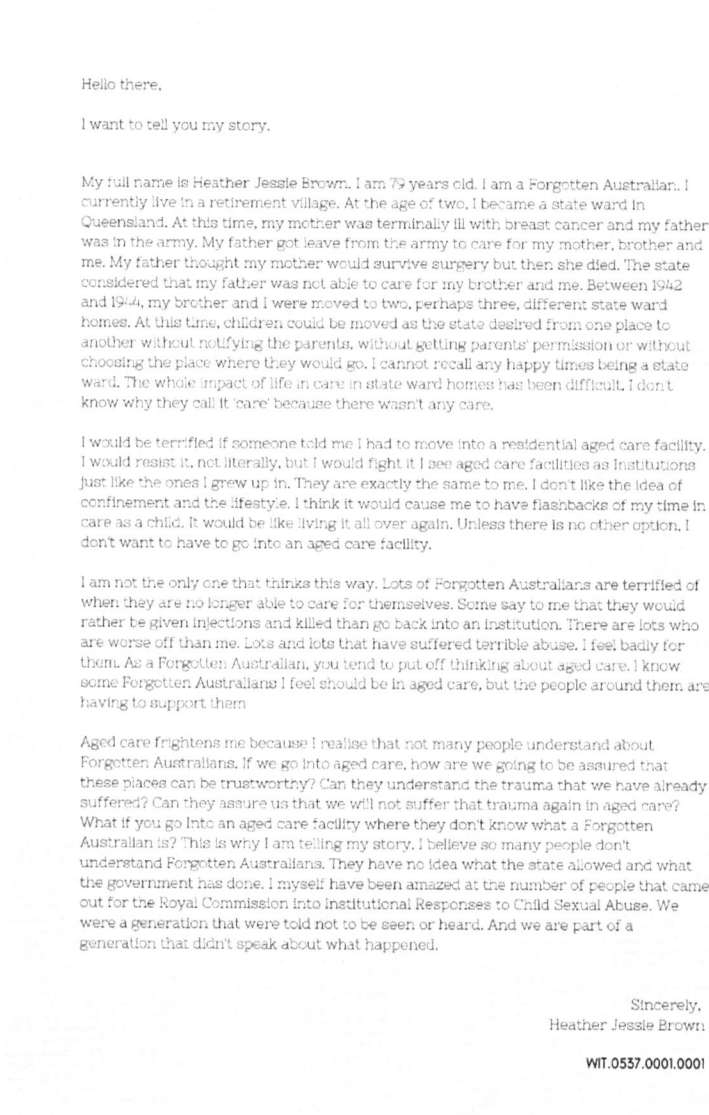

Hello there,

I want to tell you my story.

My full name is Heather Jessie Brown. I am 79 years old. I am a Forgotten Australian. I currently live in a retirement village. At the age of two, I became a state ward in Queensland. At this time, my mother was terminally ill with breast cancer and my father was in the army. My father got leave from the army to care for my mother, brother and me. My father thought my mother would survive surgery but then she died. The state considered that my father was not able to care for my brother and me. Between 1942 and 1944, my brother and I were moved to two, perhaps three, different state ward homes. At this time, children could be moved as the state desired from one place to another without notifying the parents, without getting parents' permission or without choosing the place where they would go. I cannot recall any happy times being a state ward. The whole impact of life in care in state ward homes has been difficult. I don't know why they call it 'care' because there wasn't any care.

I would be terrified if someone told me I had to move into a residential aged care facility. I would resist it, not literally, but I would fight it. I see aged care facilities as institutions just like the ones I grew up in. They are exactly the same to me. I don't like the idea of confinement and the lifestyle. I think it would cause me to have flashbacks of my time in care as a child. It would be like living it all over again. Unless there is no other option, I don't want to have to go into an aged care facility.

I am not the only one that thinks this way. Lots of Forgotten Australians are terrified of when they are no longer able to care for themselves. Some say to me that they would rather be given injections and killed than go back into an institution. There are lots who are worse off than me. Lots and lots that have suffered terrible abuse. I feel badly for them. As a Forgotten Australian, you tend to put off thinking about aged care. I know some Forgotten Australians I feel should be in aged care, but the people around them are having to support them.

Aged care frightens me because I realise that not many people understand about Forgotten Australians. If we go into aged care, how are we going to be assured that these places can be trustworthy? Can they understand the trauma that we have already suffered? Can they assure us that we will not suffer that trauma again in aged care? What if you go into an aged care facility where they don't know what a Forgotten Australian is? This is why I am telling my story. I believe so many people don't understand Forgotten Australians. They have no idea what the state allowed and what the government has done. I myself have been amazed at the number of people that came out for the Royal Commission into Institutional Responses to Child Sexual Abuse. We were a generation that were told not to be seen or heard. And we are part of a generation that didn't speak about what happened.

Sincerely,
Heather Jessie Brown

WIT.0537.0001.0001

Source: Photograph by Abigail Winter, 2024

digital screen hanging from the ceiling in the centre of the space. It was not a purpose-built exhibition space, but was often activated as one, as in the case of the Time to Listen exhibition. At first glance, you would be forgiven for thinking the exhibition we had created was quite sparse in terms of the content on display, but the reality was very different. The research coordinator's role in the exhibition space was to facilitate the exhibition experience by greeting people on arrival, situating them within the space and explaining what was on

Figure 7.2: Rose's submission

Hello there,

I want to tell you my story.

I am a woman, an Australian Ten Pound Pom. I am a daughter, sister, mother, friend, teacher, embroiderer, cook, at times quilter, painter. I have my hair cut, wear old clothes, buy new ones from a catalogue. I am a householder, would-be gardener, ratepayer, pensioner.

I wear glasses, am partially deaf, and I am arthritic. I sleep fairly well and rise to another day. I read, I write, I think, I dream, I plan, I hope, I expect. I experience joy and bear disappointment. I have a persona, habits and irritating quirks. I have values, beliefs and allegiances. I have a spirit and a soul. I am content.

I have a name.

I am 95.

Quick! Get out one of the boxes labelled OLD, perhaps the one labelled FRAGILE, THIS WAY UP, HANDLE WITH CARE or, perhaps the one labelled PAST USE BY DATE. Put me in the right box and store me, an adjective or a statistic.

Now I will have no history but an assessment. I will no longer have an opinion worth noting nor will I be expected to read substantial books, listen to good music, enjoy interesting food – in small helpings –, be open to new ideas. There will be some appropriate activities, singsongs and bingo, perhaps. There will be carers and trainees with special smiles learning to use the special voice for the OLD. "Cuppa, darling?" with a rising lilt, or the mock encouragement to exercise, "Of course, you can. One more, just for me" when I can't do it for myself, let alone anyone else! There will be the sweet inclusion "And how are we today?" We? I will not have a name, my name, but be 'Darling' or 'Sweetpea'. I will wear the clean unmatched clothes chosen for me. I will say I am sure I do understand what I am asked, and sure, too, about my reply, even about the date of my birth. I will cringe once more at being told "How wonderful you are!" and ensure "You are so lucky, you must be very grateful." And I will renew my ability and resolve not to be a nuisance but to be grateful, cooperative and obedient too.

This is not a 'submission' with capital letters, Facilities, Economics, Care Homes, Community buses, Assessments, Disabilities etc. It is about me and many like me, people, persons. We are not demented, not yet, most of us still live at home. We are individuals with histories, experience, culture, wisdom, habits, hopes, dreams, names and addresses. Perhaps, somewhere among all the discussions this could be remembered. Perhaps it could be built in and emphasised in training courses, – abolish the "Voice", or when the Capital Letters are in use and planning is being done. Community buses are no good if you need a taxi to reach the bus stop!

OLD has no recognised starting point, it is not a disease, affliction or nuisance. It is a fact of being alive, not to be deplored or feared but accepted, welcomed, enjoyed, and when necessary provided for properly for each person.

Sincerely,
Rose Thomson (pseudonym)

AWF.500.00249.0002

Source: Photograph by Abigail Winter, 2024

offer to see and experience, and inviting them to explore at their own pace. She reflected:

> It was in observing them navigate the various pieces of work that I realised how rich some of the content was and how much time it really demanded of people. Reading found poetry on the digital screen

Figure 7.3: Maria's submission

Hello there,

I want to tell you my story.

Over a period of 6 months I have had to fight for my mothers basic care needs to be addressed and resolved. I have to go to see my mother every day just to make sure she has a drink within reach and that she is dressed (including underwear) appropriately everyday. I have had to organise doctors appointments and buy her own wheelchair as the ones used in the nursing home are uncomfortable and inappropriate. I have had to go find staff members to get their attention as my mother waits for long periods as there is no one to take her to the toilet.

On the weekends there is not a single staff member on the floor, residents left unattended for hours. The home has no bus to take the residents on outings, and unless the residents are capable of walking they stay inside the facility day after day never seeing the sun or feeling the change of seasons. My mother would like to go outside but is frightened to ask just in case they forget she is outside.

Today I was informed that the physiotherapist aide who was working 5 days a week has lost 3 of those 5 days meaning that my mother will never be assisted in helping her to walk again after her stroke. The actual physiotherapist comes 1 day a month. I have no idea how this can be of any assistance at all.

My mother has had gastro many many times and the care staff make comments like 'oh what have you been eating' or 'this is the 3rd time we have had to change you today' or 'you have to understand we have other people to attend to other than you'. Humiliation and admonishment seems to be a regular part of her day and she is frightened to complain in case they do something to her when I am not around. er stroke has left her speaking Italian (her first language) she spoke and understood English very well now she is yelled at 'ENGLISH, I CAN'T UNDERSTAND YOU'. She ashamed and embarrassed and she feels like they treat her like she is doing it on purpose or that she is somehow now an idiot gibbering to them.

She is sleeping on an aid bed that deflates thus. leaving her sleeping on the metal frame of her bed. We have complained and complained to no avail. She was supposed to be turned during the night, this never happens. She is put to bed at 7:30pm flat on her back, and there she stays until 6:00am the next morning.

I have had many meetings with her case worker, the manager and the care staff on duty. I have written a formal letter of complaint and I am regularly trying to resolve issues on a day to day basis. Things are good for a few days and then it's back to be awful again. My mother is paying $125 per day for substandard treatment and I am at my wits end trying to keep. her spirits up. She asked me how long it would take for her to die if she stops eating or drinking and that is a reflection of how unhappy she is.

Sincerely,
Maria Rossi (pseudonym)

AWF.001.00964

Source: Photograph by Abigail Winter, 2024

was not just about the time it takes someone to read, but about how long the sense-making experience takes. The co-respondence letter writing activity was a perfect example of this. It was not an activity to be rushed, and often the last thing that people engaged with before they left. Knowing what was waiting for them, it was if they were waiting until they had become familiar with the space before

Figure 7.4: Co-respondence responses

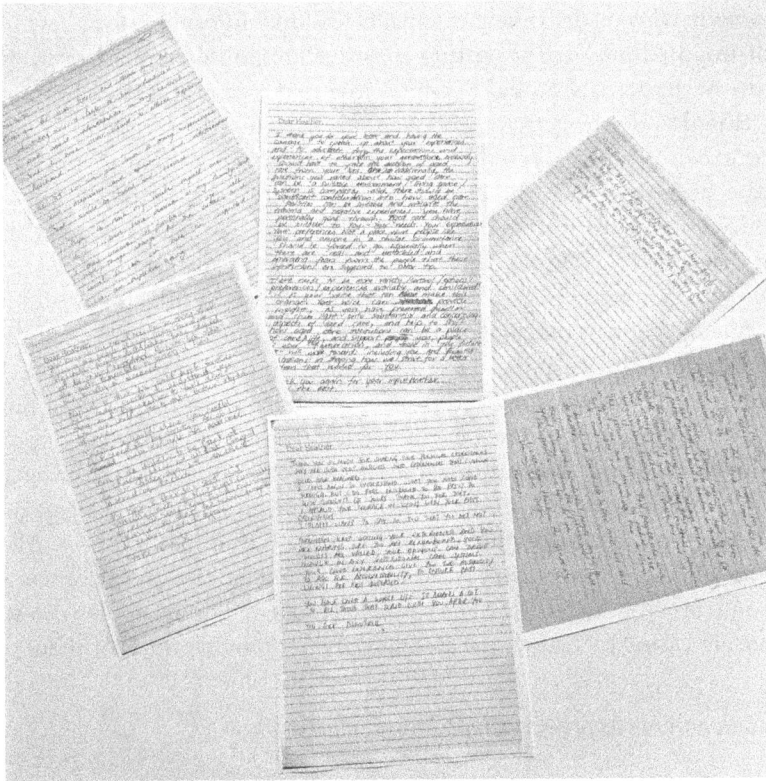

Source: Photograph by Abigail Winter, 2024

they settled in to become part of the artwork themselves. This was a big request, and one I honoured by giving them plenty of space – space to read, to integrate, to reflect and eventually respond. At that point, my role as a facilitator was to protect their space and allow it to unfold undisturbed.

One thing that surprised us during the exhibition was the response to the way the documents looked. We had reformatted the selected submissions to look like letters, starting them with 'Hello there, I want to tell you my story' and signing them with the author's name/pseudonym. We found that this formatting choice had a real influence on the way in which people interpreted the activity. Initially, all participants thought that their responses would be shared with the original author. Many shared that they felt a sense of responsibility to write a worthy response to ensure that the author of the letter felt heard and acknowledged. Some were worried that their response/reply would be inadequate – how could anything they said make up for what these people experienced? Finding out that their response would not make its way back to the original author only moderately reduced their anxiety, indicating this method's transformational, emotional power.

This activity also made some participants feel uncomfortable, for a few reasons. The self-imposed pressure of writing a 'perfect' response was part of it, but also the nature of the activity brought people close to the subject matter. Some people kindly refused to do the activity, knowing that they may be unable to get through it without being noticeably emotional. But for those willing to undertake it, they were brought into a direct one-to-one relationship with the text. They experienced a real story shared by a real person. They had to read it through enough that they could reply to it, and in doing so, many chose to reveal a part of themselves. It is one thing to read something, which in this case would involve a powerful engagement on its own, but having to respond requires a whole other level of engagement. Responding brings people into relationship. It enables the reader to demonstrate empathy and explain the impact that the text had on them.

When we read the responses later on, we felt that that all of the co-respondents had definitely read and engaged with the submissions. This meant that the activity successfully encouraged engagement, as well as meeting the broader goal of the wider research project to amplify voices from the Royal Commission. All of the co-respondents also brought in deeply reflective and emotional responses. As one co-respondent wrote to Maria: 'The system is broken. Those people who work in aged care are caring by nature; the system does not provide time for them to care.'

Case 2: Documents as art – machine learning artwork

The source document for our second arts-based knowledge translation, the machine learning artwork (Figure 7.5), was inspired by the submission from Heather, who identified as a 'Forgotten Australian' woman. Initially, the researcher-artist created a poem from the submission. The poem identified that there was a recurrence of coming back to the same (physical) place – the orphanage of her childhood became the aged care residence of her older age. There was also an underlying idea of being not 'seen' and not 'heard' (referring to Heather's words), which led to invisibility. This insight resonated, aligning with our approach to retelling stories through art to amplify the voices within written submissions that would otherwise remain archived and unseen by the broader Australian (and international) public. Following these initial inspirations, the researcher-artist used hand-drawing, focusing on negative space and outlines, to create a concrete poem about forced, abused orphans. A concrete poem uses the layout of its words to create a shape relevant to the topic of the poem (for examples, see Miller, 2021). This poem was challenging because it felt stuck in the space of the child's experience, while the document was from the woman at the other end of her life (Heather was 79 at the time of writing her submission, in 2019).

With concrete poetry, the spaces between the words matter – the words cannot be decoupled from the image; both are needed to tell the story. By playing with the phrases 'not seen' and 'not heard', the phrase 'not be' became the first layer

Figure 7.5: The *Not/Be Heard* machine learning artwork

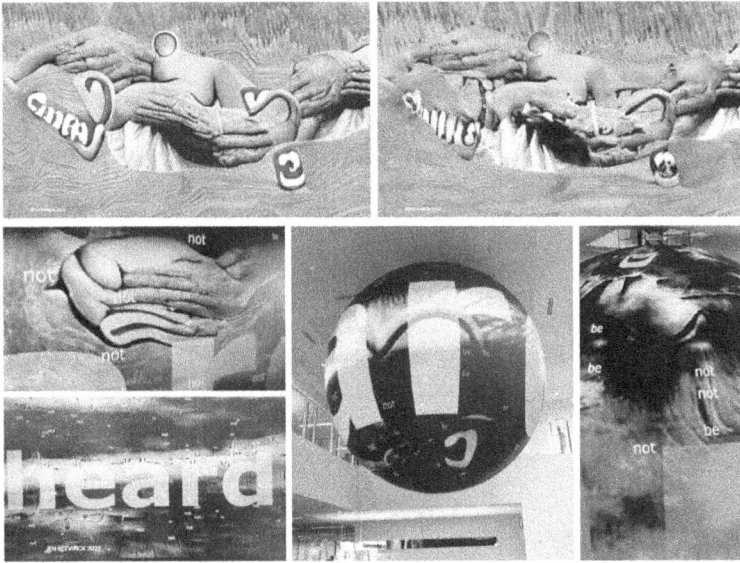

Source: Jen Seevinck, 2022, QUT Sphere

of the final artwork, which was white text on a black background. This more ambiguous phrase would balance the depressing and potentially upsetting message and better fit the artwork's location: the Sphere, a five-metre round digital screen in the middle of an education building at Queensland University of Technology in Brisbane, Australia. It is possible to walk around the Sphere from below or above – it is a physical, embodied space, supporting large-scale visuals (see the centre and bottom-right images in Figure 7.5). The black-and-white text was visually impactful as well as cryptic. We felt that adding visual imagery could increase engagement.

The researcher-artist took the opportunity to explore machine learning to create this visual content. A standard, large-scale database (ImageNet) was selected, and prompts entered through combined VQGAN and Clipit models hosted in a Google collaborative notebook.

VQGAN and Clipit are neural network models, and the combination, VQGAN + CLIP, allows for creation of images from text. This was first created by Katherine Crowsen in 2021. The machine learning algorithm iteratively created images, with incremental difference, for review. Words from the concrete poem were used initially but, as the output did not resonate artistically, the word 'carer' was added. This resulted in even more challenges in the form of problematic images, because the concept of 'carer' brought images of hands, but they were always the hands of someone who was White – reflecting the machine learning database's inherent programmed bias. This echoed the findings of a related research project within the broader one. This analysed Australian press images and also found that the visual trope of aged, wrinkled hands was the most dominant representation of the aged in aged care (Thomson et al, 2024). A key challenge, therefore, was that much of the imagery did not help to give visibility to people in aged care. In addition to race- and age-related biases, imagery created by the machine learning algorithm was often too disturbing for a public-facing exhibition, where passers-by could view it without reading about its context.

Through these and other reflections on the machine learning imagery, viewing context and image texture became points of interest for the researcher-artist. She shifted her conceptualisation of the artwork to embrace contextualised religiosity, where people standing below the Sphere would gaze upwards at the images and content on an adjacent screen would provide details. The machine learning images were heavily curated and sequenced into animations, creating an experimental, textured aesthetic that was intended to be more evocative than literal. In the final artwork (*Not/Be Heard*; Figure 7.5), this would work as an attractor to draw people to the work, while an adjacent wall screen would provide more detail.

The machine learning artwork, in the end, was an opportunity for the researcher-artist to experiment with how to give form to words that arose from the documentation provided to the royal commission. However, the challenges and inherent programmed biases in the machine learning database limited the final visualisation.

Advantages and limitations

The main advantage of the methods of using documentation that we have described in this chapter is the cost. The collection of documents from public sources, like royal commission submissions, is cost-free, because the documents are already in the public domain, making this a practical data collection method (Grant, 2019; Kara and Khoo, 2022). Also, depending on what type of publicly available documentation you select, there is likely to be a large amount of it, giving plenty of data to analyse.

An additional advantage is that this approach usually does not require ethical clearance (and the time this can cost a research project). However, that does not mean there are no ethical considerations. Kara and Khoo (2022) note the ethical questions raised by using existing documents – the potential need to obtain informed consent for their use, but also issues of confidentiality and representation. In addressing the issue of confidentiality, because the submissions are publicly available in the online repository, we used the submission number and the names of the submission authors (or pseudonyms). These enabled us to personalise the extracts and submissions, allowing for empathy for the writers. For our own research participants, we of course followed all approved ethical clearance requirements, including anonymisation, as per the informed consent forms they signed. As described earlier, we were also careful to consider the emotional and psychosocial burden on those who attended the exhibition. We left some areas of the exhibition space empty so that people could sit and think if they needed to. We also had boxes of tissues placed on tables for people to use without having to ask permission. The feedback from participants engaging in these arts-based knowledge translation activities included: '[They are] not as intimidating as regular data analysis'; 'It let me spend more time with it. So rather than just intellectually understanding what happened, I sat with the words and digested it. I feel like I have a sense of ownership over it in some way'; and 'It helped digest the experience of the source work's author. I feel like it sparked a lot of conversation and feelings to be discussed.'

The issue of representation is a harder one, because we took the words from the submissions and used them for our own arts-based transformational knowledge ends. In doing so, we were careful to remain true to the words and emotions of the submissions. Although, like all research processes, our own biases and interests guided this selection.

Our arts-based methods also address Kara and Khoo's (2022, p 250) call for research to 'create positive change'. By actively engaging members of the public with artistically modified documents, we gave the submissions an extended life. This provided engagement opportunities for people who would never have read the submissions in their original form or sought them out in the government archive.

The main limitation we found with the submissions was the time it took to download, read and select the ones we could use to amplify the voices of those who took the time to write submissions. Related to this, as already discussed, was the difficulty in selecting which submissions would be appropriate to use for our amplification methods. Finally, we obviously could not archive all of the documents that we downloaded and analysed as data sources for the project. If nothing else, they were already archived on the aged care royal commission website.[2] Instead, we have a research website summarising our work and outputs across the three-year project.

Other possible uses of this method

Like Braun and Clarke's (2022) description of inductive thematic analysis, our methods for using publicly available documents were discipline agnostic. Researchers across disciplines have been using publicly available documents as data sources for many years (McCredie et al, 2016; Grant, 2019; Tarrant and Hughes, 2022). What distinguished our approach was the consistent application of arts-based knowledge translation engagement activities. For the broader project, these included found poetry, letter writing, card game development and interactive artworks as outcomes. We also encouraged readers to experiment, something done by other researchers also – for example, Miller (2024) wrote research poems in response to a non-fiction book about natural disasters. In other contexts, we asked people to draw their experiences and reflections. We also received haikus and free verse poetry in response to our evaluations of teaching research poetry as a method.

Conclusion

While it is rare for public inquiry documents to be analysed, Cain et al (2023) used the same royal commission submissions as a data source. Their focus was specific, identifying the precursors and mediating factors that determine the use of chemical restraint of older people in residential aged care. They followed a specific process: they searched over 7,000 documents and identified seven cases, then carried out descriptive qualitative analysis. Our approach was intentionally different: we did not follow a typical formula or process for data analysis, but used the arts to creatively transform the public submissions into unique, expressive outputs that contributed to the discourse around aged care in Australia.

As many members of the public write submissions for public arenas, from submissions to royal commissions to letters to the editor, these are a rich source of information for researchers. They can serve both as data sources for traditional qualitative analysis and, as we describe here, as inspiration for arts-based transformational engagement.

The transformation of these liminal texts – documents often overlooked and left in a state of potential – into artistic expressions not only amplifies the voices within them but also fosters what Mezirow (1990; 2009) calls a transformative learning experience, where people perceive and understand the world around them differently because of the experience. By using arts-based transformative research with the royal commission submissions, we moved beyond analysis to invite a deeper connection, fostering understanding, empathy and, potentially, transformation from public documents.

Key considerations for using this method

- Any document can be a source for arts-based knowledge translation.

- Creating engaging arts-based knowledge translation provocations takes time – much more time than desk-based analysis.

- Take time and care selecting documents.

- If you are sharing publicly sourced documents, be thoughtful about what you choose. Others may not have the same interest, background, contextual knowledge or ability to read potentially confronting information.

- Be kind to your participants. Consider the psychosocial and emotional burden you may be asking them to engage with.

- Make sure your instructions to participants and the purpose(s) of the activities are clear. Help participants make an informed choice about documents and activities they engage with.

> • Think outside of usual data analysis methods. Just because the data exist as texts does not mean that your outputs need to be word-based, or presented as 'data'. Narratives, poems, plays and graphics can be transformative arts-based ways to analyse and present research outcomes from documentation.

Notes

1 The document library of the Royal Commission into Aged Care Quality and Safety is available at: http://bit.ly/rcacqs.
2 See: https://research.qut.edu.au/royalcommissionagedcare.

References

Amos, I. (2019) '"That's what they talk about when they talk about epiphanies": an invitation to engage with the process of developing found poetry to illuminate exceptional human experience', *Counselling and Psychotherapy Research*, 19(1): 16–24.

Baumgartner, L.M. (2012) 'Mezirow's theory of transformative learning from 1975 to present', in E.W. Taylor and P. Cranton (eds) *The Handbook of Transformative Learning: Theory, Research, and Practice*, John Wiley & Sons, pp 99–115.

Braun, V. and Clarke, V. (2022) *Thematic Analysis: A Practical Guide*, SAGE.

Britt, M.A., Rouet, J.-F. and Durik, A. (2017) *Literacy Beyond Text Comprehension: A Theory of Purposeful Reading*, Routledge.

Cain, P., Chejor, P. and Porock, D. (2023) 'Chemical restraint as behavioural euthanasia: case studies from the Royal Commission into Aged Care Quality and Safety', *BMC Geriatrics*, 23(1): art 444. doi: 10.1186/s12877-023-04116-5

Connolly, A. (2019) 'Aged care royal commission has had a third of the coverage of banks' bad behaviour. It doesn't add up', *ABC News*. Available from: https://www.abc.net.au/news/2019-11-03/aged-care-royal-commission-coverage-imbalance/11666490

Crowson, K. (2021) 'VQGAN+CLIP(Updated)' *Colab*. Available from: https://colab.research.google.com/github/justinjohn0306/VQGAN-CLIP/blob/main/VQGAN%2BCLIP(Updated).ipynb

Dalglish, S.L., Khalid, H. and McMahon, S.A. (2020) 'Document analysis in health policy research: the READ approach', *Health Policy and Planning*, 35(10): 1424–31. Available from: https://doi.org/10.1093/heapol/czaa064

Grant, A. (2019) *Doing Excellent Social Research with Documents: Practical Examples and Guidance for Qualitative Researchers*, Routledge.

Kara, H. and Khoo, S-M. (2022) 'Conclusion', in H. Kara and S.-M. Khoo (eds) *Qualitative and Digital Research in Times of Crisis: Methods, Reflexivity, and Ethics*, Policy Press, pp 247–52.

Kukkonen, T. and Cooper, A. (2019) 'An arts-based knowledge translation (ABKT) planning framework for researchers', *Evidence & Policy*, 15(2): 293–311.

Leavy, P. (2015) *Methods Meets Art: Arts-Based Research Practice* (2nd edn), The Guildford Press.

McCredie, B., Docherty, P., Easton, S. and Uylangco, K. (2016) 'The channels of monetary policy triggered by central bank actions and statements in the Australian equity market', *International Review of Financial Analysis*, 46: 46–61.

Mezirow, J. (1990) *Fostering Critical Reflection in Adulthood: A Guide to Transformative and Emancipatory Learning*, Jossey-Bass.

Mezirow, J. (2003) 'Transformative learning as discourse', *Journal of Transformative Education*, 1(1): 58–63.

Mezirow, J. (2009) 'Transformative learning theory', in J. Mezirow and E.W. Taylor (eds) *Transformative Learning in Practice: Insights from Community, Workplace, and Higher Education*, John Wiley & Sons, pp 18–31.

Miller, E. (2021) *Creative Arts-Based Research in Aged Care: Photovoice, Photography and Poetry in Action*, Routledge.

Miller, E. (2024) 'The Black Saturday bushfire disaster: found poetry for arts-based knowledge translation in disaster risk and climate change communication', *Arts & Health*, advance online publication. doi: 10.1080/17533015.2024.2310861

Parsons, J.A. and Boydell, K.M. (2012) 'Arts-based research and knowledge translation: Some key concerns for health-care professionals', *Journal of Interprofessional Care*, 26(3): 170–2.

Patrick, L.D. (2016) 'Found poetry: creating space for imaginative arts-based literacy research writing', *Literacy Research: Theory, Method, and Practice*, 65(1): 384–403.

Prince, C. (2022) 'Experiments in methodology: sensory and poetic threads of inquiry, resistance, and transformation', *Qualitative Inquiry*, 28(1): 94–107.

Royal Commission into Aged Care Quality and Safety (2019) *Interim Report: Neglect* (3 vols), Commonwealth of Australia. Available from: www.royalcommission.gov.au/aged-care/interim-report

Scott, J. (1990) *A Matter of Record: Documentary Sources in Social Research*, Polity Press.

Tarrant, A. and Hughes, K. (2022) 'Qualitative data re-use and secondary analysis: researching in and about a crisis', in H. Kara and S.-M. Khoo (eds) *Qualitative and Digital Research in Times of Crisis: Methods, Reflexivity, and Ethics*, Policy Press, pp 156–71.

Thomas, S. (2001) 'Reimaging inquiry, envisioning form', in L. Neilsen, A.L. Cole and J.G. Knowles (eds) *The Art of Writing Inquiry*, Backalong Books, pp 273–82.

Thomson, T.J., Miller, E., Holland-Batt, S., Seevinck, J. and Regi, S. (2024) 'Visibility and invisibility in the aged care sector: visual representation in Australian news from 2018-2021', *Media International Australia*, 190(1): 146–64.

PART III

Using official documents

8

Reflections on using charity annual reporting data to consider questions of representation

Helen Abnett

Summary

- This chapter describes the methodological approach taken in two studies exploring charities' representational strategies within their Trustees' Annual Reports and Accounts.

- Study 1 uses thematic analysis to interrogate how international development charities depict themselves and their partnerships, revealing dissonance between narrative and governance sections that suggests a strategic orientation towards legitimation rather than transparency.

- Study 2 applies qualitative content analysis to detailed expenditure data from NHS-linked charities, examining how spending choices communicate the charities' perceived roles in supplementing (providing additional services), substituting (including 'filling the gaps') or sidestepping (supporting work that takes place outside or alongside) public provision.

- The chapter offers critical insight into how a combination of methodological choices – the theoretical framework, data source and methodological approach – enabled a novel contribution to be made.

- Together, these studies demonstrate the potential of annual reporting data as a valuable, but under-used, resource for understanding charities' representational practices.

Introduction

In the UK, charitable organisations play a prominent role in society. Charities provide care in their communities, deliver services on behalf of the state, create access to music and art, advocate on behalf of different individuals and groups, and much more. While charities are prevented by law from engaging in party politics, their work is often still political in that it has public, social and economic impact (Reich, 2018; Dunning, 2022; Child, 2024). This means that the role of charities – their functions and activities as well as their positions and identities – has widespread relevance. The identities are partly constructed by and through charities' own communications. Charities' portrayals of who they are, what they do and who they serve (which I term their 'representational practices') shape wider understandings of the appropriate role of charities in relation to the state, private sector and society as a whole.

In this chapter, I describe how I and co-authors conducted two different studies on charity representations, each of which analysed data from documents. Study 1 (Abnett, 2024) used thematic analysis to explore how international development charities describe themselves, their local partners and their partnership relationships in their annual reports and accounts. Study 2 (Abnett et al, 2023) considered detailed expenditure data in charity accounts to explore the role that NHS-linked charities present themselves as playing within the NHS. By describing and comparing the two studies, this chapter demonstrates some ways in which annual reporting data can be used and outlines the advantages and limitations of these approaches.

Cordery and McConville (2023, p 110) have shown that charity annual reporting data offer a 'potential goldmine' of qualitative and quantitative data that can help us to understand 'the fundamentals of voluntary organisations and the sector at large' and to answer questions 'on matters as diverse as performance, governance, regulation and organizational practices'. Building on this learning, this chapter reflects on the use of charity annual reports and accounts to answer a different – but related – set of questions about charities' representational practices. Such questions focus on how discourses and identities are constructed within charity annual reports and accounts and reflect on the wider implications of these constructions.

The data source

What are Trustees' Annual Reports and Accounts?

In the UK, charity reporting regulations and filing requirements differ by jurisdiction, charity income size and charity registration type. In England and Wales (which, for these purposes, operates as one jurisdiction), most registered charities with a gross income of £25,000 or more and all charitable incorporated organisations, of any size, must file a Trustees' Annual Report and a set of annual accounts with the Charity Commission of England and Wales (CCEW). The CCEW publishes submitted charity Trustees' Annual Reports and Accounts for up to the last five years on their online database.

The Trustees' Annual Report and Accounts are – as the name suggests – made up of two parts, the Trustees' Annual Report and the annual accounts, published together as a single document. In practice, the Trustees' Annual Report contains within it two different types of information: a narrative part describing organisational activities and achievements, followed by information on the organisation's operational, governance and management approach. Some annual reports also include a letter from the organisation's leader summarising the organisational approach, values and attitudes. The accounts contain financial information.

The content of Trustees' Annual Reports and Accounts are partly regulatorily defined, with the charities' Statement of Recommended Practice (SORP) outlining reporting and accounting requirements. However, charities also have significant scope to shape the format and nature of these reports, to decide what to include and exclude, and to structure how they present the qualitative and quantitative information provided. Thus these documents vary greatly in length, presentation and level of itemised detail provided within their accounts. As Dhanani and Kennedy (2023, p 349) argue, this means that 'the formality of the report that offers audiences a sense of authenticity and reliability belies the more symbolic forms of legitimation that may be used to influence audience perceptions'. Researchers using annual reports and accounts must, therefore, make efforts to contextualise these documents within these broader frames of legitimation and meaning.

Using Trustees' Annual Reports and Accounts in research on representation and identity construction

A number of studies have considered issues of identity construction within the annual reports of both charities and organisations in other sectors. For example, Dhanani (2019) analysed the photographs that ten large English and Welsh international development charities included in their annual reports, while Dhanani and Kennedy (2023) similarly explored the photographs used in the annual reports of eight of the largest US-based humanitarian organisations. Kamla and Roberts examined visual images in the annual reports of companies within the Arab Gulf states, finding that these companies 'used visual images to depict and represent the possibility of a successful profitable, modern and global business that is also sympathetic to tradition and operates within the framework of Islamic principles' (2010, p 449).

Drawing on a different perspective, Heckert et al used quantitative content analysis to trace the multiple-identity constructions of one Dutch foundation in the text of their annual reports over nearly two decades, arguing that the annual reports 'are ideal for this purpose since they are official communications of the organization itself' (2020, p 130). Alternatively, Haniffa and Hudaib (2007) used content analysis to explore the communicated ethical identity (the combined Islamic and corporate identity) constructed in the annual reports of Islamic banks.

There is, therefore, a growing body of knowledge that asks innovative and interesting questions about the identities constructed by organisations through the medium of their annual reports. In the rest of this chapter, I explore in greater depth two studies I was involved with, both of which drew on Trustees' Annual Reports and Accounts in different ways to consider issues of representation and the implications of the discourses constructed.

Study 1: International development charities

Research question and theoretical framing

This research examined the Trustees' Annual Reports and Accounts of 29 international development charities (also known as international non-governmental organisations – INGOs), seeking to answer the key research questions: 'how do INGOs represent themselves, their project partners, and their partnering relationships? And what model of partnership is reflected in such descriptions?' (Abnett, 2024, p 2). To consider the findings, the study draws on *stakeholder theories*. These are theories of 'organizational management and ethics' which address 'morals and values explicitly as a central feature of managing organizations' (Phillips et al, 2003, pp 480–1). While stakeholder theories were originally developed for use by for-profit firms (Hansen, 2023), within the charity sector, they have been widely drawn on to explore accountability and representational practices.

There are two distinct approaches to stakeholder theory. Ethical stakeholder theory is premised on an understanding that organisations should treat others equally and fairly, and it contends that charities will feel a moral responsibility to be 'complete, truthful and objective' (Dhanani and Connolly, 2012, p 1144) in their representational practices. However, positive stakeholder theory (which is closely linked to legitimation theory; Chen and Roberts, 2010) argues that organisations are in competition for both resources and legitimacy. Thus, they will seek to shape their representations so as to present a particular narrative of their organisations, rather than seeking openness or transparency.

I accessed the annual reports and accounts from the CCEW database, based on a purposive sampling process that identified larger charities that had a donor-dependent income profile, published one or more letters by organisational leaders within their report and mentioned project partners within the report and accounts (see Abnett, 2024). As prior research on international development charities' representational activities has largely focused on the images used (Dhanani, 2019; Dhanani and Kennedy, 2023), in this research I drew on the text of the reports and accounts to consider how these charities represented themselves, their project partners and their partnering relationships.

Data analysis

I explored the Trustees' Annual Reports and Accounts using inductive thematic analysis. Thematic analysis is a method which looks 'for identifying themes and patterns of meaning across a dataset in relation to a research question' (Braun and Clarke, 2013, p 175). The method I chose follows a six-phase process of thematic analysis, as described by Braun and Clarke (2006; 2013). Box 8.1 outlines and briefly summarises these six phases of thematic analysis.

Box 8.1: The six phases of thematic analysis

Phase 1:   **Data familiarisation.** This involves repeated and active reading of the data.

Phase 2:   **Generating initial codes.** Preliminary codes are generated from the data in response to the research questions.

Phase 3:   **Searching for themes.** The long list of initial codes is analysed and reviewed, and codes are combined to form the overarching themes.

Phase 4:   **Reviewing and refining themes.** The codes for each theme are read to ensure consistency and validity. The robustness of the themes are considered in relation to the entire dataset.

Phase 5:   **Defining and naming themes.** This involves identifying the core meaning of each theme, determining what aspect of the data each theme captures and writing a detailed analysis of each theme.

Phase 6:   **Writing up.** This is an iterative process that enables the themes and ideas generated to be clarified while also making links to theory and the literature.

Source: Braun and Clarke, 2006; 2013

The research process in practice

To conduct the research, I uploaded each of the Trustees' Annual Report and Accounts under study to NVivo – a qualitative data analysis software package – and coded the text using this package. As outlined earlier, in line with thematic analysis, I read these Trustees' Annual Reports and Accounts a number of times in the initial phase of research to become familiar with the data. Given the research questions' focus on partners and partnership representations, I then began to focus on and generate initial codes based only on those elements of the text that described partners and the partnering relationships – an approach described by Braun and Clarke (2013, p 216) as 'selective coding'. This included coding for representations of the charity itself when they were made in a context which described their local partners and partnering relationships.

It was during these initial phases of research that I began to develop an unexpected understanding of one particular aspect of the dataset. As Braun and Clarke note, the initial stages of data familiarisation are not just about absorbing data, but about reading it '*actively, analytically* and *critically*' and 'asking questions like ... [i]n what *different* ways [do participants] make sense of the topic discussed?' (2013, p 205, emphasis in original). Applying this to my research meant asking the following question of the documents: in what different ways are partners and partnering relationships represented? Asking this type of question of the data enabled me to understand that the themes I was generating varied across the different sections of the annual reports and accounts. In particular, the patterns and themes being generated within the narrative sections diverged from those being generated within the managerial and governance sections of these documents, as well as the accounts.

The next stages of coding and analysis took account of these differences, and while searching for, reviewing, refining and defining the themes, I continued to pay attention to this discord. It was this dissonance that generated this study's key contribution. As outlined in Abnett (2024), the themes generated within the narrative sections of these reports focused on ideas of collaborative partnership and co-implementation, albeit with the INGO occupying a leading role. However, the managerial sections and accounts generated themes of a hierarchical, quasi-grant-making relationship, focusing on upwards accountability from local partners to the INGO. Drawing on the theoretical framework, these themes and ideas were crystalised to argue that the dissonance found within the reports and accounts suggest that in their reports, INGOs are not being fully open and transparent, but instead 'prioritise ... legitimation rather than authenticity' (Abnett, 2024, p 585), in line with the positive model of stakeholder theory.

Within this research, drawing on the entirety of the text of the Trustees' Annual Report and Accounts – and adopting a flexible research methodology that inductively generated codes from within the data through a detailed and repetitive reading and coding process – led to the production of novel findings. Analysing these findings through stakeholder theory enabled greater understanding of the implications of these findings. It was the combination of these choices – the theoretical framework, data source and methodological approach – that allowed this novel contribution to emerge.

Study 2: NHS-linked charities

While Study 1 used the entirety of the text of charity annual reports and accounts, Study 2[1] took a very different approach, focusing instead on the detailed expenditure information reported by charities within their accounts.

Research question and theoretical framing

This research analysed over 3,000 lines of expenditure data from 676 sets of accounts filed by 340 different charities (Abnett et al, 2023). The approach taken to the research was based on our understanding that this detailed expenditure information reflects the choices these charities make as to how to classify, record and present their spending. The expression of different types of expenditure has a specific social and symbolic value that – we argue – links to the role and identity that these charities actively choose to present for themselves.

The charities in this study largely provided funding to directly pay for goods and services for their associated NHS body or other organisation and/or to give grants to these NHS bodies or other partners. Thus, we chose to explore our findings using a theoretical framework developed by Toepler and Abramson (2021) to consider the relationship between government and grant-making foundations in the US. Drawing on this framing, we predicted that these charities' representations would project one (or more) of three roles: (1) the charities would describe their expenditure in ways that are consistent with an approach that complements and/ or supplements public provision; (2) the charities would describe their expenditure activities in ways that suggest their role is to substitute for government service provision; and (3) the charities would position themselves as supporting work that takes place outside or alongside the NHS, thus sidestepping government provision.

Data collection

The research drew on a purposive sample of annual accounts of NHS-linked charities, and analysis focused specifically on charitable and grant expenditure reported by these organisations. This data had to be extracted from the wealth of accounting information reported by these charities, which – given the volume of data under consideration – was a substantial task. The project team involved in this research thus chose to employ a specialist data entry firm, which manually extracted each individual line of accounting information. These sampling and data extraction processes were overseen by Professor John Mohan. For further details, see Abnett et al (2023).

Data cleaning and analysis

The dataset collected through this process had to be cleaned – for example, to remove spelling and typographical errors. I did this using OpenRefine, an open-source data tool for cleaning messy data. This cleaning was also important in the data familiarisation stage of the analysis. As in the familiarisation stage of Study 1, during data cleaning we began to gain an understanding of the types of expenditure items that were included within the dataset.

Once cleaned, the dataset was analysed using qualitative content analysis. Content analysis is a methodology that has been widely used to classify and interpret financial records and in accounting research more generally (Cordery and McConville, 2023). The form of content analysis we used in this study was similar to that referred to by Hsieh and Shannon (2005) as summative content analysis. Within our research, this meant considering each line of reported expenditure and coding it to one of a number of defined codes, described within a specific coding framework we developed for this study.

We constructed the coding framework abductively, meaning the process involved a combination of inductive and deductive thinking, and we took a flexible approach to generating new codes from the data. Thus, prior to the start of analysis, we explored wider guidance for charity accounting as well as specific guidance produced for NHS-linked charities. For example, guidance produced by the Healthcare Financial Management Association (2022) suggests expenditure could be coded to include distinctive categories such as 'medical research', 'purchase of new equipment', 'building and refurbishment', 'staff education and welfare' and 'patient education and welfare'. While such a breakdown provided a useful starting point for our coding structure, our data familiarisation process demonstrated that this structure could not always be applied to the annual accounts we were analysing. For example, our data did not always indicate whether education or welfare costs were for patients or staff, with many lines simply titled 'education, welfare and amenities' or similar. In addition, the data included a number of lines that fell outside the Healthcare Financial Management Association categories.

The deductive codes developed with reference to the guidance were thus combined with codes developed inductively through the data familiarisation process, to provide a draft coding framework consisting of eight discrete codes. Our coding framework included clear descriptions of the types of costs to be included within each code. Also, during the data cleaning process, we had identified 'clusters' of lines, where data with the same row description appeared five or more times, and we tested the draft coding scheme through initial block coding of these clustered lines of data and presented findings to the wider project team. This reassured us of the coding scheme's suitability for capturing the broader range of expenditure data included in our dataset, and our coding framework was finalised.

Each of the remaining expenditure lines (2,575 lines of data) were then manually coded by one of two researchers. This involved reading and considering each line of data and coding it to just one of the eight abductively developed thematic codes: for example, an expenditure line of 'ambulatory ECG monitors' was coded to 'clinical equipment', while 'clothing and teas for patients' was coded to 'education, welfare and amenities'. Each line could only be coded to one code. To ensure consistency, the two coders met regularly to discuss progress. Once coding was completed, an inter-rater reliability test (a test to measure how well the two raters agreed) was performed. A random sample of 10 per cent of the manually coded items was second-coded by the coder who had not done the initial coding, and a kappa test (a statistical test that measures inter-rater reliability) was performed. The result of the test indicated a high degree of inter-rater reliability, providing some reassurance that our approach to coding provided valid results.

Using this methodology, our research found that charities' expenditure representations cover a wide variety of different activities. Many of these expenditure lines portrayed these charities as contributing substantial funding for amenities and welfare items, including spending on flowers, newspapers, toiletry packs, toys, cushions and books. These costs can be seen as '"comforts": improving the environment for staff, patients and the wider community, but without a clear clinical aim' (Abnett et al, 2023, p 374). However, these charities also reported substantial expenditure on equipment, buildings and furniture for NHS institutions. Expenditure described within the dataset included 'funding for basic hospital equipment, such as vital signs monitors, laryngoscopes, bladder scanners, dental drills, pulse oximeters, treadmills and weighing machines. Larger pieces of equipment are also included – including x-ray machines and defibrillators' (Abnett et al, 2023, p 375). Drawing on our theoretical framework, we argued that the charities studied chose to represent themselves in ways that are consistent with being both supplementary and substitutive of state provision of healthcare. Their role was shown to be providing not just 'comforts', but also goods that are essential in comprehensive healthcare provision. This, we further argued, reinforced a blurring of the remits of charity and the state in providing a comprehensive health service in England and Wales.

Within this research, therefore, the detailed focus on one relatively small part of the charity annual reports and accounts led to interesting and novel findings. As with Study 1, it was the combination of choices – theoretical framework, data sources and methodological approach – that enabled this contribution.

Advantages and limitations of the research approaches

The two studies described in this chapter demonstrate that Trustees' Annual Reports and Accounts provide a rich and multifaceted source of data. Furthermore, I chose to highlight these two different research studies to show how this data can be analysed in different and creative ways: Study 1 compared representational activities within different sections of these documents, and Study 2 showed how a qualitative analysis of financial data can generate new insight, furthering our understanding of the role played by charities in the English and Welsh healthcare system.

The advantages of using both thematic analysis and qualitative content analysis as described include that these are well-accepted methods that have been used extensively in research. The different methods used were also appropriate to the different types of research conducted: the flexibility of thematic analysis and the focus on patterns enabled the novel findings outlined in Study 1, while the more rigid approach to summative qualitative content analysis outlined in Study 2 enabled large volumes of data to be summarised and coded.

These choices also reflect my positionality as a pragmatic researcher. My pragmatic approach foregrounds the situatedness of the documents themselves and takes from epistemic heterogeneity – which contends that 'no single philosophic approach [to research methodologies] can drive out all the others' (Riccucci, 2010, p 117) – a sense that documents are not objects to be unlocked, but artefacts to be interpreted. It is the research questions (as well as the research purpose) that guides the selection of a research approach (White, 1999; Riccucci, 2010). Within such an approach, research methods are seen as tools rather than as indicators of a particular type of knowledge claim. This allows the freedom to choose the research methods and approaches that are most appropriate to the research questions. As described, it was the combination of these choices – the theoretical framework adopted, the specific aspect of the report and accounts considered and the methodological approach chosen – that enabled each study's contribution.

There are of course challenges with, and limitations to, these data sources and methodologies. In particular, both of the methods described involved summarising the data into codes or themes. This means some of the intricate and specific details of the data were not conveyed through the research processes and writing up. It has also been argued that both these methods can also potentially lead to issues with subjectivity or interpretation (Cordery and McConville, 2023, p 119).

While in Study 2, this was partly addressed through triangulation between two researchers and wider team working, the analysis in Study 1 largely reflected my own understanding of the documents and themes. I sought to ensure the research was robust by drawing on a well-accepted and detailed methodology, clearly defining and presenting the themes and revisiting and reviewing these themes over a prolonged period of time. The work was also tested through presentations at seminars and conferences as well as through the peer review process.

In terms of the limitations of Trustees' Annual Reports and Accounts as a data source, it must be recognised that these documents can only provide a partial account. Moreover, in Study 2, a notable proportion of the data we considered was presented and coded as 'miscellaneous' or 'other'. We regarded this data as extraneous or otherwise ancillary to our study. In addition, coding such documents represents a significant time burden, particularly when much of the data will be excluded from analysis. Such exclusions are themselves clearly worthy of critical evaluation and reflection. Another limitation, as described in Abnett (2024), is that these data sources provide a top-down account, presenting the perspectives and voices of charity leadership, the 'elite' (see Ho et al, 2023), rather than the views of others within or outside charities. Thus, while Study 1 reflected on partnership representation, the voices of the partners were excluded. The limited nature of these documents must be considered in any consideration of findings.

Ethical considerations

The studies described here reinforce Cordery and McConville's (2023) description of charity annual reports and accounts as a potential goldmine of qualitative and quantitative data that – as yet – has not been fully explored. Drawing on these documents as data sources has an ethical advantage compared to other methods. Using this extant and publicly available source can enable researchers to answer important research questions without imposing the 'burden of participation', in terms of time, financial and labour costs, on potential interview subjects or survey respondents (Ruggiano and Perry, 2019, p 83). This is particularly relevant when working with charity organisations, whose time and resources are often tight and whose workers might face more frequent and more acute emotional demands and burdens.

In considering the ethics of the sources and methods used, it is, of course, not sufficient to simply compare the use of documents to other methods. These annual reports and accounts are publicly available documents, but as Grant (2019, pp 55–6) notes, simply being in the public domain does not mean such documents are automatically 'fair game' for researchers. We must also consider the appropriateness of the research and questions of data protection and privacy (Grant, 2019, p 56).

A perhaps more complex ethical consideration related to these documents is the question of anonymity. Neither study anonymised organisations. In particular, Study 1 listed the names of organisations and included substantial extracts from the reports of the named organisations. This opens up a number of ethical issues, including the risk of reputational harm for named organisations. While the decision not to anonymise was taken with the recognition that anonymity would likely never be truly achievable (due to the public nature of the documents), the primary motivating factor was data transparency. Being open about the organisations studied means the research findings can be better interrogated by others, including – if they wish – the charities themselves. In addition, given the paper called for international development charities to 'be more consistent and transparent when describing their partnering relationships' (Abnett, 2024, p 594), naming these organisations was also an intentional act to encourage the charities to reflect on their own practice.

Conclusion

The research studies described here focus specifically on the annual reports and accounts of larger registered charitable organisations in England and Wales. However, the approaches outlined have the potential to be used in a number of other contexts. This might involve charities of different sizes and in different jurisdictions, or it might involve other types of organisation, including those in the private and state sectors.

The methods also have the potential to be expanded in a number of ways. As we describe in Abnett et al (2023), at the time when Study 2 was conducted, we felt that computational social science approaches did not have the capacity to robustly analyse the dataset. Yet, constant developments in computational methods may mean that future research could perhaps take better advantage of machine learning methods, which would allow for analysis of substantially larger datasets. I nevertheless remain cautious of the potential for such methods to understand the nuance and detail of such data. As a researcher, I have learned that spending time with data through detailed coding processes means I develop a richer relationship with the documents that form the datasets I use, which I believe enables deeper insight and reduces the risk of 'unknown unknowns'.

As outlined earlier, a limitation of the use of annual reports and accounts is that they only represent one voice – generally considered to be that of the charities' leadership. Research such as that outlined here could be furthered with analysis of responses to and reflections on these representations by those who charities state they seek to reach, as well as others within the charities. This has the potential to raise other voices and consider the wider implications of charity representations – as Bhati and Eikenberry (2016) do in their research on how children feel about their portrayal in the images of fundraising campaigns, and as Breeze and Dean (2012) do in their exploration of the views of young homeless people regarding the images of homelessness that appear in major charity campaigns.

In addition, analysing these annual reports and accounts in comparison to other internal or external documents produced by charities (such as their websites, fundraising materials and strategy documents) could drive forward our understanding of the relationship between charities' internal organisational practice and their external representational activities. This would not only aid our understanding of how these organisations work, but also help us think about how any dissonance found – due to legitimation practices, for example – could be overcome so that charities can better meet their responsibilities of openness and transparency.

Key considerations for using this method

- In analysis of documents, it is the combination of theory, method and data source that enables novel contributions to be made. Pay attention to all three of these elements of the research process and consider how they might lead to different ways of answering the research question.

- You may find yourself using a range of analysis methods and approaches. This should not be feared – it can add substantial value to your research!

- The thematic analysis and qualitative content analysis approaches described in this chapter are time-consuming and require detailed reading and re-reading of the data, which is then summarised into broader themes, patterns and codes. You should ensure your chosen approach is the best way of answering your research question. Also, consider whether your coding framework should be developed inductively, deductively or abductively.

- Pay attention to positionality and subjectivity. Think about how they might impact on the research and how you could address them if necessary.

- Finally, in the use of documents, remember whose voice you are considering – and whose you are excluding – and the implications of this for your ability to answer your research questions.

Note

[1] For Study 2, 'Border crossings: charity and voluntarism in Britain's mixed economy of healthcare since 1948', we gratefully acknowledge the support of the Wellcome Trust (Grant 219901/Z/19/Z).

References

Abnett, H. (2024) 'Collaborator or quasi–grant maker? Revealing the dissonance in international development charities' partnership representations', *Development in Practice*, 34(5): 585–96.

Abnett, H., Bowles, J. and Mohan, J. (2023) 'The role of charitable funding in the provision of public services: the case of the English and Welsh National Health Service', *Policy & Politics*, 51(2): 362–84.

Bhati, A. and Eikenberry, A.M. (2016) 'Faces of the needy: the portrayal of destitute children in the fundraising campaigns of NGOs in India', *International Journal of Nonprofit and Voluntary Sector Marketing*, 21(1): 31–42.

Braun, V. and Clarke, V. (2006) 'Using thematic analysis in psychology', *Qualitative Research in Psychology*, 3(2): 77–101.

Braun, V. and Clarke, V. (2013) *Successful Qualitative Research: A Practical Guide for Beginners*, SAGE.

Breeze, B. and Dean, J. (2012) 'Pictures of me: user views on their representation in homelessness fundraising appeals', *International Journal of Nonprofit and Voluntary Sector Marketing*, 17(2): 132–43.

Chen, J.C. and Roberts, R.W. (2010) 'Toward a more coherent understanding of the organization–society relationship: a theoretical consideration for social and environmental accounting research', *Journal of Business Ethics*, 97: 651–65.

Child, C. (2024) 'An overview of nonprofit sector theories' in E. Witesman and C. Child (eds) *Reimagining Nonprofits: Sector Theory in the Twenty-First Century*, Cambridge University Press, pp 17–40.

Cordery, C. and McConville, D. (2023) 'Annual reporting in voluntary organisations: opportunities for content analysis research', in J. Dean and E. Hogg (eds) *Researching Voluntary Action: Innovations and Challenges*, Policy Press, pp 110–21.

Dhanani, A. (2019) 'Identity constructions in the annual reports of international development NGOs: preserving institutional interests?', *Critical Perspectives on Accounting*, 59: 1–31.

Dhanani, A. and Connolly, C. (2012) 'Discharging not-for-profit accountability: UK charities and public discourse', *Accounting, Auditing & Accountability Journal*, 25(7): 1140–69.

Dhanani, A. and Kennedy, D. (2023) 'Envisioning legitimacy: visual dimensions of NGO annual reports', *Accounting, Auditing & Accountability Journal*, 36(1): 348–77.

Dunning, C. (2022) *Nonprofit Neighborhoods: An Urban History of Inequality and the American State*, The University of Chicago Press.

Grant, A. (2019) *Doing Excellent Social Research with Documents: Practical Examples and Guidance for Qualitative Researchers*, Routledge.

Haniffa, R. and Hudaib, M. (2007) 'Exploring the ethical identity of Islamic banks via communication in annual reports', *Journal of Business Ethics*, 76(1): 97–116.

Hansen, R.K. (2023) 'Applying a stakeholder management approach to ethics in charitable fundraising', *Journal of Philanthropy and Marketing*, 28(4): art e1731. doi: 10.1002/nvsm.1731

Healthcare Financial Management Association (2022) *Example NHS Charity Annual Report And Accounts 2021/22*, HFMA. Available from: www.hfma.org.uk/sys tem/files/nhs-charitable-funds-example-ara-202122.pdf

Heckert, R., Boumans, J. and Vliegenthart, R. (2020) 'How to nail the multiple identities of an organization? A content analysis of projected identity', *Voluntas: International Journal of Voluntary and Nonprofit Organizations*, 31(1): 129–41.

Ho, M.-H., Duffy, B. and Benjamin, L.M. (2023) 'Documents in a field of action: using documents to address research questions about nonprofit and voluntary organizations', *Voluntas: International Journal of Voluntary and Nonprofit Organizations*, 34(1): 133–9.

Hsieh, H.-F. and Shannon, S. E. (2005) 'Three approaches to qualitative content analysis', *Qualitative Health Research*, 15(9): 1277–88.

Kamla, R. and Roberts, C. (2010) 'The global and the local: Arabian Gulf States and imagery in annual reports', *Accounting, Auditing & Accountability Journal*, 23(4): 449–81.

Phillips, R., Freeman, R.E. and Wicks, A.C. (2003) 'What stakeholder theory is not', *Business Ethics Quarterly*, 13(4): 479–502.

Reich, R. (2018) *Just Giving: Why Philanthropy Is Failing Democracy and How It Can Do Better*, Princeton University Press.

Riccucci, N.M. (2010) *Public Administration: Traditions of Inquiry and Philosophies of Knowledge*, Georgetown University Press.

Ruggiano, N. and Perry, T.E. (2019) 'Conducting secondary analysis of qualitative data: should we, can we, and how?', *Qualitative Social Work*, 18(1): 81–97.

Toepler, S. and Abramson, A. (2021) 'Government/foundation relations: a conceptual framework and evidence from the U.S. federal government's partnership efforts', *Voluntas: International Journal of Voluntary and Nonprofit Organizations*, 32(2): 220–33.

White, J.D. (1999) *Taking Language Seriously: The Narrative Foundations of Public Administration Research*, Georgetown University Press.

9

Unequal bureaucracies in practice: analysing documents using Institutional Ethnography

Órla Meadhbh Murray

Summary

- This chapter provides an overview of Institutional Ethnography (IE), which is an interdisciplinary feminist approach to research that provides a way to analyse bureaucratic documents in practice as well as their potentially unequal effects.

- Drawing on a five-year IE of UK university audit processes, the chapter focuses on how to do a close analysis of one document with the 'text' method, using the National Student Survey as a case study.

Introduction

Institutional life is full of digital and print documents – application forms, online systems, policy papers, books, manuals, guidelines – which we read, write and perform in our everyday lives as workers, clients, patients and students. Institutional Ethnography (IE), an interdisciplinary feminist approach to research developed by feminist Marxian sociologist Dorothy E. Smith (1926–2022), conceptualises such institutional documents as 'texts' that organise our everyday lives and provide a material manifestation of institutions (Smith, 2005; Smith and Turner, 2014; Smith and Griffith, 2022). In IE, a text is defined as a replicable material object that carries messages across time and space, organising the everyday work of people into institutional processes that extend far beyond where they are situated (Smith and Turner, 2014). Through reading, writing and speaking about institutional texts, people are required to translate everyday life into institutional formats, doing interpretive work to fit ourselves, and the messiness of life, into the textual reality of the institution. However, this often results in a gap between textual reality and actuality (where people are living and existing before they encounter a particular institutional text). This disjuncture between lived experience and what is captured in institutional texts is where IE research begins, with researchers often reflecting on their own, or discussing others', experiences of institutional processes as a starting point for tracing and analysing institutional processes and how people navigate texts throughout such processes. The focus of IE research is often on explaining how things work and examining who is included or excluded by seemingly neutral bureaucratic processes, which often have unequal effects, echoing broader discussions about epistemic injustice, as described by Victoria Pagan in Chapter 5.

In this chapter, I outline how I analysed documents in my PhD project, a five-year IE of UK university audit processes (Murray, 2019). While the IE concept of texts is more expansive than just documents, my analysis focused on bureaucratic documents. During the PhD, based on exemplars from Dorothy E. Smith's work, I developed a three-part typology of text analysis methods within an IE framework: text, process, discourse (Murray, 2020b). In this chapter, I focus on the 'text' method – which involves a close analysis of one text or a small array of texts – using my analysis of the National Student Survey (NSS) as a case study. I begin with a brief overview of IE and how I used it to analyse documents related to UK higher education (HE). Then I focus on the NSS example, explaining what it is and how I analysed it. Finally, I reflect on the advantages, limitations and broader applicability of this method.

Institutional Ethnography: a sociology for people

As Smith and Griffith (2022, p xiv) explain:

> Institutional ethnography is a sociology that takes up a stance in people's experience in the local sites of their bodily being and seeks to discover what can't be grasped from within that experience, namely the social relations that are implicit in its organization. It calls on sociologists to discover just how the everyday/everynight worlds we participate in are being put together in people's local activities, including, of course, our own.

Dorothy E. Smith developed IE from the 1970s onwards in collaboration with colleagues and students in Canada and the US. Over the last decade, IE has become increasingly popular in Europe, particularly in the UK and Nordic countries. It is difficult to succinctly explain what IE is and how it works because it is such a broad and wide-ranging interdisciplinary field. Researchers are united by a specific ontology of the social – a theory of how the social world works – and use IE in various ways depending on their disciplinary background, context, research foci and methods. The huge variation within the field is demonstrated by the wide array of approaches covered in IE edited collections (for example, Smith, 2006; Griffith and Smith, 2014; Lund and Nilsen, 2020; Luken and Vaughan, 2021). As such, it is difficult to summarise and often misunderstood as merely a method or a conventional ethnography of an institution. Rather, IE is an entire approach to doing sociology 'that begins and always stays with actual people and their doings; it seeks to discover just how actual people's doings are coordinated with others' (Smith and Griffith, 2022, p 3). To contextualise my focus on how I used documents in my text-focused IE of UK university audit processes, I briefly explain the overall approach and some key aspects of how IE conceptualises texts.

IE begins with (often marginalised) people's experiences, examining how everyday life is coordinated by institutional texts and language that originate from elsewhere and elsewhen, connecting people across contexts (Smith, 2005; Smith and Turner, 2014). Many IE projects, including the project presented here, consider how people navigate institutional texts, processes and discourses with the aim of producing 'maps' – visual diagrams or written explanations of how institutions or specific processes work in practice. By beginning with people and their unequal experiences of institutions, IE can provide an excellent problem-solving approach to changing institutions, informed by people's perspectives from 'below'. Through starting with people's everyday experiences and asking how things work in practice, IE research can identify structural issues in precise ways, highlighting which seemingly neutral bureaucratic texts and processes are exclusionary. For example, George W. Smith's study, first published in 1988, of police raids on gay bath houses in Toronto focused on identifying how homophobic policing was textually justified (see Smith, 2014). G.W. Smith examined the police report of a raid and showed that it produced an account of the raid that was legitimised with reference to higher-level legal texts. This IE analysis (though that terminology was not as widely used at the time) focuses on what is discriminatory at an institutional level rather than on individual homophobic police officers, identifying potential interventions and information that is useful for people wishing to enact change.

The focus on the institutional is done through analysing replicable institutional texts and associated language, which organise across contexts. Replicable texts appear as if they are the 'same' text, bringing ideas and institutional frameworks into many people's everyday lives and organising them into chains of connected institutional activity. For example, a passport application process involves strict rules and regulations about what counts in the application, and there are many people involved in the process, such as the applicant writing the application and the front-line worker checking the application against the guidelines. While different readers might engage with the same text (here, the passport application) in different ways – agreeing or disagreeing with it, (mis)interpreting it, trying to ignore it, skim-reading it or even not reading it – they are all being organised by the 'same' text and there are consequences (for example, being denied or granted a passport) as a result of one's response. IE focuses on examining texts ethnographically, understanding them as they are used in practice, 'as they actually enter into actively coordinating people's doings' (Smith and Griffith, 2022, p 31) in complex bureaucratic chains of activity connecting people in different places and times through texts.

Smith (2005, pp 101–21) conceptualises reading texts as the text–reader conversation. A person reads in a particular time and place and makes sense of the text in relation to their experiences, other texts and discussions with other people.

In this process of reading, the text becomes 'activated' by the reader, whereby the act of reading 'inserts the text's message into the local setting and the sequence of action in which it is read', regardless of the reader's response (Smith, 2005, p 105). With institutional processes such as passport applications, the text–reader conversation for an applicant involves translating oneself and one's work into institutionally recognisable formats, selectively including or excluding information; this is called 'institutional capture' (Smith, 2005, p 119).

Thus, institutional texts are partial representations, selectively put together to fit institutional logics and requirements, often by making (in)visible different aspects of peoples' experiences according to institutional requirements and logics. As such, institutional texts and processes perpetuate inequalities through including some things and people and excluding others, and through assuming certain subjects and not others. For example, non-binary people are unable to translate themselves into a passport application, or other bureaucratic processes, if there are only binary gender options, and as such they must participate in institutional capture or else be excluded from the process. The critical focus on institutional texts and language in IE aims to make sense of structural inequalities and absences built into institutional texts, such as passport application processes, with the hope of informing change.

IE foregrounds how documents (conceptualised as texts) are used *in practice* by people in their everyday lives, requiring them to translate themselves into institutionally legible textual representations as part of institutional processes. Much IE research focuses on the gap between people's actual lives and these textual representations of them within institutions. By asking questions about who the presumed subject of an institutional process is or who or what is rendered (in)visible in the translation of life into institutional texts, IE can highlight the exclusionary effects of institutions.

The project and researcher positionality

This section looks at how UK university audit processes work in practice from the standpoint of an early-career academic. My PhD research (2013–18; Murray, 2019) used IE to analyse UK university audit processes, asking: how do texts organise UK universities, specifically from the standpoint of academics? I was particularly interested in how academics exert interpretative agency through (mis)interpreting and sometimes subverting or avoiding audit processes. Through formal interviews and informal chats with UK university academics and professional service staff involved in implementing audit processes, I developed a working understanding of how audit processes operate in practice. I put these experiences into conversation with institutional texts (policy documents, application forms and guidance, and surveys) through extensive text analysis of the official processes. In short, I examined how key audit processes worked in practice, how much interpretive leeway academics had in implementing them and whether these processes could be done differently by focusing on the dynamics between everyday reading, writing and speaking about audit-related texts by academics and other workers in UK HE.

During this early period of the project, I was trying to work out how to do IE text analysis in practice, which proved difficult due to the lack of methodological specificity in much of the IE literature at that time around how to choose and analyse texts. Thus, I spent a large part of my early PhD process reading Smith's key books where she developed IE as an approach (Smith, 1987; 1990a; 1990b; 1999; 2005; 2006; Griffith and Smith, 2014; Smith and Turner, 2014). I identified exemplars of how Smith conducted IE text analysis and used these to develop a typology of IE text analysis methods (Murray, 2020b), as discussed later in this chapter. Simultaneously, I developed my general understanding of how UK HE worked. Beginning with my own experience, I reflected on my everyday working life as a PhD student in sociology and an hourly paid teacher in the social sciences at the University of Edinburgh. I had stayed in the same department where I completed my undergraduate degree, having secured research funding to continue as a master's and PhD student with a proposal to examine the ongoing neoliberalisation of UK HE through an intersectional feminist lens using IE. I got involved with my local University and College Union branch, briefly becoming a postgraduate rep in the branch committee, which gave me further insight into the university and the broader sector.

My experience of the sector is impacted by my positionality in terms of the specific university I am at, the discipline I work in, my position in the hierarchy of job security and seniority in academia, my ideological commitments and my intersecting structural identities. My Whiteness and middle-class background smooth my experience of academia as I fit into the racialised and classed expectations of the UK academy, while my being queer, femme, disabled and Irish complicate this in ways that vary across context. As I discuss elsewhere, identity and positionality are situated and relational rather than static, fixed or deterministic (Murray, 2018; 2020a), but the brief positioning provided here gives a general sense of how I move through academic spaces and the propelling and limiting structural factors.

Focusing the project on three audit processes and developing methods

IE is an iterative process of learning about the field of study and then continually adjusting the research focus in response to what you learn. I spent a long time developing my general understanding of IE and the UK HE sector through reading academic literature, speaking informally with academic friends and colleagues across universities and disciplines, and reading media commentary and social media discussions among academics and other commentators on how IE and UK universities work. To identify specific audit processes to analyse in my project, I began actively listening and looking out for audit-related discussion in my everyday life in academic spaces. I listened out for frequently used jargon, academics' anxious discussions about audit processes and audit-related texts which were being negotiated in academics' everyday working lives. In particular, I was interested in finding general, and generalising, audit processes that were organising academic life at a sector-wide level, which were usually publicly available online. I decided to focus only on publicly available documents because it helped avoid ethical and legal concerns around non-public documents for myself and any informants who might experience reputational or legal sanction if using non-public documents. This also meant my analysis could be easily checked by readers, who can access the full documents online via links in my references and draw their own conclusions or disagree with my interpretations; this fits with a broader feminist ethic of reflexivity and accountability (Murray, 2020b; 2025).

Based on my initial autoethnographic reflections, reading and observations, I chose three key audit processes that I argue are central to the UK-wide organisation of academic work – that is, audit processes that academics actually enacted in their everyday work and which were required across all UK universities; these inform the distribution of funding and prestige to universities, departments and individual academics. The three audit processes were:

- the NSS, which is a yearly UK student satisfaction survey for final-year undergraduates that informs university league tables, the Teaching Excellence Framework, course comparison websites and university branding;
- the UK Research and Innovation government research funding processes, specifically the Economic and Social Research Council research grant application process, which funds social science research projects;
- the Research Excellence Framework, which is the UK government audit process for academic research which informs the distribution of government research funding and is used in university league tables and branding.

There are many other important audit processes in UK HE, and these are not the only relevant ones, but they fitted my criteria of sector-wide, publicly available audit processes that were commonly discussed by academics in their everyday working lives. In terms of choosing the actual documents to analyse and people to speak with, this was more complicated because of how many documents surrounded these audit processes. Here, my IE text analysis methods became important in narrowing down the focus of my analysis. The three-part typology of IE text analysis methods that I developed through my PhD (Murray, 2020b) – text, process, discourse – provides different approaches to analysing documents within an IE framework:

- Text involves close reading of a single text or a small array of texts.
- Process focuses on how multiple texts fit together into an institutional process of interlocking texts.
- Discourse involves naming a discourse rooted in multiple, often disparate, texts that organises how people interpret and enact texts and textually mediated processes, often focusing more on language and how people talk in relation to texts.

These three ways of conceptualising IE text analysis are based on examples of Smith's text analysis, and I discuss them in more detail elsewhere (Murray, 2020b; 2025). In this chapter, due to limited space, I focus only on the first method – text – and my analysis of the NSS.

Choosing the NSS

In 2014, when I started analysing the NSS, it was widely discussed in the sector. Anxieties about 'low scores' or 'feedback concerns' were prevalent in my everyday life as a postgraduate tutor at the University of Edinburgh, and there was much commentary in UK HE academic literature and media commentary. As a UK-wide survey aimed at all final-year undergraduate students, the NSS provided an important regulatory text across the sector. The format and language of the survey generalised across the sector and provided regulatory frameworks through which to perceive and assess student experiences. In the academic literature on UK HE, the NSS was often discussed as part of a broader critique of the neoliberalisation of HE in this context. The NSS, as a student satisfaction survey, repositioned students as consumers of education, who were to be satisfied for fear of bad NSS scores and the potential negative impact on university reputations and subsequent income. I argue that this regulatory power is largely due to the NSS informing the evaluation and ranking of university courses, and thus student decisions around where to study, through its use in university league tables, the Teaching Excellence Framework and the UK government-run degree comparison website, Discover Uni. Initially, I was particularly interested in how the language and format of the NSS and its results were shaping teaching and student support provision, and I used my experience at the University of Edinburgh to inform a critical reading of the survey itself and how it framed 'the student experience' in limited, and limiting, ways.

My analysis of the NSS began by developing what Smith (2005, pp 151–2, 210) calls 'work knowledges' – peoples' experiences of their own work and how it is coordinated with others' work – using a generous conceptualisation of work (anything that takes time and effort). I began with autoethnographic reflections on my own experiences as an undergraduate student who had completed the NSS at the end of my degree and, subsequently, as a postgraduate tutor on the same degree programme. I began to actively listen and look for references to the NSS in my everyday academic life. The term 'feedback' came up a lot in staff meetings, tutor training sessions, official emails and informal conversations between staff. The 'feedback problem' was a source of stress, with student feedback (both staff feedback on student assessments and student feedback on teaching provision) conceptualised as something we needed to improve. I noticed increasing amounts of work and staff stress related to this idea of improving 'feedback' in response to the perception that our NSS scores for assessment and feedback were low. These reflections informed both my decision to focus on the NSS and my initial analysis of the survey itself.

Identifying specific documents

Initially, I accessed the NSS website and downloaded the 2014 survey questions, which were in a publicly available PDF. While the PDF is different to how students encounter the survey in practice (the NSS is now mostly completed as an online survey, which is more interactive than the PDF version), my focus was on the content, format and structuring of questions and how they produced (new) areas of concern in the sector and ways of conceptualising 'the student experience'. Additionally, the online survey form was not accessible to non-students. I considered interviewing and/or observing students completing the NSS, but this was complicated ethically as my presence might have impacted students' responses and constituted 'inappropriate influence' according to the NSS guidance (Ipsos MORI, 2017). Thus, I decided to use my 'text' method of doing a close reading of one text, focusing on the NSS PDF. I initially conceptualised this as reading from the standpoint of an undergraduate at the University of Edinburgh, drawing on my experiences as an undergraduate student (2008–12) and general knowledge of that context to identify disjunctures between actual student experiences at the University of Edinburgh and the textual reality of the survey.

To contextualise my reading of the survey, I also conducted six informal interviews with workers and student representatives who were, or had been, involved in NSS-related work at the University of Edinburgh and in Scottish HE more broadly. The interviews showed me how people were actually using the NSS survey and its results at the University of Edinburgh and in the Scottish HE context as well as the new types of NSS-related work that were being created by the survey. Alongside this, I read many additional documents about the NSS, including all the web pages on the NSS website and related policy documents, reports and other guidance, which I cited when referring to them in my analysis. These were used as contextual information to inform my close reading of the survey PDFs.

In 2018, while finalising my PhD research, I updated my analysis to include the 2017 NSS survey PDF, as the questions had changed. I detailed the shifts in language and structure and connected this to broader changes in the sector. Such ongoing changes highlight the importance of downloading and screenshotting online texts at the time of analysis in case the online version disappears or is changed over time. While some defunct websites or older versions of web pages may be available via the Internet Archive's Wayback Machine, it is more reliable to create your own digital archive.

Using reading frames to analyse documents

When analysing the NSS survey PDFs, I initially numbered each line on the survey to ensure precise referencing in my analysis. My approach to doing the analysis drew on two exemplars from Smith (1990a, pp 12–51, 120–58), in which she detailed IE analysis of one text and a small array of texts. Both exemplars involve Smith showing how texts are put together in order to achieve particular aims, whether that be to convince the reader of a particular interpretation of an event or to produce what she calls 'facticity', or being seen to be 'factual'. This helped me to make sense of the NSS as a survey, which I argued was centrally concerned with producing a legitimate, factual account of student experiences in UK HE. Smith explains that to examine how a text is put together, it is necessary to look at how it is structured and worded in ways that organise people and their readings. This is quite a complex thing to replicate, so I developed a list of things to look out for when analysing the NSS PDFs – this 'reading frame' is 'a structured set of points, to think systematically about examples of actual research' (Stanley and Wise, 2008, p 5). This structured my analysis and helped me to explain my 'in the head' methods of reading – the text–reader conversation I was having in my analysis.

My initial reading frame had an overarching question: how does this text organise the reader, other people and other texts? It also included a list of five specific things to look for, based on my reading of Smith's (1990a, pp 12–51, 120–58) two exemplars:

- the spatio-temporal position of the text and my reading (the context of the text and my reading; who I am; and how I made sense of the text);
- the positioning of people and objects in the text (the structure/categories used; any judgements or comparisons between people and objects);
- the structuring of the text;
- the intertextualities (references, either explicitly or implicitly, to other texts);
- the text-act-text sequences (whether it is part of an organisational process or chain of activity).

This list was an attempt to summarise key ideas from Smith and IE more broadly in order to structure my reading and help me describe my methods of analysis. However, when I used this reading frame on the 2014 NSS survey PDF, it produced a very abstract and superficial analysis that seemed to reproduce my pre-existing assumptions about the NSS rather than helping me focus on the how the text itself was structured and what it was doing. I realised I needed to create a more detailed reading frame to hone my reading and help me focus more on the details of the text itself rather than merely projecting my pre-existing assumptions about the text onto my analysis.

This second reading frame was based on Liz Stanley's (2017) practical guidance on how to analyse documents in detail, which itself drew on Smith's ideas about active texts – namely, texts which organise people and often ask people to do things such as 'sign here' or 'please email the completed form to …'. Stanley (2017, para 1.4) explains that to analyse a text in action reminds researchers to focus on 'the contexts of that production, distribution and effects, as well as to specific content', which she does through a temporal framework (Stanley, 2017, para 1.5):

- *Context.* Documents emerge in a general context for specific reasons.
- *Pre-text.* Texts have a more specific origin (the before of the text) – for example, the author(s) may have produced the text in a specific institution for a particular

purpose or process. The text may then be found by the researcher in a specific place, such as an archive or institutional website.

- *Text and its meta-data, content and structure, and its intertexts.* Here, the attention is on the text itself, or the analysis of the document, which focuses on close reading of the content and structure and any explicit or implicit references to other texts.
- *Post-text.* The 'after' of the text focuses on how it is used or linked to other texts and activities in institutional processes.
- *Context 2: The next context that arises.* It represents whether the text has an impact on the broader sociopolitical or institutional context after its production, publication and circulation.

This temporal approach to understanding a text helped me to be more precise about where my ideas were coming from when reading a text – was it my understanding of the author and their social context when producing the text, was it from a close analysis of the text itself, or was it from the impact or aftermath of the text?

I tried to keep the question 'how do I know that?' at the forefront of my thinking when using this second reading frame, to encourage me to identify supporting evidence for different claims – specifically, to distinguish between whether the text itself says something or I know something from other texts or interviews with people who use the text. I used Stanley's (2017, para 1.4) five temporal moments in the life cycle of a text in action to structure this second reading. I then added lists of things to think about or questions to ask myself about the text, as follows:

- *Context.* Broader socio-historical context; Institutional context, i.e. UK higher education; Organisational context e.g. the specific university; Situating my choice and reading of the text.
- *Pre-text or before.* Where did I get it from and where is it stored/accessible? Origin story of text – what text(s) lead to production of the text under analysis? Was there an organisational process that led to its creation? Authorship – if known, is it a single/multiple/group/institutional author? If more than one author, what are their different roles and responsibilities in producing the text? What impact might the authorship or origin have on intended readership if known? For example, through media coverage and other discussion of the text, prior to production.
- *Text or during.* Content/message of the text – what is it and how is it conveyed? Authorship – how is it configured? E.g. Stated/unstated/implied? Narrative tone/voice; Positioning of people in the text; Readership: is an intended readership implied or stated? What activities are required or asked of readership by the text? What knowledge is needed to interpret the text? Structure: format; genre; use of colour and images; Language use, specifically things that all attention to themselves, e.g. unusual vocabulary; repeated

words; Intertextualities: regulatory or boss texts referenced; interlocking texts mentioned.

- *Post-text or after.* Official institutional processes: e.g. text-act-text sequences such as storage, archiving, circulation, and origin of text; Interlocking texts and other texts that are regulated by this text; Unofficial or unintended textual uses and misuses: performances or invocations of the text; Absences/ silences – reading different ideologies into the text, who and what is excluded or side-lined?
- *Context 2.* Broader context of usage and commentary on text; Organisational context; Institutional context; My interpretation of broader impact of text. (Murray, 2019, p 283, originally in table form)

This detailed list of things I wanted to consider was based on my extensive reading of IE literature and other text analysis reading, as detailed more precisely in my thesis (Murray, 2019). This second reading frame is not exhaustive or necessarily relevant for all texts. I developed it specifically for my purposes in analysing the NSS. If you wish to use a similar method, I encourage you to create your own reading frame, bringing together different questions, concepts and things to look for that are rooted in your own research context, questions and the text(s) under analysis.

Based on the second reading frame, I wrote a very long and, in my view, quite boring line-by-line analysis of the NSS survey PDF. To turn this writing into my final PhD chapter involved stepping back and thinking about which parts were most analytically important when trying to explain how the NSS works in practice. And so, I rewrote it, producing a more succinct, analytically organised argument that identified precise examples from my in-depth text analysis and contextualised these through references to my informal interviews and further reading of academic literature and other texts related to the NSS (for example, UK HE blogs, media coverage and website information). The focus was always on explaining how the NSS works in practice, and I continually asked myself: How do I know that? Where is my evidence for that claim?

Conclusion

If you are interested in understanding how people use texts and respond to bureaucratic processes in practice, then this method may be of interest. It is highly flexible and responsive to different purposes and the research context itself. While my second reading frame was extremely in-depth and worked well when analysing a small array of short documents, it would be too time-consuming to do with longer documents or a larger array of documents. However, my other two IE textual analysis approaches – process and discourse – provide ways to analyse larger sets of documents, analysing in less in-depth detail but at scale, as I discuss elsewhere (Murray, 2020b; 2025).

The IE approach is also very focused on how documents organise people and how they are used in practice, so it concentrates more on institutions and the 'structural' rather than individual people's experiences, which does not work for all research projects and interests. While some may be drawn to the feminist orientation of IE, it does not focus on gender or intersecting inequalities in the way one might expect. Instead, the feminist orientation is more ontological and epistemological; it takes experiential expertise seriously (particularly that of marginalised groups) and then uses such experience to identify how seemingly neutral institutional processes and documents can exclude certain groups (Smith, 2005; Murray, 2020b; 2025).

What makes this method difficult is that it involves developing a working knowledge of IE concepts and its underpinning ontology, which can be time-consuming. If you are unfamiliar with IE, I would recommend Smith and Griffith's (2022) introductory book, the overview of IE by Smith (2005) and the edited collection titled *Incorporating Texts into Institutional Ethnographies* (Smith and Turner, 2014). While you might use specific concepts or practical ideas, such as Stanley's reading frame approach, or repurpose specific bits of my reading frame for your own purposes, this should be done carefully to ensure it fits within your ontological, epistemological and methodological approach to research.

Key considerations for using this method

- Understanding IE often takes a lot of time. You need to read the foundational IE books and grapple with the theoretical and conceptual aspects as well as deciding which methodological direction to go in given the wide array of options in this field. Allow yourself sufficient time to familiarise yourself with the IE literature.

- Documents are often conceptualised as texts in IE, with texts being understood as materially replicable objects that carry messages across contexts, allowing many people across time and place to read 'the same' message. Thus, the focus is on *how* they work in practice when people actually use them in a particular context. A key question to ask is: how does this text organise me, the reader, other people and other texts?

- Analysing documents within IE is about focusing on how people actually use the documents in practice, which usually requires reflecting on your own use of the documents or your observations of others' use of the documents, or discussions with other people who use the documents.

- Coming back to the question 'how do I know that?' and using a reading frame (a list of things to look out for when analysing the document) will help you to explain 'in the head' analysis work clearly and identify where the evidence for your knowledge claims is coming from.

References

Griffith, A.I. and Smith, D.E. (eds) (2014) *Under New Public Management: Institutional Ethnographies of Changing Front-Line Work*, University of Toronto Press.

Ipsos MORI (2017) *The National Student Survey Good Practice Guide*, Ipsos MORI. Available from: www.hefce.ac.uk/media/HEFCE,2014/Content/Learn ing,and,teaching/NSS/Allegati ons/NSS-2018-Good-Practice-Guide.pdf

Luken, P.C. and Vaughan, S. (eds) (2021) *The Palgrave Handbook of Institutional Ethnography*, Palgrave Macmillan.

Lund, R.W.B. and Nilsen, A.C.E. (eds) (2020) *Institutional Ethnography in the Nordic Region*, Routledge.

Murray, Ó.M. (2018) 'Feel the fear and killjoy anyway: being a challenging feminist presence in precarious academia', in Y. Taylor and K. Lahad (eds) *Feeling Academic in the Neoliberal University: Feminist Flights, Fights and Failures*, Palgrave Macmillan, pp 163–89.

Murray, Ó.M. (2019) *Doing Feminist Text-Focused Institutional Ethnography in UK Universities*, PhD thesis, University of Edinburgh, Available from: http://hdl.han dle.net/1842/35719

Murray, Ó.M. (2020a) 'Beyond confession: doing holistic reflexivity and accountability', in R. Govinda, F. Mackay, K. Menon and R. Sen (eds) *Doing Feminisms in the Academy: Identity, Institutional Pedagogy and Critical Classrooms in India and the UK*, Zubaan Books, pp 222–32.

Murray, Ó.M. (2020b) 'Text, process, discourse: doing feminist text analysis in institutional ethnography', *International Journal of Social Research Methodology*, 25(1): 45–57.

Murray, Ó.M. (2025) *University Audit Cultures and Feminist Praxis: An Institutional Ethnography*, Bristol University Press.

Smith, D.E. (1987) *The Everyday World as Problematic: A Feminist Sociology*, University of Toronto Press.

Smith, D.E. (1990a) *Texts, Facts, and Femininity: Exploring the Relations of Ruling*, Routledge.

Smith, D.E. (1990b) *The Conceptual Practices of Power: A Feminist Sociology of Knowledge*, University of Toronto Press.

Smith, D.E. (1999) *Writing the Social: Critique, Theory, and Investigations*, University of Toronto Press.

Smith, D.E. (2005) *Institutional Ethnography: A Sociology for People*, AltaMira Press.

Smith, D.E. (ed) (2006) *Institutional Ethnography as Practice*, Rowman & Littlefield.

Smith, D.E. and Turner, S.M. (eds) (2014) *Incorporating Texts into Institutional Ethnographies*, University of Toronto Press.

Smith, D.E. and Griffith, A.I. (2022) *Simply Institutional Ethnography: Creating a Sociology for People*, University of Toronto Press.

Smith, G.W. (2014) 'Policing the gay community: an inquiry into textually-mediated social relations', in D.E. Smith and S.M. Turner (eds) *Incorporating Texts into Institutional Ethnographies*, University of Toronto Press, pp 17–40.

Stanley, L. (2017) 'How to analyse a document in detail', *Whites Writing Whiteness*. Available from: www.whiteswritingwhiteness.ed.ac.uk/how-to/how-to-analyse-a-document-in-detail

Stanley, L. and Wise, S. (2008) 'Feminist methodology matters!', in D. Richardson and V. Robinson (eds) *Gender and Women's Studies*, Palgrave Macmillan, pp 221–43.

10

Using documents in research during periods of conflict and political turbulence

Anna J. Davis

Summary

- This chapter provides a guide to navigating the complexities of using official documents for research that is focused on areas experiencing conflict and political turbulence.

- Shifting geopolitical conditions – like war, government censorship and protests – can disrupt access to data and require researchers to adapt quickly.

- The chapter describes the author's journey of researching Belarus, Ukraine and Armenia during 2020–24, a time when all three states were experiencing conflict and political turbulence.

- It offers a grounded look at the realities of fieldwork complications while doing research with official documents.

- Factors such as nationality, gender and institutional affiliation can shape both access to information and interpretation of data, and the reader is encouraged to reflect on the influence of their own identity and positionality.

Introduction

The use of documents to inform academic and scholarly inquiry always comes with challenges. This is especially true when the geopolitical stage is continually shifting, as this affects documents produced by the state or housed in state-owned facilities. Researchers studying areas experiencing conflict and political turbulence face challenges in locating and analysing documents for their research in addition to the challenge of situating the data appropriately despite a changing reality.

In this chapter, I highlight the complexities and practicalities involved in analysing official texts for scholarly inquiry in contexts of conflict and political turbulence, drawing on my experiences while conducting doctoral research using official documents from Belarus, Ukraine and Armenia during 2020–24. The time period under analysis was 1991 to 2020. My research took place during ongoing government repressions in Belarus, during conflict between Armenia and Azerbaijan, which has fluctuated in intensity since the late 1980s, and during Russia's full-scale invasion of Ukraine since 2022.

To provide an example of using documents in research, I begin the chapter with an explanation of my doctoral research process and theoretical approach. Then, I discuss what an official document is and why selecting certain types of documents is important. I then explain my decision to analyse documents and texts using critical discourse analysis and the process I used. In the remainder of the chapter, I connect these methodological and theoretical discussions to my own experiences of conducting research using documents during periods of conflict and political turbulence. I explain the situations of this kind that occurred during my research, discuss important considerations of positionality and outline the main lessons learned from the practical and ethical challenges I encountered during the research. These are presented in such a way that they can be accessed and applied by other researchers at any stage in their scholarly journey.

The research process: constructing case studies

Before considering how to use documents in research during periods of conflict and political turbulence, it is important to understand how to formulate a research design that uses documents as the primary data source. One common approach is case study research design, where a case or set of cases is investigated (Yin, 2018). Case studies are crafted by the researcher to organise and analyse an observed phenomenon or phenomena. That phenomenon represents a 'concrete entity' and exists independently of the method used (Yin, 2018, p 349). In my doctoral research, I used a case study design to answer the following question: given their varying commitments to bilateral relations with Russia, how are the post-Soviet international identities of Belarus, Ukraine and Armenia developed using long-term cooperation and integration in the form of civil nuclear relationships with Russia in the period since 1991?

The cases under investigation in my doctoral research were the civil nuclear relationships that Belarus, Ukraine and Armenia pursued in order to advance foreign policy goals. I constructed case studies with a defined time period (1991 to 2020). The main reason for starting with 1991 was that this was the year the Soviet Union collapsed and Belarus, Ukraine and Armenia (along with the other former republics of the Union of Soviet Socialist Republics – USSR) gained independence. The decision to conclude the period of study in 2020 was based on the impact of the conflict and political turbulence that was escalating in Belarus on my ability to compare these three states in a fair way.

The case studies were constructed as three separate instances of post-Soviet identity formation. They were selected because Belarus, Ukraine and Armenia were the only members of the former USSR with operational nuclear power plants, all of which were supported, either entirely or to some extent, by the Russian state-owned energy complex. In addition, all three cases were non-Russian former

Soviet republics and were using nuclear discourses in foreign policy. However, the intensity of conflict and political turbulence in each of these countries during the research process made it impossible to access data as planned.

Theoretical approach

In addition to research design, the theoretical approach is an important element in my discipline of area studies and international relations. To analyse the case studies and substantiate my argument, I drew on conventional social constructivism, which is used in international relations and considers the meanings of material objects to be relative, based on a number of ideational factors. It emphasises how narratives, expressed in discourse and language, provide foreign policies with social roles (Hopf, 1998; 2012; Hansen, 2006). Furthermore, in international relations, social constructivism typically considers the relationship between Russia and former Soviet states as competing, evolving and synergetic over time and varying across states. This was promising because I wanted to understand and tell the story of how Belarus, Ukraine and Armenia expressed their international identities and social roles through civil nuclear cooperation while also negotiating their relationships with Russia. Finally, this approach provided a unique way to understand the potential applications of a *material* capability, such as nuclear energy, in foreign policy and identity construction.

What is an official document and how is it used for research?

As noted in other chapters in this book, before beginning a research project using documents, it is important to determine the type or types of documents that are most suitable for the study. In social science research, documents are not just 'containers of content', but are themselves expressions, products and functions of social contexts (Prior, 2003, p 17). As such, documents are a form of discourse. Discourse is 'an organisation of talk or text that does something, in the broad social world, or in the immediate interaction, or in both' (Antaki, 2008, p 431). This makes documents a valuable resource in studies that attempt to understand human behaviour over time.

The type of document that is most suitable for your research depends on the research question, your argument and the actors and level of analysis, among other things (see Helen Abnett, Chapter 8, for more on this). For my doctoral research, I chose to use official documents. The term 'official document', which I use throughout this chapter, describes texts that are produced by a government, legal or other state authority or public official. I define official discourse in the same way for all my case studies: strategic narratives in official texts provided by the state and by individuals or organisations representing the state.

The reason I only considered texts produced by state and regional authorities was that these are the actors involved in overseeing nuclear-related activities and accounting for and controlling materials for nuclear fission and radioactive materials (International Atomic Energy Agency – IAEA, 2006; 2019). This was especially important because the nuclear industries in Belarus, Ukraine, Armenia and Russia were not just financially backed by their respective states, but owned by them.[1] The types of official documents I used and analysed included:

- policy papers
- government reports and strategies
- intergovernmental agreements
- legislation
- international treaties
- government responses
- transcripts of official meetings or events
- government press releases
- text on official websites

I also included texts produced by state officials, as opposed to state bodies or organisations. This allowed for inclusion of documents written or containing statements by individuals employed or otherwise representing the state as well as those produced by corporations and organisations owned by and representing state policy. For example, a news article containing a quote by a state official could be included even though this type of document is not classified as official. General text on nuclear energy with no official connection was not considered because this did not reflect the state's position.

Finding documents

The locations of the documents I used in my doctoral research depended on the time period under analysis. Those produced during the 1990s or earlier were largely located in some sort of archival database. Those produced from the 2000s onwards were mostly accessible on official government websites and archives of those websites. The latter varied across case studies, as some governments updated their websites with every new administration or periodically (every five years, for example).

Legislation was available in the documents and archives sections of the official web pages of the Belarusian, Ukrainian and Armenian nuclear power plants, the official embassy websites for Belarus, Ukraine, Armenia and Russia, the official websites of the nuclear regulator in each of the four states and the official presidential and government websites of each of the four states. Official press releases were accessed via the press, news, updates and archives sections on government websites, which also held copies of official texts, transcripts and accounts of official interviews and statements. Statements by officials were collected from texts that did not fall into the categories of legislation or press releases but, nonetheless, expressed an official view on the civil nuclear relationship with Russia. This included recorded video statements and speeches, transcripts of official meetings, industry conferences, and event presentations, and remarks in the public domain.

Analysing documents

The qualitative analytical method I selected for my case studies was critical discourse analysis. Discourse analysis (the broader method incorporating critical discourse analysis) allows us to examine how 'knowledge, identities and social positions are discursively construed' (Gruber, 2024, pp 4–5). When the purpose of analysing documents is to focus on the 'role of discourse in the (re)production and challenge of dominance', we use the umbrella term, critical discourse analysis (Van Dijk, 1993).[2]

The choice of critical discourse analysis as a methodological tool centred on (1) its compatibility with an international relations conventional constructivist study of identity and (2) the unique way in which discourse analysis combined with this particular international relations approach views materiality.

To the first point, critical discourse analysis places a spotlight on the power, or agency, of language itself and focuses on how meaning is generated through language (Howarth, 1998; Hansen, 2016). It is naturally associated with constructivist scholarship largely because discourse analysis scholars introduced this practice to both international relations and its subfield, foreign policy analysis (Hansen, 2016). In doing so, international relations constructivism has contributed a different way of understanding language by asking 'not whether statements are true or not, but which values, norms, and identities are being created in language' (Hansen, 2016, p 96).

Second, critical discourse analysis is important for understanding various meanings associated with materiality. As, in international relations, conventional constructivism allows for these different meanings to exist, critical discourse analysis provides a means to discover those meanings during the research process because of its unique consideration of context, actors, audience and presence of intention and strategy associated with language, words and discourse.

Adapting to conflict and political turbulence

A strong research design is a core enabler of one's ability to adapt when conflict and political turbulence occur. In this section, I connect the situations I encountered during my doctoral research with maintaining the integrity of the research and the overall design and with navigating my own positionality as the researcher.

Political turbulence in Belarus

In 2019, I began researching the Belarusian case study for my master's thesis. I explored how Belarusian foreign policy and its international identity[3] have been afforded various benefits through civil nuclear cooperation with Russia.

By the time I was prepared to conduct fieldwork in Belarus, the COVID-19 pandemic was beginning to spread to Europe. This delayed my travel plans for March 2020. My approved travel risk assessments and ethics reviews applications subsequently expired. I created new travel plans and underwent new ethical and risk assessments for summer 2020. This was interrupted again, this time by mass political demonstrations and protests against the Belarusian government and the illegitimate presidential election of Aliaksandr Lukashenka. These events saw the Belarusian government detain thousands of peaceful protestors and ban American citizens, which I am, from travelling to Belarus. At the time of writing, the US Department of State advises against all travel to Belarus. In the meantime, the Belarusian government continues to stifle political opposition, imprison activists, journalists and political figures, and engage in human rights abuses. Therefore, conflict and political turbulence made it impossible to conduct research for my doctoral programme in Belarus.

Conflict in Ukraine

When I began my doctoral research in 2020, I incorporated two additional case studies, Armenia and Ukraine, in the same context of civil nuclear cooperation with Russia and foreign policy advantages. In my second year, once the appropriate ethics and travel risk assessments were complete, I planned to conduct fieldwork in Ukraine during March 2022. This was interrupted by Russia's full-scale invasion of Ukraine on 24 February 2022, which continues at the time of writing. Ethics and travel risk approval would not be granted to someone in my position wishing to visit Ukraine to conduct research on official policy while the country experiences a full-scale invasion. It was therefore impossible for me to travel to Ukraine to conduct fieldwork for my PhD research.

Conflict and political turbulence in Armenia

Given that fieldwork in Belarus and Ukraine became impossible, I gained ethics and risk assessment approval from my university to conduct research in Armenia. In September 2022, I was finally able to travel to Yerevan, the capital of Armenia. However, this trip was plagued with complications from the start. When I arrived in Yerevan, a number of police blockades were present in the main intersections and streets. I learned from my taxi driver that the reason for this increased security presence was the eruption of military clashes along the border with Azerbaijan the night before. Officials in both countries blamed the other side for instigating these latest clashes, which resulted in an estimated 200 Armenian and 80 Azerbaijani deaths (Caprile and Przetacznik, 2023).

After notifying my university of the updated situation regarding conflict and political turbulence, I made the decision to stay in Armenia, as the capital city remained relatively peaceful. The next day, the Russian government claimed that it had negotiated a peace deal between Armenia and Azerbaijan. I continued with my plan of interviewing officials and experts on Armenia's civil nuclear relationship with Russia. As the conflict on the border appeared to subside, I decided to take the 23-mile (37-kilometre) drive from Yerevan to Metsamor, the small town which is home to Armenia's nuclear power plant. Since this was the subject of my research, I was determined to see the Metsamor nuclear power plant.[4]

The plant is visible for miles around the town, and it is located just off of the main highway, the M5. Thus, its location is no secret. However, this did not stop the security forces at the plant from detaining me and my travel companion for a few hours because we pulled our car over to the side of the road to take a photo of the plant. Dressed in military uniforms with automatic rifles strapped around their shoulders, six men, who spoke only Armenian and Russian, questioned us (fortunately, I speak some Russian and my colleague is fluent). They examined and photographed our passports, travel documents (they appeared particularly concerned about my American passport) and my itinerary of interviews, and they inspected and filmed our car. They then waited for approval from their superiors, with whom they communicated over the phone in Russian, and finally they allowed us to leave.

After we were released, we returned to our hotel and I contacted the American embassy in Yerevan and my supervisor at the University of Oxford to update them. That evening, I witnessed the eruption of mass protests in the main square calling for the prime minister's resignation for his communications over a potential peace deal with Azerbaijan. The protestors attempted to forcibly access the parliament building, but were stopped from doing so by the authorities. The American embassy in Yerevan later informed me of the possibility of an investigation by the Armenian government into my presence at the Metsamor nuclear power plant. Based on this information, combined with the factors mentioned earlier, I decided to return to the UK and continue data collection and analysis remotely.

Positionality in conflict and political turbulence

The positionality of the researcher is a critical component of any analytical process, but may be considered particularly relevant when using critical discourse analysis and especially so when investigating subjects that are politically contentious. Positionality in this sense refers to the effects that the researcher's own biases, experiences and interpretations may have on the analysis of data. My own positionality while conducting my doctoral research centred on my identity as a female, western (American) scholar at the University of Oxford, at the early stage of my career. Each of these elements of my positionality influenced the research process.

The first point to emphasise regarding my positionality was the impact of my identity as both an American and a scholar from a university outside the countries I was studying. This was important because of the presence of conflict and political turbulence in these countries while I was completing the research and the relations, positive or negative, between their governments and my own.

On a number of occasions, I became frustrated because access to the data was being affected by protests, website blocking and, of course, the inability to travel to analyse documents in person. I learned the necessity of empathy with my interlocutors during this process. The priority of those being directly affected by conflict and political turbulence was not to direct me to the location of the documents I required, but to ensure their own safety and well-being and, in the case of protests, to respond to the violations of their respective governments. Therefore, I had to place myself in their position when asking for support in locating or gaining access to certain documents or collections.

In some circumstances, my position as a female junior scholar affected the interactions between myself and interlocutors. Although this was primarily a feature of the interviews I conducted, it affected other data collection to a lesser, but still noteworthy, extent. Most of my interlocutors were Belarusian, Ukrainian and Armenian men, at least ten years older than me and well-established experts in their respective fields. The differences between us were stark. Gender and age differences combined with my junior position as an early-career researcher meant that my knowledge and expertise could be perceived as inferior to that of my interlocutors. However, this perceived inferiority was beneficial when it led to interlocutors explaining nuances and details which they thought I did not understand or was not aware of, since this provided me with further insight into what they considered important, basic or fundamental to the topics we were discussing.

Still, when my interlocutors offered to provide access to data, it was important for me to ensure boundaries had been established in such a way that guaranteed no expectation of reward or reciprocity. The first notice of this boundary was in the research information sheet, which all my interlocutors received prior to our interviews. Further to this, when offers were made after the interview to provide me with publications and other documents or to put me in contact with other individuals who could provide additional materials, it was important for me to reiterate that there was no expectation or requirement for my interlocutor to do this and that they were more than welcome to send any materials of their own accord. This latter point is important for periods of conflict and political turbulence because there can be no expectation on the part of interlocutors that they will receive any benefits from a researcher from a country that may be perceived as able to supply aid or refuge.

Aside from interactions with individuals in the process of obtaining the necessary documents, it was important for me to be aware of my own biases in interpreting and analysing those documents. At this point, I must explain the potential impact of presentism on research conducted during or after conflict and political turbulence, before discussing how the aspects of my own positionality came into play. Presentism is defined as 'a bias towards the present or present-day attitudes, especially in the interpretation of history' (Oxford English Dictionary, nd). We can think of presentism as judging the past with the values and perspectives of the present. This does not mean that presentism is an inherently negative feature of conducting research with documents, but that we must be aware of any impact it may have on the data. Data collection should produce a reconstruction of 'the past without distorting effects of the present' (Armitage, 2022, p 45). Therefore, we need to be aware that conflict and political turbulence can influence memory and perceptions of the past in such a way that might change the researcher's results compared to if they had conducted the research a few years prior.

In my own doctoral research experience, presentism held potential to exacerbate my biases because of the additional factor of ongoing conflict and political turbulence in each of my three case studies. Caution was necessary on my part to analyse these documents, as much as possible, in the contexts in which they occurred rather than with the new realities of the present. Relations worsened drastically between the US (my country of citizenship), the UK (where I was completing my PhD) and two of the countries I was studying (Belarus and Russia) as I carried out data collection and analysis. Therefore, it was possible that my own presentism would influence my analysis of the data collected from Belarusian and Russian sources in such a way that they would be reflected negatively, particularly for those sources that were published prior to the deterioration of relations. The opposite was true for Ukraine and Armenia, as relations between these two states with the UK and the US was generally positive, especially for Ukraine, during the time when I was conducting the research. Therefore, presentism may have created a tendency on my part to always reflect Ukraine and Armenia positively rather than be objective.

Researchers must be aware of potential presentism in research with all types of documents, not just official ones. This is because 'the content of a document is never fixed and static, not least because documents have always to be read, and reading implies that the content of a document will be situated' (Prior, 2003, p 18). This was the case during my research as the point of view expressed in the official texts I analysed was held *at the time of their creation*, not necessarily at the time when I was analysing them. An important exception to this was certain official documents that could be amended over time, such as legislation. These documents contain several different versions, but these should not be considered separately. Rather, they should be considered as a collective whole in order to understand the degree to which conflict and political turbulence have or have not affected their meanings, purposes or audiences. For example, with respect to my doctoral research data, state energy policies were released every 5, 10 or 15 years, and each new version built on the prior one and responded to the events at the time of writing, although I found that new releases did not necessarily mention those events explicitly.

Lessons learned from practical and ethical challenges

From conducting my doctoral research using documents during periods of conflict and political turbulence, I learned how to navigate lack of physical access to individuals and institutions, the value of resourcefulness to gain virtual access to blocked official websites and archives, and the importance of triangulating documents across languages. These are examined in turn.

Navigating lack of physical access to individuals and institutions

Due to travel constraints, visiting research institutions and archives in the countries which comprised my case studies required a good deal of creativity and resourcefulness. As discussed earlier in relation to my experiences in Armenia, it is important to recognise when it becomes necessary to leave the area and continue data collection remotely. That said, it is possible to conduct in-person research with documents in a different location than originally planned. In such cases, it is important for the researcher to be open to opportunities. By reaching out to new points of contact who might have access to or know of alternative sources of data, we can begin to accommodate for, as much as possible, the inaccessibility of other in-country data due to conflict and political turbulence.

One example from my doctoral research of allowing for alternative in-person opportunities to present themselves relates to my choice to pursue interviews and informal conversations with experts and current and former officials. In some cases, these interviews pointed me in the direction of, or gave me access to, in-person resources. One of my interviews led me to discover a Belarusian library located in London. The library is not widely publicised, and it is only open to scholars for scheduled visits, so I initially missed it as a potential source of data. However, I soon discovered a treasure trove of unique texts and documents that either contextualised or were directly related to my research. This discovery was an important lesson that access to documents during periods of conflict and political turbulence can still be facilitated in person, although in ways we might not think to look for at first.

Another example involved an unplanned trip to the IAEA in Vienna after connecting virtually with experts on LinkedIn. Although the visit was unofficial and I did not have time to obtain approval to use the information I gathered in my thesis, the experience helped to inform my personal approach and appreciation of a number of nuanced realities between the IAEA and the states in my case studies.

These examples support the claim that even if the researcher is not planning to conduct interviews, speaking with other scholars and experts, as I did, is worth exploring as a means of leaving no stone unturned when conflict and political turbulence disrupt the research process. This approach is likely to have value in many empirical areas of study beyond conflict and political turbulence.

Being resourceful to gain virtual access to blocked official websites and archives

Beyond in-person access to documents and officials, accessing online documents proved challenging as conflict and political turbulence occurred in Belarus in 2020 and with Russia's full-scale invasion of Ukraine in 2022. Censorship by the Belarusian and Russian governments of various official websites and archival databases has become much more frequent in recent years than it was prior to 2020. At several points in 2020 and 2021, access to Belarusian government websites was impossible. Circumventing this challenge required a number of strategies. The first obvious step was to use a virtual private network (known as a VPN). This essentially led Belarusian and Russian servers to provide access as if I were inside the country. However, this did not always work, as some websites were blocked inside the country.

In the case that the web link, or URL, for the data was available but not the actual web page containing the associated document, I relied on the non-profit digital library Internet Archive. This service holds some 916 billion web pages. Here, I would often find at least one version of a web page I needed to access in order to read or download documents. As noted by Órla Meadhbh Murray (Chapter 9), it is important to save, and properly reference, online data when and where possible (typically, these are saved as a PDF). This ensures that should data become blocked or inaccessible due to conflict and political turbulence, the researcher can still access the corpus.

In other cases, when a document necessary for my research was no longer available because it was on a blocked web page, I had occasional success locating a duplicate or another version on a different government or other official website. For example, international agreements between states are retained by all parties involved, and the copies held by the other parties usually contained all versions of the agreement (in the case that the agreement was in more than one language). Although a number of official agreements held by Belarus were not accessible from sources in that country from 2020, I was able to locate and download them, in Belarusian (or Russian, as is often used in official texts) and usually in English, via other governments' databases.

Triangulating documents across languages

It is important to note the ethical challenges of analysing documents where the text is presented in one language but the researcher is writing about it in another language. In some cases, I had access to 'duplicate' copies of official documents in English, Russian and either Belarusian, Ukrainian or Armenian. However, in many cases, these contained slight variations in presentation, and sometimes chunks of paragraphs were missing or quotes were provided in one and not another.

Tracing and analysing the different versions of the same text is referred to as triangulation. This is different from textual collation, which typically means comparing different versions of the same text in order to establish a sort of truth of 'what really happened'. Instead, for my research purposes, triangulating different linguistic versions of official documents was intended to shed light on the intentions of the discursive agent – the state or the state representative – in presenting the topic of nuclear capabilities in whatever way they did. During this process, I considered key questions such as: Why did they present it one way in one language, to a given audience, and a different way in another language, to a different audience? What might be the benefit gained?

Thus, I recognised that multiple realities might be true at once depending on the language and the audience. When possible, it is useful to locate all versions of the same text (such as press releases or meeting transcripts), if they exist, in order to capture the whole nature of the discourse. As duplicate copies sometimes existed and other times did not, it was my responsibility as the researcher to explain this and offer analysis of similarities and discrepancies where they did exist.

Conclusion

Navigating research endeavours during periods of conflict and political turbulence presents formidable challenges. As areas of the world continue to experience increased political repression, violence and war, it is more important than ever for researchers to be equipped with the skills and knowledge necessary to continue exploring and understanding the issues and experiences surrounding these events. Both context and positionality in situations of conflict and political turbulence can force adaptation of research plans and introduce emotional, historical and interpersonal dynamics that disrupt ideas of research as neutral or detached. Scholarship on using documents for research can be further developed by taking such challenges into account and offering guidance for researchers on how to navigate them. This chapter has provided a step in this direction by highlighting the complexities and practicalities involved in analysing official texts for scholarly inquiry in such contexts, drawing on my experiences of conducting research with official documents during continued government repressions in Belarus, during the ongoing conflict between Armenia and Azerbaijan and since Russia's full-scale invasion of Ukraine began in 2022. Further expansion of scholarship on the method and practice of using documents for research during periods of conflict and political turbulence is called for. The challenges of such research serve as a timely reminder of the resilience and adaptability required of researchers in confronting the complexities of contemporary scholarship.

Key considerations for using this method

- When undertaking research using official documents, remember that they reflect the social construction of reality of the author(s)/creator(s) and are directed towards certain audiences and intended for particular functions.

- Official discourse includes narratives promoted by the state and by official state representatives. Analyse how these narratives are constructed and what agendas they may serve.

- The meaning and function of official documents can shift over time. Re-evaluate their relevance and use in light of new political or social developments.

- Changing contexts may negatively affect and, in some cases, prohibit your ability to access official documents, so be sure to download and save copies of all documents when you first access them.

- Consider any shifts in understandings and interpretations of documents over time. Just because a document was meant to convey a certain message when it was written does not mean this is how we understand it today. Reflect on how your own background, position or assumptions might influence your understanding of the document.

- If your original research location becomes inaccessible, stay open to conducting fieldwork elsewhere. New opportunities may arise in nearby areas or through different access points – stay flexible.

- Although conflict and political turbulence can disrupt your research plan, being persistent, adaptable and creative with your methods will help you to keep your work moving forward and overcome any challenges that may come your way.

Notes

[1] It is not uncommon for companies in the civil nuclear industry to receive funding from the state – in fact, it is argued by some that state backing is essential for a healthy civil nuclear industry, as this means it can afford to innovate and develop improved and new technologies. However, it is not always the case that the state owns the entire nuclear industry in a country as it does in Russia. Canada, Japan, the UK and the US are just a few examples of countries where nuclear power plants are primarily privately owned, investor-owned utilities or under mixed ownership. Meanwhile regulation and waste management are almost always the responsibility of government agencies and organisations. Nuclear research and development are typically a mix between public and private organisations.

[2] For a guide on how to do critical discourse analysis, see Grant (2019, chapter 4).

[3] International identity is defined in my doctoral research as a narrative constructed by the state of itself and its originality positioned within a certain social structure of states and authenticated by association with dominant norms and social meanings.

[4] This was a calculated risk, as I had visited a number of nuclear power plants before, although none of them were in former Soviet states. As I later learned, it was unofficial knowledge that Russia had a unique degree of management authority at the Armenian nuclear power plants, and Russian security forces were responsible for maintaining security at the plant despite it being officially owned by the Armenian government.

References

Armitage, D. (2023) 'In defense of presentism', in D.M. McMahon (ed) *History and Human Flourishing*, Oxford University Press, pp 59–84.

Caprile, A. and Przetacznik, J. (2023) *Armenia and Azerbaijan: Between War and Peace*, European Parliamentary Research Service. Available from: www.europarl.europa.eu/RegData/etudes/BRIE/2023/747919/EPRS_BRI(2023)747919_EN.pdf

Grant, A. (2019) *Doing Excellent Social Research with Documents*, Routledge.

Gruber, H. (2024) 'Snyder and Habermas on the war in Ukraine: a critical discourse analysis of elite media discourse in Germany', *Critical Discourse Studies*, advance online publication. doi: 10.1080/17405904.2024.2331164

Hansen, L. (2006) *Security as Practice: Discourse Analysis and the Bosnian War*, Routledge.

Hansen, L. (2016) 'Discourse analysis, post-structuralism, and foreign policy', in S. Smith, A. Hadfield and T. Dunne (eds) *Foreign Policy: Theories, Actors, Cases* (3rd edn), Oxford University Press, pp 95–111.

Hopf, T. (1998) 'Constructivism in international relations theory', *International Security*, 23(1): 171–200.

Hopf, T. (2012) *Reconstructing the Cold War: The Early Years, 1945–1958*, Oxford University Press.

Howarth, D. (1998) 'Discourse theory and political analysis', in E. Scarbrough and E. Tanenbaum (eds) *Research Strategies in the Social Sciences*, Oxford University Press, pp 268–93.

IAEA (International Atomic Energy Agency) (2006) *Basic Infrastructure for a Nuclear Power Project* (IAEA-TECDOC-1513), IAEA. Available from: www-pub.iaea. org/MTCD/Publications/PDF/TE_1513_web.pdf

IAEA (International Atomic Energy Agency) (2019) *IAEA Annual Report 2019*, IAEA.

Oxford English Dictionary (nd) 'Presentism', *Oxford English Dictionary*. Available from: www.oed.com/dictionary/presentism_n?tab=meaning_and_use (accessed 3 May 2024).

Prior, L. (2003) *Using Documents in Social Research*, SAGE.

Van Dijk, T.A. (1993) 'Principles of critical discourse analysis', *Discourse & Society*, 4(2): 249–83. doi:10.1177/0957926593004002006

Yin, R.K. (2018) *Case Study Research and Applications: Design and Methods* (6th edn), SAGE.

PART IV

Exploring the personal

11

Impactful inquiry: how insider knowledge enhances the real-world relevance of research with documents

Ella Houston

Summary

- Drawing on perspectives from cultural disability studies, the chapter focuses on a co-analysis of representations of disability in advertising with disabled participants.

- A case study featuring a 2014 print advertisement for US fashion retailer Nordstrom is presented to demonstrate an application of textual analysis and semi-structured interviews as research methods.

- Textual analysis and semi-structured interviews are highlighted as useful research methods for developing analyses of documents that aim to address social justice issues.

- Reflecting researcher positionality and ethical considerations, guidance is provided on making research more respectful and inclusive for disabled participants.

- The research shows that representation of disability in advertising is a complex issue and that disabled people draw on their personal experiences when challenging advertisements that portray disability and diversity in tokenistic ways.

Introduction

As well as reflecting how societies and cultures respond to diversity, representations of disability in documents (from advertisements to government reports) influence understandings of disability. However, the ways that documents impact people's perspectives towards disability cannot be easily predicted. Individuals interpret 'slightly, or even vastly' different meanings from the words, phrases, sounds and visual content that documents contain (Grant, 2019, p 13). In any case, an ongoing problem is that stereotype-laden approaches to disability are promoted over disabled people's personal narratives across masses of documents (Bolt, 2021).

This chapter focuses on my co-analysis of representations of disability in advertising with disabled participants, highlighting how their 'insider' perspectives illuminate the power of documents to reinforce and challenge the societal inequalities they face. I present a case study featuring a print advertisement for Nordstrom in 2014, demonstrating my application of textual analysis and semi-structured interviews as research methods. Nordstrom is a well-known US retailer of fashion for adults and children.

The next section details my research process, highlighting how data gathered via textual analysis and semi-structured interviews with disabled participants facilitated in-depth analysis of representations of disability in advertising. I also discuss my positionality and ethical considerations in relation to the research. This is followed by a description of the case study and a concluding discussion.

The interdisciplinary research I present combines perspectives from cultural studies and disability studies, thus contributing to the field of cultural disability studies. Cultural studies explores how beliefs, customs and prejudices are circulated throughout society via cultural texts (a term which refers broadly to documents, practices and products that are 'capable of transmitting or generating meaning'; Hoad, 2022, p 153). Cultural studies theory recognises that rather than being manipulated by popular culture into how to think and act, individuals' responses to television programmes, films, advertisements and so on are complex (Hall, 1973). Meanwhile, disability studies highlights how popular representations of disability 'lodge in [disabled people's] subjectivities, sometimes with profoundly exclusionary consequences', damaging their self-esteem (Thomas, 1999, p 47). Even though there seems to be more awareness of disability and diversity in recent advertising, tokenistic approaches towards inclusion are still rife (Houston and Haller, 2022). Analyses of advertisements informed by cultural disability studies theory emphasise in-depth, critical approaches (Haller and Ralph, 2006; Bolt, 2014; 2016; Loebner, 2022; Shek-Noble, 2022). Engaging with disabled people's perspectives enriches the process of analysing advertisements, bringing more depth and meaning to research with documents.

Combining theoretical and embodied perspectives towards advertising

Textual analysis

Since texts provide evidence for theories about 'social structures, relations and processes' (Kovala, 2002, p 4), textual analysis is a popular research method in cultural disability studies. After all, this field seeks to uncover and 'destabilize our dominant ways of knowing disability' (Snyder and Mitchell, 2006, p 4). Textual analysis enables researchers to explore how texts reflect ideologies that are prevalent across 'particular historical and cultural moment[s]' (Fürsich, 2018). This method reveals the potential of texts to influence how we think about our surrounding worlds. For instance, analysing how texts such as television programmes and newspapers frame messages about societal issues develops our understanding of popular culture's role in influencing public attitudes. As the general public absorbs messages about disability from mass-produced texts, such as advertisements, newspapers, magazines, television programmes and films, cultural disability studies explores how such texts 'influence our [ways] of imagining human differences' (Snyder and Mitchell, 2006, p 202).

Textual analysis attends to 'subtle subtexts[s]' in documents, exploring how messages are communicated via 'allusion, the unspoken, ambiguity, equivocation, implicitness, innuendo, a second level' (Pernot, 2021, p vii). As such, it is important not to accept the content of documents on face value. For example, an advertisement might feature written and verbal messages claiming that a brand seeks to empower disabled people. These messages could be enhanced by uplifting music, bright colours and models who appear happy and confident. However, if the advertisement only includes images of disabled people whose impairments are only slightly visible, it could be inferred that these messages reflect superficial approaches to inclusion. When applying textual analysis to documents that contain written, audio and visual content, researchers should avoid treating written and verbal messages as the most important forms of communication.

Semi-structured interviews

Complementing textual analysis' potential for revealing intricate and subtle features of documents, semi-structured interviews enable researchers to gather 'in-depth data' from participants in a relatively short amount of time (Karatsareas, 2022, p 101). While structured interviews involve a set itinerary of questions, semi-structured interviews use some preset prompts for discussion but also enable interviewers to ask 'follow-up questions' (Hall, 2020, p 77). Semi-structured interviews include 'both open-ended and more theoretically driven questions' (Galletta, 2013, p 45). Open-ended questions begin with expansive phrases, such as 'to what extent do you think that …' or 'have you ever experienced …', encouraging interviewees to guide discussions. This type of question enables participants to highlight issues they believe are most relevant to the research topic, which may include issues that had not been anticipated by researchers. Theoretically driven questions prompt interviewees to consider the extent to which academic theory and concepts relate to their everyday lives. For example, asking disabled participants whether and how they believe that charity advertisements promote disabling stereotypes enables cultural disability studies researchers to test the theory that the charity industry objectifies disabled people (Longmore, 2016).

Disabled people are often suspicious of research that explores issues surrounding disability. There is a long history of research that prioritises the interests of non-disabled researchers and funding agencies led by non-disabled people (Kitchin, 2000). One of the biggest problems associated with the charity advertising industry is that the capital it generates has historically '[funded] medical research' and interventions that have 'nothing to do with disabled people or disability' (Barnes,

1992, p 23; Waltz, 2012). Although medical research is automatically praised as a force for good, disabled people are typically given few opportunities to steer research processes, highlighting the political, environmental and attitudinal barriers they face. As research can sideline issues that matter most to disabled people, opportunities should be created for direct input from disabled participants. In addition to promoting accessibility by allowing interviewees to guide the style and pace of conversations (Aidley and Fearon, 2021), semi-structured interviews enable disabled participants to focus on the issues they are most concerned about.

My practical application of the research methods

In the study discussed here, I followed a triangulated approach, which involved using multiple research methods and data sources to develop critiques of advertisements. My research examined portrayals of mental health issues, mobility and sensory impairments in advertising (Houston, 2017). However, this chapter focuses mainly on a case study featuring a print advertisement produced by Nordstrom in 2014, providing deeper insights into my application of textual analysis alongside research participants' responses to the advertisement. This case study exemplifies how disabled participants generate multilayered responses to representations of disability. Participants discussed subtle features of the advertisements, identifying meanings, values and emotions that are subtly associated with disability.

During the first phase of the research, I applied textual analysis to a sample of nine television and print advertisements produced post 2000. Textual analysis recognises that a 'vast amount [of] phenomena' convey meanings (Bergström and Boréus, 2017, p 5). With this in mind, I analysed multiple modes of communication across television and print advertising – including written and spoken messages, music, sounds and visual content – alongside studying characters' facial expressions and behaviours. While some of the advertisements were produced in the US, the research was conducted in the UK. I found advertisements via Google searches, using search terms such as '*disab*★ AND *advert*★', and I selected the most popular results for analysis. To meet the inclusion criteria, advertisements had to be produced post 2000 in either the UK or the US, as the research focused on Anglo-American advertising. Advertisements had to feature disabled women as either the sole or main character. Instead of developing an exhaustive list of advertisements featuring disabled women, I sought to gather a sample of advertising across a diverse range of sectors, and the selected advertisements covered commercial and pharmaceutical companies as well as charities and public health organisations.

Following my selection of the sample, I made detailed notes for each advertisement, referring to explicit messages, characters and scenes depicted. I developed my preliminary notes later on as I recorded more subtle aspects, such as implicit messages and veiled assumptions. For example, I analysed a pharmaceutical advertisement for the antidepressant Wellbutrin XL that contained the tag line 'I'm ready to experience life' positioned next to a smiling woman and the medication's logo. The indirect message is that the woman is now able to enjoy life as Wellbutrin XL has supposedly 'cured' her depression. The veiled and problematic assumption is that people who have depression lead static, unfulfilling lives. I created a table for each advertisement, using the overarching themes I uncovered as headings, and I stored relevant notes in the corresponding columns. Besides helping me to develop in-depth understandings of the advertisements, this rigorous approach mitigated the potential issue of 'cherry-picking' advertising content that fit with my personal and academic beliefs. Table 11.1 is an excerpt of the table I created to organise my notes on Nordstrom's advertisement.

During the second phase of the research, I conducted semi-structured interviews with 15 participants who self-identified as disabled women and were aged 18+ and living in the UK or the US. Participants were recruited via online disability community mailing lists. Each participant completed one audio-recorded interview, which included a small number of open-ended questions and lasted for approximately an hour. During the interviews, I used advertisements from my sample as prompts for discussion, asking participants to describe their responses to how disability is represented. Alongside including participants in the process of analysis, this approach 'creatively enhanced the interviewing process' (Kara, 2020, p 107). It prompted participants to share stories and perspectives that might not otherwise have sprung to mind. The open-ended questions I asked invited participants to consider:

- whether they had experienced anything similar to the scenarios depicted in the advertisements;
- the extent to which they believed the representations of disability were empowering or disempowering;
- whether they believed that the advertisements could have included any other aspects or details surrounding disability;
- whether and how the advertising content impacted their sense of self.

Table 11.1: Excerpt of data gathered via an application of textual analysis to Nordstrom's 2014 advertisement featuring Jillian Mercado

Theme 1: Toughness	Theme 2: Punk/rebellion	Theme 3: Synthesis of body and wheelchair
Mercado wears a thick leather jacket.	She has dyed, spiky purple hair.	The black leather jacket and boots are the same colour as her wheelchair.
Her power wheelchair has signs of rust and wear on the wheels.	She wears black leather clothes.	Mercado is sitting on the wheelchair and holding one handle – she appears to be relaxed and in sync with her wheelchair.
She wears chunky leather boots.	Although her body is in a sideways position, she turns her head to stare directly at the camera – challenging the audience's gaze.	

After I transcribed the audio recordings, I applied narrative analysis to the interview data. This approach focuses on the meanings that participants attach to the personal stories and experiences they share during interviews. Using printed copies of interview transcripts, I followed a colour-coding approach, highlighting participants' references to their personal perspectives and stories in specific colours. For instance, I used the colour blue whenever a participant shared an experience of being stigmatised by other people. I created a table for each participant, with the titles of overarching narrative themes featuring as headings and the corroborating data from the transcript stored in the corresponding columns.

Recognising my positionality

Disability studies plays an important role in my life both in and beyond academia. My undergraduate and master's degrees are in disability studies, and my doctoral research combined perspectives from feminism and disability studies to examine disability and gender in contemporary advertising. Moreover, I am a senior lecturer in disability studies and a core member of the Centre for Culture and Disability Studies at Liverpool Hope University. As someone who identifies as disabled, disability studies has brought new meanings to my educational experiences, career and personal relationships. It also increases my awareness of how disability intersects with other aspects of my identity. As a White woman who is in permanent employment and whose impairment and health conditions are not immediately noticeable, I appreciate that my experiences of disability are privileged in various ways. My positionality is important to consider in relation to the case study discussed in the chapter, which focuses on an advertisement featuring Jillian Mercado – a disabled Latinx model and actor. I recognise that as a White researcher, I am less aware of issues facing disabled women who are part of marginalised racial and ethnic groups. I acknowledge this limitation as a way of challenging the 'whitewash[ing]' of disability studies (Bell, 2017, p 407).

Disability studies underpins my approach to research, from my commitment to investigating issues that impact disabled people to my alignment with constructivist perspectives. I believe that disability is socially and culturally constructed – understandings of disability vary across geographical locations, time periods and communities (Shuttleworth and Kasnitz, 2006). Rather than believing that there is a universal definition of *disability*, I believe that people's perceptions of this concept are shaped by cultural knowledge systems, from language to representations.

Ethical considerations

Anyone who is interested in researching issues surrounding disability should be mindful of the oppressive history of 'parasitical' researchers who consume disabled people's time and energy to 'serve their own professional interests' (Hunt, 1981, pp 43, 46). Analysing documents enables researchers to explore and challenge cultural attitudes towards disability in ways that make demands of 'no one other than the researcher' (Snyder and Mitchell, 2006, pp 202–3). However, I involved disabled people in the co-analysis of advertisements as I was aware that by relying only on my own interpretations, I would fail to do justice to disabled people's diverse opinions about representations of disability.

When conducting interviews with participants (following ethical approval from Lancaster University's Faculty of Health and Medicine research ethics committee), I was mindful that advantages associated with this research method can pose ethical issues. Semi-structured interviews generate 'relaxed, open and honest' discussions, with participants often sharing personal anecdotes (Morris, 2015, p 5). This benefit also presents a potential ethical issue, as participants can be 'seduced' by the informal nature of semi-structured interviews into 'say[ing] "too much"' (Brinkmann, 2020, p 452). I advised participants – via a research information sheet and at the beginning of interviews – to only share stories and perspectives they felt comfortable contributing to the research. In addition, for a period of four weeks following their interview, participants could withdraw any of their data from the research.

When inviting participants to analyse documents, researchers should be mindful that the content could cause upset or discomfort for individuals. It is impossible to predict what kind of content might stir troublesome memories or emotions for another person. For instance, when I conducted interviews with women who have mobility impairments, all participants praised the portrayal in the Nordstrom advertisement of Jillian Mercado as a confident disabled woman. However, one participant appeared sad, explaining that she was unable to be as comfortable in her own skin as Mercado seemed to be. Engaging with Nordstrom's advertisement reminded her of being excluded from feminine 'rites of passage', such as practising applying make-up and getting ready to go out, when she was growing up. If participants seem upset when analysing documents, they should be invited to take a break and reminded of their right to withdraw from the research. It is also helpful to provide participants with information about relevant support organisations and resources.

Taking a rigorous and transparent approach to analysing data from documents helps researchers to avoid 'falsifying, distorting, suppressing, selectively reporting or sensationalising their research evidence or findings' (British Educational Research Association, 2024, para 75). Developing a robust research design and allowing space for reflecting on your data analysis promotes an ethical approach to research with documents. During my analysis of advertisements, I stored my detailed notes in a separate table for each advertisement, ensuring that I was able to revisit and check the accuracy of the data I collected.

Having considered key methodological aspects of the research design, the chapter now moves on to discuss the case study. Drawing together data gathered via textual analysis and semi-structured interviews, the case study explored how Nordstrom's advertisement presented a bold challenge to patronising portrayals of disability. The advertisement drew on aspects of the punk genre to reflect disability as a cool and desirable aspect of identity, defying pitying attitudes towards disabled people.

The case study: a co-analysis of Nordstrom's advertisement featuring Jillian Mercado

Contemporary advertising increasingly recognises disability as an aspect of everyday life and identity for many people. Key principles of the Disabled People's Movement, such as 'rights not charity' and 'disability pride', are filtering into social consciousness, influencing how disability is represented in advertisements. Nordstrom's 2014 advertisement featuring disabled model, actor and advocate Jillian Mercado illustrated how advertising gradually reflects a more culturally sensitive society. The advertisement focused on an image of Mercado sitting in her power wheelchair (which was facing sideways, while her face was turned directly towards the camera), modelling Nordstrom's biker-style boots. The bare background placed the spotlight on her spiky, purple hair, her black leather jacket and boots, her black, lightly patterned skirt and her slightly scuffed power wheelchair.

Commercial advertising, which ultimately aims to promote profit-driven brands, frequently misconstrues disability activism and identity. Tokenism occurs when advertisers take the bare minimum approach to depicting disability, such as including one person whose impairment, mobility aid or prosthesis is immediately noticeable among a crowd of non-disabled people. My application of textual analysis to Nordstrom's advertisement demonstrates how subtle features contributed to a dynamic portrayal of disability, avoiding the promotion of tokenism. On first impressions, the advertisement – which did not contain any quotes from Mercado or 'pro-diversity' statements – appeared to say little about disability. However, closer inspection uncovered how it attended to disabled people's calls for greater 'depth, range [and] nuance to disability representation' (Wong, 2020, p xxi).

Nordstrom's advertisement drew on colour and texture as 'semiotic resources' that are evocative of punk subculture (Aiello and Parry, 2020, p 143). In advertising, semiotic resources include language, imagery, sounds, logos and actors' body language, as they are used to convey meanings and emotions to audiences. Mercado's black leather jacket and boots, alongside her purple hair, brought to mind punk fashion. Since the punk movement resists 'condescending social conventions and traditions [that are] stiflingly oppressive' (Bolt, 2024, p 72), the advertisement hinted at her defiance towards ableism. Her punkish style challenged the ableist assumption that disabled people are desperate to blend into the crowd and conform to societal 'norms'. Mercado was featured on her own, unaccompanied by clichéd messages about 'inclusion'. In doing so, the advertisement was reminiscent of the disability activist Cripple Punk movement's rejection of 'inspiration porn-y' representations 'made by [non-disabled] people trying to profit off of us' (Ash, cited in Fraser, 2022).

When using textual analysis, researchers should remain mindful of the 'social, political, cognitive, moral and material [effects]' associated with documents (Fairclough, 2003, p 14). The ideas and messages reflected in documents have the potential to reinforce and/or challenge societal inequalities and taken-for-granted ways of thinking. Nordstrom's representation of a punkish disabled woman resisted condescending societal attitudes towards disability. Focusing on a single image of Mercado (who some might recognise for her advocacy work, such as founding Black Disabled Creatives in 2020), the advertisement recognised how a person's 'appearance [can] make politically charged statements' (Singh, 2021, p 41). The participant data further reflected advertising's ability to subtly communicate powerful messages about disability. Louise (pseudonyms are used for all participants) suggested that the advertisement quietly yet effectively challenged exclusionary 'norm[s]' inherent in the fashion industry:

> I've actually never seen an advertising campaign from a big store like Nordstrom that is showing a disabled person with so much of their wheelchair. I actually think it's a step in the right direction because, you know, we're slowly getting away from the norm that we've had for so long of stick-thin people who are six or seven foot tall. [...] They're kind of showing that there is no right or wrong – you can be different and still do what you have to do, and you don't have to let the impairment dictate where you shop or how you dress. For me, the simplicity of the image is the big thing, because they haven't got words depicting what they're trying to get across. They're letting the image do the talking and I thought that was quite important.

Louise believed that the advertisement showed how disability can be part of – rather than hinder – an individual's sense of style. As she explained, dynamic representations of disabled models challenge exclusionary beauty 'norms' in the fashion industry. Exploring participants' responses enabled me to address a potential limitation of textual analysis, which is that the data it generates are 'unlikely to be as powerful as hearing the voices of disabled people themselves' (Shakespeare, 2014, p 52). Textual analysis can be, and in cultural disability studies often is, carried out by disabled researchers, thus somewhat mitigating this criticism. However, as argued by eminent disability studies scholar Carol Thomas (1999, p 5), the personal accounts of disabled people are 'singular in their power to illustrate and illuminate' societal issues.

Involving disabled people in the co-analysis of advertisements enabled me to uncover their opinions regarding how representations of disability influence the societal attitudes and barriers they encounter. 'Human reactions' should not be conflated with 'chemical reactions', as individuals often share complex and conflicting interpretations of documents (McKee, 2003, p 120). 'Objectivist' approaches, which claim to produce unbiased research findings that can be easily replicated to check for so-called accuracy, fail to recognise that sociocultural phenomena cannot be reduced to 'objective facts' (Green, 2016, p 190; Meekosha and Shuttleworth, 2009, p 47). By considering diverse interpretations of advertisements, I approach the analysis of documents as an 'argumentative activity' (Dow, 1996, cited in Fürsich, 2009, p 244). I recommend that anyone who is interested in carrying out similar research approach documents as springboards for developing critical and complex understandings of marginalised people's experiences in society.

Reflecting on Nordstrom's portrayal of Mercado as a cool and dynamic character, participants shared personal stories highlighting their frustration with being treated as 'different' by non-disabled strangers. As individuals 'assign meanings to [their experiences] through storytelling' (Smith and Sparkes, 2008, p 18), people who are oppressed are often keen to share stories about their lives in their own words. However, research has a 'dismal track record' in representing oppressed populations. For example, in many cases qualitative researchers have misinterpreted 'Black people's lived experiences through a White worldview or through one-dimensional representation' (Walton et al, 2022, p 2). When sharing my research findings with wider audiences, I draw on lengthy excerpts from interview data, mitigating the potential issue of distorting perspectives shared by participants. Studying the context of participants' reactions to advertisements deepens understandings of the feelings and meanings they attach to representations of disability. The next excerpt, for instance, captures how Helen's appreciation of Nordstrom's advertisement was underpinned by her belief that it challenged ableist attitudes she has experienced:

> The fact that [Mercado is] portrayed as a party-going, electronic wheelchair user is quite a big step forward. Her jacket matches the colour of her wheelchair, and she looks rather confident. [...] It's quite nice because leather jackets and purple-bluish dyed hair is usually associated with a subversive, rebellious subculture and wheelchair users are not usually perceived as rebellious. It's nice that that's part of her identity and she might just be going to a rock concert, just like anyone else would. [...] I think sometimes people are surprised when we're out on our own. I mean, less and less so, and I wouldn't say I've got lots of discriminatory experiences, but whenever I travel by train or go anywhere, people ask 'is someone meeting you?' or 'do you have an assistant with you?' [...] And, just seeing [Mercado] in the rock, punk concert clothing and portrayed on her own as a legitimate, independent person [can] be quite empowering because it shows that we're in charge of our own lives, we develop our own tastes and preferences, and have our favourite rock bands.

As well as showing how representations of disability impact on disabled people's 'sense of personhood' (Thomas, 1999, p 47), Helen's response illustrates how documents are 'perspective-dependent' (Kovala, 2002, p 5). Her analysis was enhanced by her embodied experiences of ableism, which prompted her to consider the potential ripple effects of the advertisement. Helen highlighted the advertisement's potential to challenge outdated attitudes towards disability, such as assumptions that disabled people are helpless. Her standpoint as a disabled woman enabled her to decipher meanings from the advertisement in deeper ways. Inasmuch as representations of disability can have detrimental impacts on individuals' self-esteem, Helen's response illustrates how they can also have affirming qualities. Referring to Mercado's punkish style, she suggested that 'wheelchair users are not usually perceived as rebellious', appreciating how using a wheelchair is simply portrayed as 'part of her identity'. While many audiences might recognise Nordstrom's attempt to move away from patronising portrayals of disability, disabled people's 'insider reading[s]' reveal nuanced messages that will likely go unnoticed by non-disabled people (Tsai, 2012, p 48).

Conclusion

Perspectives shared by disabled participants make the 'real world' significance of data gathered via textual analysis more explicit. Meanwhile, textual analysis facilitates comprehensive and critically informed understandings of advertisements, which can be missed by researchers who focus solely on participants' reactions to advertising. I recommend that researchers taking a similar approach avoid privileging one method over another. Instead, bringing together both research methods helps to cultivate critiques that are responsive to issues that matter to disabled people. The sort of research presented in this chapter could be developed further by having participants access advertisements in advance of interviews. This would afford them more time to reflect on – as opposed to sharing their immediate reactions to – key issues surrounding disability and advertising.

When discussing my research findings, I avoid making generalisations about disability and advertising. Sweeping claims about how marginalised identity groups 'should' be represented undermines the diverse nature of human experiences and perspectives. For instance, while participants spoke at length about how the portrayal of Mercado challenges disabling attitudes, none of them mentioned the ocularcentric nature of Nordstrom's advertisement. Visual imagery is a powerful way of communicating multiple messages at a single glance. However, communicating messages solely in 'visual terms' hinders accessibility for audiences who are visually impaired (Bolt, 2014, p 30). Acknowledging that it is not possible for a single research project to capture how the entire population of disabled people respond to advertisements, this point serves as a reminder of the 'perspective-dependent' nature of documents (Kovala, 2002, p 5).

Combining theoretical, conceptual and embodied knowledge, the approach I take to analysing documents is well suited to disciplines oriented to social justice. A key focus in African studies, for example, is examining 'the concept of ontological appropriation in colonial Africa' (Eybers, 2023, p 47). Research that combines Africanist analyses of documents, such as artworks and films, with narratives shared by African people has the potential to highlight the ongoing ramifications of the Global North's extraction of African culture. Academic critiques enriched by embodied knowledge serve as powerful reminders of issues that continue to reverberate among marginalised populations despite being brushed aside by wider society.

> ## Key considerations for using this method
>
> - As triangulated approaches can generate lots of data, it is useful to draw on a focused sample of documents and a small participant sample.
>
> - When co-analysing documents, participants should not feel pressured into discussing their personal beliefs or experiences if they are not comfortable doing so.
>
> - Accessibility should be a top priority when inviting people to co-analyse documents. Ensure that accessibility features, such as written and/or verbal descriptions of visual content, are available.
>
> - It is useful to provide clear prompts that remind participants of the research aims and help 'demystify' the process of analysing documents. Prompts could encourage participants to consider how visual, verbal and/or written content contributes to messages communicated by documents.
>
> - Invite participants to elaborate on the insights they share. When participants remark that they like or dislike aspects of documents, or if they make a broad comment, ask them to elaborate further.

References

Aidley, D. and Fearon, K. (2021) *Doing Accessible Social Research: A Practical Guide*, Policy Press.

Aiello, G. and Parry, K. (2020) *Visual Communication: Understanding Images in Media Culture*, SAGE.

Barnes, C. (1992) *Disabling Imagery and the Media: An Exploration of the Principles for Media Representations of Disabled People*, The British Council of Organisations of Disabled People and Ryburn.

Bell, C. (2017) 'Is disability studies actually white disability studies?', in L. Davis (ed) *The Disability Studies Reader*, Routledge, pp 406–16.

Bergström, G. and Boréus, K. (2017) 'Analysing text and discourse in the social sciences', in K. Boréus and G. Bergström (eds) *Analyzing Text and Discourse*, SAGE, pp 1–26.

Bolt, D. (2014) 'An advertising aesthetic: real beauty and visual impairment', *The British Journal of Visual Impairment*, 32(1): 25–32.

Bolt, D. (2016) 'Negative to the extreme: the problematics of the RNIB's See the Need campaign', *Disability & Society*, 31(9): 1161–74.

Bolt, D. (2021) *Metanarratives of Disability: Culture, Assumed Authority, and the Normative Social Order*, Routledge.

Bolt, D. (2024) *Disability Duplicity and the Formative Cultural Identity Politics of Generation X*, Routledge.

Brinkmann, S. (2020) 'Unstructured and semi-structured interviewing', in P. Leavy (ed) *The Oxford Handbook of Qualitative Research*, Oxford University Press, pp 424–57.

British Educational Research Association (2024) *Ethical Guidelines for Educational Research* (5th edn), British Educational Research Association. Available from: www.bera.ac.uk/publication/ethical-guidelines-for-educational-research-fifth-edition-2024-online

Eybers, O.O. (2023) 'Coloniality as appropriation of Indigenous ontologies: insights from South Africa and Ethiopia', *Journal of Black Studies*, 54(1): 45–61.

Fairclough, N. (2003) *Analysing Discourse: Textual Analysis for Social Research*, Routledge.

Fraser, C. (2022) 'Cripple punk: the disabled young people smashing ableism', *Vice*, 18 July. Available from: www.vice.com/en/article/akevzj/what-is-cripple-punk

Fürsich, E. (2009) 'In defense of textual analysis: restoring a challenged method for journalism and media studies', *Journalism Studies*, 10(2): 238–52.

Fürsich, E. (2018) 'Textual analysis and communication', *Oxford Bibliographies*. Available from: www.oxfordbibliographies.com/display/document/obo-978019 9756841/obo-9780199756841-0216.xml#:~:text=The%20method%20is%20lin ked%20closely,cultural%20assumptions%20of%20a%20text

Galletta, A. (2013) *Mastering the Semi-Structured Interview and Beyond: From Research Design to Analysis and Publication*, New York University Press.

Grant, A. (2019) *Doing Excellent Social Research with Documents: Practical Examples and Guidance for Qualitative Researchers*, Routledge.

Green, M. (2016) 'Neoliberalism and management scholarship: educational implications', *Philosophy of Management*, 15(1): 183–201.

Hall, R. (2020) *Mixing Methods in Social Research: Qualitative, Quantitative and Combined Methods*, SAGE.

Hall, S. (1973) *Encoding and Decoding in the Television Discourse*, Centre for Contemporary Cultural Studies, University of Birmingham.

Haller, B. and Ralph, S. (2006) 'Are disability images in advertising becoming bold and daring? An analysis of prominent themes in US and UK campaigns', *Disability Studies Quarterly*, 26(3). doi: 10.18061/dsq.v26i3.716

Hoad, C. (2022) '"Images and Words": textual analysis and its uses for metal music studies', in A. Bennett (ed) *The Bloomsbury Handbook of Popular Music and Youth Culture*, Bloomsbury, pp 151–71.

Houston, E. (2017) *The Representation of Disabled Women in Anglo-American Advertising: Examining How Cultural Disability Tropes Impact on the Subjective Wellbeing pf Disabled Women*, Doctoral thesis, Lancaster University.

Houston, E. and Haller, B. (2022) 'Introduction. Advertising and diversity: the framing of disability in promotional spaces', *Journal of Literary & Cultural Disability Studies*, 16(4): 361–8.

Hunt, J. (1981) 'Settling accounts with the parasite people', in Disability Challenge, Union of the Physically Impaired Against Segregation, pp 37–50.

Kara, H. (2020) *Creative Research Methods: A Practical Guide* (2nd edn), Policy Press.

Karatsareas, P. (2022) 'Semi-structured interviews', in R. Kircher and L. Zipp (eds) *Research Methods in Language Attitudes*, Cambridge University Press, pp 99–113.

Kitchin, R. (2000) 'The researched opinions on research: disabled people and disability research', *Disability & Society*, 15(1): 25–47.

Kovala, U. (2002) 'Cultural studies and cultural text analysis', *CLCWeb: Comparative Literature and Culture*, 4(4): 1–7.

Loebner, J. (2022) 'Crip theory and creative briefs: interpreting disability in the creative process', *Journal of Literary & Cultural Disability Studies*, 16(4): 369–86.

Longmore, P. (2016) *Telethons: Spectacle, Disability, and the Business of Charity*, Oxford University Press.

McKee, A. (2003) *Textual Analysis: A Beginner's Guide*, SAGE.

Meekosha, H. and Shuttleworth, R. (2009) 'What's so "critical" about critical disability studies?', *Australian Journal of Human Rights*, 15(1): 47–75.

Morris, A. (2015) *A Practical Introduction to In-Depth Interviewing*, SAGE.

Nordstrom (2014) Print advertisement featuring Jillian Mercado. Available from: https://models.com/work/nordstrom-summer-sale

Pernot, L. (2021) *The Subtle Subtext: Hidden Meanings in Literature and Life* (trans W.E. Higgins), Penn State University Press.

Shakespeare, T. (2014) *Disability Rights and Wrongs Revisited* (2nd edn), Routledge.

Shek-Noble, L. (2022) 'Supercrip in motion: a critical visual analysis of promotional materials for the Tokyo 2020 Paralympic Games', *Journal of Literary & Cultural Disability Studies*, 16(4): 405–22.

Shuttleworth, R. and Kasnitz, D. (2006) 'The cultural context of disability', in G. Albrecht (ed) *Encyclopedia of Disability* (Vol 1), SAGE, pp 330–6.

Singh, S. (2021) 'Queer hair semiotics: analysis of the select LGBTIQ documentaries', *dialog*, 38: 30–48.

Smith, B. and Sparkes, A.C. (2008) 'Narrative and its potential contribution to disability studies', *Disability & Society*, 23(1): 17–28.

Snyder, S.L. and Mitchell, D.T. (2006) *Cultural Locations of Disability*, The University of Chicago Press.

Thomas, C. (1999) *Female Forms: Experiencing and Understanding Disability*, Open University Press.

Tsai, W.S. (2012) 'Political issues in advertising polysemy: the case of gay window advertising', *Consumptions Markets & Culture*, 15(1): 41–62.

Walton, Q.L., Kennedy, P.P., Oyewuwo, O.B. and Allen, P. (2022) '"This person is safe": an exemplar of conducting individual interviews in qualitative research with Black women', *International Journal of Qualitative Methods*, 21(1): 1–14.

Waltz, M. (2012) 'Images and narratives of autism within charity discourses', *Disability & Society*, 27(2): 219–33.

Wong, A. (2020) 'Introduction', in A. Wong (ed) *Disability Visibility: First-Person Stories from the Twenty-First Century*, Vintage Books, pp xv–xxii.

12

The social conditions of possibility: reading medical records as documents of practice

Max Edward Perry

Summary

- This chapter outlines an approach to using documents that is characteristic of contemporary science and technology studies.

- It argues that documents should be understood as social artefacts, things produced through social practices, and thus they should be located and triangulated within their social milieu.

- Viewing documents through an 'epistemographic' lens allows for proper consideration of the social contingency of a document's text/image/surface.

- A case study of an outpatient clinic letter is provided from research into medical records.

- The chapter shows that researchers using documents should develop techniques of 'triangulation' (of documents), 'maximalisation' (of empirical material) and 'slantwise writing' (as analysis).

Introduction

This chapter reflects on my use of documents as empirical material in a research project exploring the sociology of medical records. My hope is that these reflections provide for you, the reader, a useful examination of the epistemological matters at stake when using documents for social science research. As such, this account pursues the questions of how knowledge claims can be made from the examination of documentary material and how such claims might be better buttressed through the careful labour of the social scientist conducting the work. Because of this, I focus less on the practicalities of acquiring, sampling and managing documents in the process of research and more on the practicalities of coordinating knowledge from the examination of documents already acquired.

Medical records are bureaucratic instruments used within healthcare to orient, transmit and make visible information regarding patients and healthcare work. Previous sociological inquiry has shown that while medical records can be said to be made 'of' documents, their constitution and form mark them out as distinct technologies which require bespoke understanding (see Berg and Bowker, 1997; Timmermans and Berg, 2003). That is, the documents within medical records are made, used and designed to perform functions in the social world. My inquiry looked to add to this work by producing a historical and sociological account of medical records that addressed their digitalisation, particularly in the context of the NHS in England since 2002. My interest, thus, was to use documents and other empirical material – both *within* and *in orbit of* medical records – to produce knowledge about the social shaping of the medical record as a technology[1] and knowledge about the new and emergent digital forms of medical record being pursued – what we could call the social life of the medical record.

It is important to state here that the documents forming medical records provide vital empirical matter from which to build an account of the life of a medical record. However, they are insufficient in and of themselves to account for the social life of records. Documents, from a sociological perspective, are artefacts of social life; thus, by themselves, they are rarely sufficient for rounded social scientific accounts of life. Because of that, important acts of contextualisation must be performed to produce social scientific understandings from documents. More broadly, I want to argue that the use of documents as empirical material in social scientific research requires one to understand that documents are not things to be read and decoded, but artefacts that should be rendered intelligible through investigative labour. This might sound a superficial distinction, but it is at the heart of this chapter and is a distinction I return to at its end.

I start with my best account of the technology of the medical record in operation. I do so because, aside from providing context for my own approach, it usefully demonstrates how a document can be read and interpreted differently, how a document can be made to work in this way or that, depending on its social contexts. This leads to my argument that the meaning of documents is an emergent, practice-based reality and that this – when properly reckoned with – is an advantage for using documents in social science research. Following this, I discuss the epistemics of using documents in such research. I explain my own 'epistemographic' (Dear, 2001) approach to the labour of investigation. Then – through a discussion of outpatient clinic letters – I provide more direct instruction on the practicalities of drawing out a social scientific knowledge from documents. The final substantive section, 'An ethic of maximalisation', reflectively explores the challenges of choosing *how* to investigate documents when their meaning can be so potently multiple. I make a broad proposition regarding the epistemological ethics of research practices, I propose three broad methodological practices: 'triangulation' of documents, 'maximalisation' of empirical material and 'slantwise writing' as analysis.

Medical records

To better understand the medical record as technology, let me sketch a typical NHS outpatient appointment as organised in England.[2] To become an outpatient, a patient must be 'referred', usually by their general practitioner (GP). Typically, this is done via a 'referral letter' sent from the GP to a specialist team based at a hospital. The referral contains a bespoke written request for an appointment for the patient (for example, 'Please will you see my patient Ms X, who …'), which will include a summary of the reasons for referral alongside some clinical history (recent prescriptions, known allergies and so on). This referral will be reviewed (triaged) by someone at the hospital. Triage is done to ensure the referral is appropriate and to determine the kind of appointment required. This work is normally done with just the referral letter, so the document is optimised for triage work; it must concisely transmit key information, trigger actions and withstand a critical scrutiny.

Assuming the referral is appropriate, the patient is booked into a clinic. Once a patient is booked into an outpatient clinic, they are sent an appointment letter advising them of the relevant logistical details. After a few days, weeks or months, the patient arrives at the outpatient department, often – as requested – carrying their own appointment letter, ready to register at the department.

Clinician practices in outpatient clinics vary, but from my observations, most clinicians' abilities to prepare in advance of their outpatient clinics are limited by operational demands and practical considerations (time and access to relevant lists and records). I found that clinicians usually arrive in their clinic with only a very broad idea about who might walk through their door. Outpatient clinics also often work at (or above) an already constricted capacity, so time in clinic is a precious and oversubscribed resource. This is particularly so for the time between seeing patients – that time when the clinician is alone. These are the moments used to carry out associated administrative tasks (ordering tests, updating prescriptions, making records), but also to discover information about patients. Such work is achieved, to a large degree, via writing and reading medical records. Again, this requires great efficiency from medical record technologies.

Medical record work must be done as quickly as possible to minimise the time between patient arrival and departure and, thus, maximise the time the clinician can spend with each patient. During my observations, I was struck by how skilled clinicians were at this administration and information extraction. If we focus on the latter, I noted how their eyes moved so quickly across pages, how their capacity to identify and memorise key information was faster than I was used to. Within moments, clinicians could wield information from a vast set of medical records, of 200 plus pages, which had been rapidly collaged together to produce a picture of the next patient's case.

All this work can be achieved because the medical record has been shaped by the realities of outpatient clinic medicine. Key information is placed at the top of letters; when dictating letters, clinicians use phrases like 'otherwise well' to denote patients that have uncomplicated medical histories. The architecture of the medical record is through such acts designed to shape, complement and augment clinical work. In paper records, some pages are colour-coded to alert clinicians to their presence, and others are made slightly larger than A4 so their edges can be quickly located with fingertips brushed across the fore-edge. Indeed, many of the issues experienced with digitising records are due to a lack of attention to the reading practices of clinicians (see, for example, Gawande, 2018; Sheills et al, 2020; Johnson et al, 2021).

By the time an outpatient clinic finishes, a clinician may have communed with thousands of documents, each one curated and managed within these technological machines, within medical records, to maximise the process of communion. The clinician will have read, touched, moved and added to medical records. They will have operated, activated and calibrated a technology.

The medical record thus envelops the reality of the documents it contains, it presents them, and it contextualises their meaning. As the saying goes, 'the medium is the message' (McLuhan, 2001 [1964]). Thus, the medium becomes vital for any understanding of the documents that one might find inside the medical record. What is one to make of the set of documents that is five millimetres wider than standard A4 paper if one has not seen the practised fingertip of a clinician run down the fore-edge of a medical record?

Epistemography of documents

This attention to the social shaping of documents has come to characterise science and technology studies (STS). Scholars in STS[3] foreground the socialness of knowledge claims, and technological objects, by focusing on the labours that produce them (see, for example, Shapin and Schaffer, 1985; Latour, 1999; Mol, 2002). In the case of documents, STS scholars are primed to treat documents as *artefacts of documentation practices* (see Shankar et al, 2016). Thus, they do not treat documents as texts to be subjected to exegeses, but as materials which might usefully inform researchers about the practices that came to produce them. As Shankar et al (2016, p 59) put it: 'Scholars should be reluctant to separate the artifact (a text) from the practices (which are documented), the noun from the verb.' Contextualisation of the image/text of the document is critical to such work; context places the image/text within the social world that came to produce it. On the one hand, this represents a challenge for scholarship, because we cannot simply take documents to be self-evident objects to be unambiguously read. However, it also represents a significant opportunity. The document becomes a potential potent social artefact of practices which can speak much more profoundly than text/image. That is, researchers can, through judicious investigation of documentary material, hope to discover the social reality of the worlds that those documents record.

So much of the life of a document comes from its place within a broader context of social organisation. STS researchers have built a reputation for providing valuable, social scientific insight into the worlds of technology and science through the careful uncovering of these social organisations.[4] STS scholars, for this reason, rarely limit themselves to documents as their only empirical material. Consider again the medical record – if we want to understand the practices of medical records, and their role in the work of medicine, the documents (the referral letter, the clinic letter and so on) must be placed in the context of their use and production.

This approach thus asks us to take a historical sensibility when regarding the document. It asks us to accept the document as a brute fact and to make its sociality subject to investigation. In this way, I want to describe (and argue for) an approach to documents that follows what historian of science Peter Dear (2001) has called an 'epistemography'. Through such an epistemography, the text/image is not subjected to epistemological true/false scrutiny, but to a sort of biographical and geographical reading. Such an approach is interested in the story of the document, its contexts, its raison d'être, its contingencies, its social shaping and its history. Thus, epistemography asks that Kantian question 'what are the conditions of existence for …?'[5] and applies it to documents as 'what are the conditions of possibility for this document to exist as it does?'

We can say that in an epistemographic account of documents, the task is not to explain whether the text/image on the page is pointing this way or that, nor whether it is accurate or wrong, nor even whether it really means what it seems to mean. Instead, the task is to describe how the document fits into a wider social world, a landscape of social practices that would produce *this* document and not *some other* document instead – a task that asks questions such as: How it is that this document comes to be printed in plain English and not a more formal clinical language? How it is that this document asks one particular question and not another? How it is that this document came to be blue when others are white? How it is that a referral document comes to contain the age of the patient but not their weight, their marital status but not their height, their ethnicity but not their blood type?

Such a concern with the conditions of possibility for a document need not be limited to the study of science or technology. Indeed, STS has come to establish itself as a useful field of knowledge production precisely because its methods remain agnostic to the 'scientism' of scientific claims. That is, STS has crafted in the study of science a method for utilising the work of scientists to talk about social worlds, and the method works also in other fields of human life where one hopes to inquire about the social *conditions of possibility*.

In Shapin and Schaffer's path-breaking *Leviathan and the Air-Pump* (a foundational STS text), this linking of science with wider bureaucratic forms is made explicit. In it, they say:

> Any institutionalized method for producing knowledge has its foundations in social conventions: conventions concerning how

knowledge is to be produced, about what may be questioned and what may not, about what is normally expected and what counts as an anomaly, about what is to be regarded as evidence and proof. (Shapin and Schaffer, 1985, p 225)

In the passage, the authors unambiguously separate the epistemological and sociological questions regarding knowledge claims. For my own work as a sociologist interested in medical records, I thus try to avoid reading documents in such a way that asks epistemic questions regarding the truth or validity of the clinical knowledge claims they make (for example, is it *right* to record weight for diabetic patients?). Instead, my target is to understand the social conventions that scaffold these knowledge claims (for example, under what conditions does the need to record weight for diabetic patients emerge?). Such questions would concern the conventions around knowledge production, the conventions about evidence, refutation and abnormality, and the systematisation of these conventions through documentation.

Triangulating an outpatient clinic letter template

We can make this epistemographic account of documents clearer through an example. Figure 12.1 shows an outpatient clinic letter template, published by the Professional Records Standards Body. The template has been produced as guidance on how to format and write a clinic letter according to a set of mandated standards. Note that the patient details are all fabricated.

An epistemographic account starts by locating the document in its context of production. This is a 'model' letter intended to guide and instruct others on best practice. Like drawings in Vesalius' 16th-century anatomical textbooks, it represents an ideal, designed as didactic tool; the text is directed towards abstraction. This didactic context calls for a particular manner of investigation that questions how medical information in the abstract, rather than the specific, is rendered valuable.

The letter masquerades as the product of a gastroenterology clinic, containing realistic accounts of the patient's bowel movements and skin condition, a limitation in the clinician's diagnostic capacity (that is, 'Performed to the limit of view at 20cm') and so on. It is not the presentation of an idealised patient (where everything has gone well and the patient is cured), but of an idealised outpatient clinic (where things have been done *properly*). As such, the idealisation includes uncertainties, further labours of clinical investigation and previous treatments which have proved 'unresponsive'. The patient is clearly not a 'model' – the information capture is.

Thus, to approach an epistemographic reading, we must locate the text within a discursive regime of medicine and ask questions regarding the conditions of possibility for this kind of clinical information transmission. For example, we might ask: In what way is alcohol intake considered to be a part of a 'social' and not a 'clinical' context? Why does smoking status represent a specific heading when so few members of the population smoke? Why is the name of the person who requested the sigmoidoscopy important for a clinic letter addressed to the GP and the patient?

Figure 12.1: Example gastroenterology outpatient clinic letter

Gastroenterology Department, St Crispin's Hospital, Donaldstown, DO5 7TP   (01234) 567890
Dr. Ruth Jones, Consultant Gastroenterologist   gd@stcrispins.nhs.uk

Outpatient letter to General Practitioner

Patient demographics		Attendance details	
Patient name	Ms. Agatha Critchard	Date of appointment/contact	01/05/2017
Date of birth	01/02/1964	Contact type	First appointment
Gender	Female	Consultation method	Face-to-face
NHS number.	124356789	Seen by	Dr. Ruth Jones, Consultant Gastroenterologist
Hospital ID	TL89765		(01234) 562170
Patient address	30 Acacia Road, BM9 6PL	Care professionals present	Mrs. N Bryant, IBD specialist nurse
		Outcome of patient attendance	Appointment to be made at a later date
Patient email address	frances@delatour.net	**GP practice**	
Patient telephone number.	077 1234 7777	GP practice identifier	A111111
		GP name	Dr C. O'Reilly
		GP details	Canvas Health Centre, 27 Acacia Road, BM9 6PM (01234) 956412

Dear Dr. O'Reilly

Diagnoses: 1. Proctitis, 2. dyspepsia   Problems and issues: Bloody diarrhoea, weight loss

Thank you for referring Ms. Critchard to the gastroenterology outpatient clinic.

History
Ms. Critchard presents with ongoing symptoms of bloody diarrhoea, weight loss, and abdominal discomfort that are unresponsive to treatment. She has a 2 month history of bloody diarrhoea. Her bowels open 5-6 per day with 1-2 nocturnal episodes. Ms. Critchard has experienced weight loss of 1 stone over the same period. She experiences a crampy left iliac fossa pain intermittently.

She has no history of travel, unwell contacts or previous similar symptoms. She has longstanding mild dyspepsia for which she takes antacid as necessary. It has never been investigated.

Family history: Ms. Critchard has no family history of I.B.D.

Social context:
Household composition: Ms. Critchard lives with her boyfriend.
Occupational history: Baker
Smoking: Ex-smoker, stopped 2 years
Alcohol intake: 10-14 units of alcohol per week.

Allergies and adverse reactions
Causative agent: amoxicillin
Description of reaction: urticarial rash in the form of a generalised severe rash
Probability of recurrence: likely
Date first experienced: She first experienced a reaction aged 12

(continued)

Figure 12.1: Example gastroenterology outpatient clinic letter (continued)

Examination findings: The abdomen was found to be soft but mainly tender in the left iliac fossa. There was no guarding or rebound and bowel sounds normal.

Investigation results: Faecal calprotein levels were 247mcg/g faeces (normal <50)

Procedure
Procedure: Rigid sigmoidoscopy.
Comment: Performed to the limit of view at 20cm. It showed inflamed and ulcerated mucosa with contact bleeding to about 15cm. Proximally appears to improve.

Clinical summary
Findings are suggestive of IBD. Rigid sigmoidoscopy looks like Ulcerative Colitis. 5ASA treatment commenced today pending further investigation.

Plan and requested actions

Actions for healthcare professionals
A flexible sigmoidoscopy has been requested on an urgent basis by Ruth Jones on 01/05/17. FBC, U&E, LFT and CRP are to be measured, the patient was provided with a form at the appointment. Stool MC&S plus C. diff are to be taken, the patient was given forms and collections points at the appointment.

Changes to medications and medical devices
(only changes to medications and medical devices as a result of the outpatient encounter are included)

Medications and medical devices
(only changes to medications and medical devices as a result of the outpatient encounter are included)

Medication name	Asacol
Form	Tablet
Route	Oral
Dose amount	3 x 800mg
Dose timing	Once a day
Course details	
Status	Added
Start datetime	01/05/17
End datetime	Ongoing
Indication	Treat symptoms
Comment/recommendation	A 14xday course was prescribed in clinic, please renew in 2xweeks time.

Yours faithfully,

Person completing record Dr. Ruth Jones, Consultant Gastroenterologist Date: 01/05/17: 16:42

Distribution list: Ms. Agatha Critchard (patient)

2

Note: This example was developed by clinicians as part of an NHS Digital project. The details are fabricated.

Source: Professional Record Standards Body, 2017

It may be tempting to leave these questions to a clinician. Surely, whether alcohol intake is a clinical matter or a social matter is a question for a gastroenterologist? However, as discussed earlier, methods of knowing take place and are enacted in the social world. What is more, this is a didactic tool *for* gastroenterologists – it instructs them what is important and what is not. A gastroenterologist is being taught through the document that alcohol intake is a social and not a clinical matter. It is this social process of epistemological and normative structuring that is of interest to us. I am not concerned to ask the text to answer the question of whether it *should* be social or clinical – I am using the document to open the question of how alcohol intake came to be 'social' and not 'clinical'.

Let us consider more closely another question from this style of reading: why it is that smoking is considered an important routine statistic to record but, for example, 'exercise tolerance' is not? We could – perhaps – say that this is because smoking status is a straightforward binary measure (smoker/non-smoker), while exercise tolerance is a more complex qualitative measure that is less easily recorded in this way. However, even in this idealised letter, smoking status is not 'smoker' or 'non-smoker', but 'Ex-smoker, stopped 2 years'. What is more, a binary measure for exercise tolerance is not hard to imagine – it could be 'patient regularly active: yes/no'. Indeed, for patients who pass through critical care, the NHS uses a clinical frailty scale, which provides a score (from 1 to 6) to indicate how 'frail' or 'fit' a patient is, particularly regarding their mobility. Such a score could easily be added to the clinic letter and could add valuable clinical context for clinicians. So, we must ask, under what conditions did smoking information come to be regarded as more vital for capture than, for example, 'patient is fully mobile and exercises regularly'?

Why smoking is important to a gastroenterology letter while exercise tolerance is not is a question that cannot be easily resolved by reference to a domain of 'clinical expertise'. Instead, we are forced to consider the cultural history attached to smoking, the infrastructure of the healthcare service and its information technology, and the existing bureaucracy around 'smoking' that heightens its discursive transmissibility. We might also wish to consider time constraints in the outpatient clinic and how easily the consultant can dispense with a conversation regarding smoking ('you should stop smoking … here have this leaflet'). 'You should exercise more' is a much more fraught conversation than 'you should stop smoking', for myriad complex social and cultural reasons that concern the history of ideas much more than the anatomy of bodies.

What I am attempting to demonstrate is not a specific mechanism through which such questions can be resolved (clearly, I have not here resolved the question of smoking and exercise tolerance). Instead, I am attempting to demonstrate how, through epistemographic examination, a thread can be pulled – a thread which leads to questions regarding the social conditions of the document. What has been revealed in the gastroenterology letter is not that 'Agatha Critchard' has an upcoming sigmoidoscopy (not least because no such patient exists). Instead, by pulling a sociological thread, we have revealed certain tacit realities of the document. Let the gastroenterologist interpret the sigmoidoscopy, and let the social scientist investigate the social conditions of the document.

By treating a document as an artefact of practice, a triangulation is required to bring the document into the world of social practices. The context of the document is important and must be prioritised in social scientific investigation. Such a contextualisation must consider the document's intended audience and use, its actual audience and use, its relationship to other existing documents, its author(s), its materiality, its temporality and so on. These may seem to be obvious questions for us to ask of a document being used for research, but we cannot imagine them to be routine operations performed as rote; instead, they are the specific modes of investigation which are used to unsettle the solidity of the document. Documents present an unnatural permanence through solidity, and this obscures their contingencies, their iterations and their palimpsestic being. To make this context present requires one to follow a document outside of its text/image/surface – that is, to observe its use, to see where it appears, to see what other documents it emulates, to see which other documents it looks to eclipse. This, I call, for ease of reference within this chapter, *triangulation*.

For my own part, using documents in research was part of a wider ethnography of the medical record. My use of documents was triangulated alongside observational techniques, interviews and other ethnographic incursions into the field. There was no social scientific understanding to be found in a medical record without its strangeness and peculiarity being made visible through its sociality. A social science of medical records thus pursues how each record's pages come together and function as one and how the record becomes social. Each document it contains represents a point at which the medical record is in relation to the world. These points must be examined epistemographically through triangulation.

Placing a document in relationship with the world need not involve a fixed and delimited set of methodological tools (the ethnography, the interview, the survey and so on). Instead, I want to suggest this as a logic of inquiry that sees a document as fundamentally social. Triangulation can be done through historical or comparative work, through untypical forms of reading (that is, through a purely typographical reading) or through interviews, ethnographic observation and other typical social scientific tools.

The specific methods used are less important than this logic of triangulation which focuses on treating documents as subjects themselves. Triangulation is thus a process of subjecting documents to laborious investigation which places them within a social milieu, attending to what Foucault (2002 [1972]) refers to as the 'rules of formation'. Investigating documents through triangulation is an attempt to identify the rules that set a document within a wider discursive unity. I have attempted to show how, from a document, we can begin to ask questions about clinical talk as a discursive unity from which there are certain rules about smoking, about alcohol, about appropriate limits, about efficiency and so on, which can be probed by the social scientist. As Foucault describes it, the task for us is to identify 'conditions of existence (but also of coexistence, maintenance, modification, and disappearance)' (Foucault, 2002 [1972], p 42). To do so, we should avoid *reading* documents and instead *triangulate* them.

An ethic of maximalisation

From this, we can say that the most difficult task for those of us engaged in using documents for research is how to find a (or *the*) appropriate way to contradict the document under investigation through triangulation. Two broad practical issues are presented when following a logic of triangulation. The first is the problem of locating and isolating which documents to subject to such analysis, and the second is knowing *how* to triangulate the sociality of a document in research – how to decide on what we could call the *forms of triangulation*. I cannot provide a fixed schema for such things. Ultimately, these will be decisions for each research project. I can, however, offer some reflections from my own work.

The documents I used in my research were not selected according to set criteria. I used medical record documents, policy documents, best practice guidance, internal hospital memoranda, emails, journal articles and many other documents. Each document *emerged* as part of my wider engagement with the field. Some documents were referenced in interviews I conducted; others I saw being used during ethnographic observation; others I happened across by total luck; others I found as part of a specific point of interest that required me to seek out written reports. In short, I needed to place myself in the field first to maximise my chances of encounter and to develop the questions that might help me search for documents.

On forms of triangulation, I found a similar theme. Some documents I had to see in use; others I had to ask people about during interviews; others I needed to place into a historical context. Some I spent time writing descriptions for, trying to render their materiality strange through excessive description; others I had to watch being cut apart before their strangeness became apparent – I am thinking, specifically, of the way that blood test results were mounted on a sheet of cardboard with glue, which made their deconstruction intensely difficult. The only systematism in my approach was in its total openness to finding new techniques of triangulation.

Thus, from my own work, in place of a fixed criterion for the identification of documents, or the techniques of triangulation, I offer an *ethic of maximalisation*. Maximalisation, in this sense, means widening your interests as far as possible and committing to remain deeply curious about the field under investigation. One need not perform ethnographic work to build a context for each document, but one does need to envelop oneself in the field to find ways of making sense of things, of building triangulations.

We can see this maximalisation as a practice of dissociating the researcher from their own subjectivities through exposure to as much empirical content from the field as possible. I use the word 'maximalisation' in direct reference to philosopher-scientist and epistemological anarchist Paul Feyerabend. Of pursuing research, Feyerabend said: 'A scientist who wishes to maximise the empirical content of the views he holds and who wants to understand them as clearly as he possibly can must therefore introduce other views; that is, he must adopt a *pluralistic methodology.*' (Feyerabend, 2010 p 13, emphasis in original). Such a pluralistic methodology applies as firmly to using documents in social scientific research as it does to the examination of atoms in physics.

The problematisation of and the methods of inquiry a researcher chooses to apply to a document used in research involve choices about how the world should be unsettled. For my own work, I was interested in the ways that bureaucratic, rationalised logics shaped clinical work, and my analysis focused on critically approaching documents to uncover these forces. I explored questions such as: How does decision support technology limit the capacity for clinicians and patients to explore the novel domain of a patient's sickness? How are drives towards the production of 'structured data' limiting clinical vocabulary? Such questions, to some degree, idealise the work of doctors by focusing critique on the ways bureaucracy limit them. Thus, my analysis did not pursue the very present dangers of clinician negligence, paternalism, unintended error and malpractice – dangers which bureaucracy is so frequently designed to guard against (see Turner, 1987; Collins and Pinch, 2014).

Maximalisation, perhaps, offers a route to greater reflexivity regarding the empirical material under investigation. By maximalising empirical content, and by concerning ourselves with the development of new ways of reading documents askance, we can allow space for the politics of analysis to be disrupted, for the subjects of our critique to speak back, to push us in new directions, for us to be reminded that doctors are not unproblematic figures and that bureaucracy has its own good faith champions.

Maximalisation, I want to suggest, can and should be pursued not just through empirics but also through writing. Amoore (2008) compellingly describes a mode of writing 'slantwise', in which researchers take positions strategically and then disavow them once analysis is produced. We can see how slantwise writing might fit as an ethic within this broader model of maximalisation (of empirical material) and triangulation (through empirical analysis) via a continual, iterative and recursive unsettling of researcher, research problematisation and research material. To maximalise in this way is to take many different positions in our analysis.

One can see that these careful procedures of inquiry are laborious. They require close, attentive, deep, contextualised and critical engagement with one's empirical material. The need to triangulate and maximalise in the ways I have described, because of their *slantwisedness*, precludes the kinds of automated or scalable readings that are being pursued in computational sociology (Margetts and Dorobantu, 2023). There are interesting investigations into the use of machine learning technologies – which may be capable of differentiating the contextual and cultural meaning of statements (see, for example, Gupta 2024; 2025) – but these represent profoundly different forms of incursion to those I have advocated here. I have described a form of inquiry that subjects documents (and other empirical material) to prolonged, detailed, undulating engagement. Such inquiries are cautious and reflective, and they are strategic about claims. The more easily scalable methods of subjecting documents to scrutiny – up to and including those that purport, through automation, to resemble 'human readings' – require certain conclusions be extended into speculative abstraction across documents. This is not to say that such techniques of knowing are not (or cannot be) useful to productive sociological insight (social science, like all science, can work at different scales); it is only to say that I have found there to be value in maintaining a close and reflective relationship with documents. There is, I maintain, value in this type of triangulated, maximalised, slantwise research, as laborious as it may be.

Conclusion

In this chapter, I have outlined an approach to the use of documents in research that foregrounds their social contingency. I have argued for a particular epistemographic approach that foregrounds maximalised triangulation and slantwise analysis. My hope is that the chapter provides a way of considering how to approach research with documents not as a practical guide but as an epistemological ethic.

In many ways, the chapter is an attempt to dissuade researchers from considering documents as simple things. It is easy to consider a document as self-evident, as containing all its meaning on its surface. In life, documents can and do operate as a mechanism for transmitting information – (one hopes) rather successfully. For example, if I am to hope that this chapter has any effect on its reader, I must hope that it has been approached as a text, the meaning of which can be decoded from the words, syntax and grammar I have used. There is, then, a difference between taking a document on its own terms and using it for research. If this chapter is to succeed, then my ideas must be transmitted to you the reader; if you are to use this chapter to find out about the society that produced it, you will need a different approach. This chapter has been about the latter.

If, in a hundred years, a social science researcher wanted to understand this chapter, and this whole collected volume, they would do well to consider it alongside the university and publishing system. They would ask questions about publishing incentives, about 'demand', about incentives in the university system, about accepted social scientific practices, about cultures of ethics, about all manner of other social properties of life that shape and characterise the text contained in these pages. For social scientists using documents in research, the text/image is not enough – we must aim to subject the document (in all its materiality) to an epistemographic, triangulated, maximal and slantwise labour of investigation. Viewed as didact, I simply hope it is read.

Key considerations for using this method

- When using documents in social sciences research, go beyond surface readings and towards an understanding of documents as things that act in the world.

- To understand a document as a thing that acts in the world, locate it within the context of its production. Doing so requires you to understand its audience (both intended and actual), which documents and practices it relates to and its histories and contingencies.

- Social scientists should concern themselves more with the real operations of a document than with whether the statements made in the document are 'true' or 'false'. That is, rather than focusing on critiquing the veracity of a document, social scientists should critically map its deployments in the social world.

- Documentary analysis can be usefully allied with other social science methodologies, particularly ethnographic observation and in-depth interviews. Doing so allows researchers to ask and observe the operations of a document and to contextualise its production.

- Do not limit your documentary research to well-established 'documents'. Policy documents, meeting minutes, books, magazine articles and blog posts are all valuable. Also consider text- and image-based artifacts that are less permanent, such as emails, handwritten notes, Excel spreadsheets, to-do lists and whiteboards. To a sufficiently curious social scientist, even the most transitory documents can prove to be valuable empirical material.

Notes

[1] The 'social shaping of technology' is a term I borrow from an influential paper by Pinch and Bijker (1984), which was seminal to the development of social scientific approaches to technology.

[2] This description is based on extensive fieldwork and ten years of previous experience in the field. The description is purposefully broad and is only intended to illuminate a general sense of medical record activities.

[3] I am including some scholars, such as sociologist Harry Collins, who may be reticent to be referred to as STS scholars. I do so only because STS is now the most well-established banner under which scholars who attend to social practices of science and technology gather and because the unifying claims I make regarding science and technology do not, I hope, come into conflict with the sociology of scientific knowledge, the social construction of technology or any other unifying projects like the 'strong programme' – all of which I include under STS. Though these may be brought into epistemological conflict, I hope that is not the case over the claims I make here.

[4] For an interesting reflection on the progress STS has made in this, see Ziewitz (2025) on STS and valuation studies. This usefully considers the ways STS has exposed the normativities of supposedly objective scientific knowledge claims.

[5] I am thinking specifically of Kant's inquiry into reason in his 'first critique' (Kant, 2015 [1781]). Though as Deleuze (2008 [1963]) has shown, this question can be subverted, not to locate and

describe the *eternal* (eternal reason) but to identify the material and the singular conditions under which new *things* are born.

References

Amoore, L. (2008) 'Foucault against the grain', *International Political Sociology*, 2(3): 274–6.

Berg, M. and Bowker, G. (1997) 'The multiple bodies of the medical record: toward a sociology of an artifact', *The Sociological Quarterly*, 38(3): 513–37.

Collins, H. and Pinch, T. (2014) *Dr. Golem: How to Think about Medicine*, Cambridge University Press.

Dear, P. (2001) 'Science studies as epistemography', in J. Labinger and H. Collins (eds) *The One Culture? A Conversation about Science*, The University of Chicago Press, pp 128–41.

Deleuze, G. (2008 [1963]) *Kant's Critical Philosophy: The Doctrine of the Faculties*, Continuum.

Feyerabend, P. (2010) *Against Method, Fourth Edition*. Verso.

Foucault, M. (2002 [1972]) *Archaeology of Knowledge* (2nd edn), Routledge.

Gawande, A. (2018) 'Why doctors hate their computers', *New Yorker*, 5 November. Available from: www.newyorker.com/magazine/2018/11/12/why-doctors-hate-their-computers

Gupta, A. (2024) 'Polysemy and the sociolinguistics of policy ideas: resilience, sustainability and wellbeing 2000–2020', *Journal of Computational Social Science*, 7: 331–60.

Gupta, A. (2025) *The Pragmatics of Governmental Discourse: Resilience, Sustainability and Wellbeing*, Routledge.

Johnson, K.B., Neuss, M.J. and Detmer, D.E. (2021) 'Electronic health records and clinician burnout: a story of three eras', *Journal of the American Medical Informatics Association*, 28(5): 967–73.

Kant, I. (2015 [1781]) *The Critique of Pure Reason*, Philosophical Library/Open Road.

Latour, B. (1999) *Pandora's Hope: Essays on the Reality of Science Studies*, Harvard University Press.

Margetts, H. and Dorobantu, C. (2023) 'Computational social science for public policy', in E. Bertoni, M. Fontana, L. Gabrielli, S. Signorelli and M. Vespe (eds) *Handbook of Computational Social Science for Policy* (1st edn), Springer Nature, pp 3–18.

McLuhan, M. (2001 [1964]) *Understanding Media: The Extensions of Man*, Routledge.

Mol, A. (2002) *The Body Multiple: Ontology in Medical Practice*, Duke University Press.

Pinch, T. and Bijker, W. (1984) 'The social construction of facts and artefacts: or how the sociology of science and the sociology of technology might benefit each other', *Social Studies of Science*, 14(3): 399–441. doi: 10.1177/030631284014003004

Professional Record Standards Body (2017) *Outpatient Letter Standard Example Letters*, Professional Record Standards Body. Available from: https://theprsb.org/wp-content/uploads/2018/02/Outpatient-Letter-Examples.pdf

Shankar, K. Hakken, D. and Østerlun, C. (2016) 'Rethinking documents', in U. Felt, R. Fouché, C.A. Miller and L. Smith-Doerr (eds) *The Handbook of Science and Technology Studies*, The MIT Press, pp 59–86.

Shapin, S. and Schaffer, S. (1985) *Leviathan and the Air-Pump: Hobbes, Boyle, and the Experimental Life*, Princeton University Press.

Shiells, K., Diaz Baquero, A.A., Štěpánková, O. and Holmerová, I. (2020) 'Staff perspectives on the usability of electronic patient records for planning and delivering dementia care in nursing homes: a multiple case study', *BMC Medical Informatics and Decision Making*, 20(1): 159. doi: 10.1186/s12911-020-01160-8

Timmermans, S. and Berg, M. (2003) *The Gold Standard: The Challenge of Evidence-Based Medicine and Standardization in Health Care*, Temple University Press.

Turner, B. (1987) *Medical Power and Social Knowledge*, SAGE.

Ziewitz, M. (2025) 'On STS and valuation', in A.K. Krüger, T. Peetz and H. Schäfer (eds) *The Routledge International Handbook of Valuation and Society*, Routledge, pp 43–53.

13

Curating COVID-19: creating an illustrated digital archive with diary and interview research data

Kate Carruthers Thomas

Summary

- This chapter outlines an example of working with diary entries and interview transcripts to create a public access, illustrated digital archive.

- It describes processes of gathering, analysing, curating, structuring and illustrating data.

- It includes a case study with excerpts and lessons for using this method in other disciplines.

Introduction

In this chapter, I discuss my experience of working with documents to create an illustrated digital archive (Carruthers Thomas, 2023) as a means of research dissemination. The documents in question comprise 50 diary entries and 25 interview transcripts recording the experiences of 25 female academics in the UK over the first 18 months of the COVID-19 pandemic. The documents were gathered as part of the research project titled 'Dear Diary: equality implications for female academics of changes to working practices in lockdown and beyond' (Carruthers Thomas, 2022). The digital archive presents curated, anonymised extracts from these documents, structured thematically and with accompanying illustrations. The archive is open access, meaning project findings are accessible to a public audience beyond the academic context.

Researching gender, higher education and COVID-19

I am a UK-based female academic whose research focuses on the way gender operates within the higher education workforce and how women's experiences of the spaces of the university workplace are shaped by gender operating as a geography of power. This approach is underpinned by Massey's (1993; 2007) concept of power geometry – that is, the differential positions of groups and individuals in relation to flows of power within particular spaces. The COVID-19 pandemic and sudden shift to working from home in March 2020 wrought profound changes in academics' working practices. Initially assumed to be a short-term measure, working from home and teaching and meeting online became new norms, albeit in hybrid forms across institutions and roles as the pandemic evolved. An aim of the 'Dear Diary' project was to investigate my peers' experiences of the shift of paid labour into the domestic/household space, given an already unevenly distributed burden of care (Hochschild and Machung, 1989). Another aim was to consider the differential gender impacts and longer-term implications of the COVID-19 pandemic for gender equality and career progression in the higher education sector. Contemporary academic careers are highly dependent on research income generation and peer-reviewed publications, and any reduction in research capacity and productivity presents a risk for female career progression in a sector already structured by female under-representation (Advance HE, 2023).

Prior online survey research conducted with academic and professional services staff of all genders (n = 534) in my own university in June 2020 (Carruthers Thomas, 2020) gathered data about experiences of living and working through the first UK COVID-19 lockdown. Findings show that female academics and professional services staff were more likely than their male counterparts to take primary or sole responsibility for home-schooling, household tasks and others' care needs and less likely to have dedicated working space at home. In the case of female academics in the survey, those with school-age children and/or care responsibilities for older people reported working from home in the lockdown had a negative impact on their capacity to carry out research-related tasks, including applying for research funding, conducting research projects and writing for publication. Pebdani et al (2023) reports similar findings in Australia.

I successfully applied for one year's project funding from the Society for Research into Higher Education to investigate further. The Dear Diary research design proposed a hybrid methodology, the diary, diary-interview method, or DDIM (see, for example, Zimmerman and Wieder, 1977; Latham, 2003; Kenten, 2010). The solicited diary method is used across disciplines to explore a range of human phenomena, enabling diarists to record 'an ever-changing present' (Elliott, 1997, para 2.4). It 'provides vehicles for participants to observe situations which researchers cannot access' (Elliott, 1997, para 2.4). In DDIM, the interview method is employed to contextualise, clarify and corroborate diary entries − or as Latham (2003, p 2005) describes it, a 'reaccounting or a reperformance' which also reduces the potential for analytical misinterpretation. DDIM is, therefore, aligned with an interpretivist approach that uses subjective and situated knowledge to understand social phenomena. The research proposal also included the dissemination of findings through selected, curated and illustrated data from diary and transcript documents in an open access illustrated digital archive. While acting as a form of repository, this archive 'would be more than a passive storehouse of old stuff' (Schwartz and Cooke, 2002, p 1). The digital aspect utilises advances in and the ubiquity of digital culture to 'promote engagement, wider impact and a potentiality for change beyond the academic article' (Mannay, 2019, p 659). The inclusion of researcher-generated illustrations drew on my own graphic social science practice – that is, use of graphics and/ or other visuals to communicate social research (Carrigan, 2017). This was an opportunity to approach the analysis of data in the documents from creative angles and to distil findings in visual form.

Gathering data

I used purposive and snowball sampling to recruit 30 female academics employed at UK universities and research institutes. Purposive sampling involves intentional selection of participants based on researcher expertise. and it is suitable for small populations with a clear research purpose. Snowball sampling involves the researcher using their social networks to establish initial links, who then recommend potentially willing participants (Parker et al, 2019). Participant information and consent forms set boundaries for the use of research documents, informing participants of their right to anonymity and data protection and that they could withdraw from the study at any stage. Five participants did withdraw during the project's early stages, meaning data were gathered from 25 women in total. Participants worked in a range of academic disciplines and occupied roles across the academic career spectrum. They were aged between 25 and 59 years old, and their personal and domestic circumstances included living alone, in partnership and in a range of family circumstances. Eleven participants had children of school age or younger in the household, and four had care responsibilities for elderly dependents.

Data gathering took place over a period of five months (May–September 2021). Participants were asked to submit two diary entries in any format: a retrospective one, Diary 1 (May 2021), and a contemporaneous one, Diary 2 (July/August 2021). I supplied separate prompts for each entry. The Diary 1 prompt was as follows:

> This piece should be **retrospective and reflective**; an account of any aspect of your experience of living and working during the COVID-19 pandemic to date (March 2020–May 2021). In thinking back over a long period of changing and challenging circumstances, you might wish to consult your own diary/calendar, messages, social media, photographs or playlists from this period. Perhaps specific dates or events played an important role for you? You can write in detail about one element or experience or widely about many.

The open focus allowed participants' 'leeway to write about what was important to them and to structure as they felt appropriate' (Elliott, 1997, para 4.2). Participants were also free to choose their diary medium, including but not restricted to text, audio, video and visual/photograph. A 500-word minimum but no upper limit was suggested for text pieces.

The Diary 2 prompt again invited participants to submit their entries in any format, but the guidance was different.

> This piece should provide a **contemporary** account of your working practices. You might choose to:
>
> • identify a specific day or days on which you will create your entry/ies
> • base your account on a theme or themes – perhaps something arising from Diary 1?
> • use 'A Day in the Life of' format.

In practice, the majority of diary entries were submitted as text files, with two audio files and one video file. The two participants submitting audio and video diary entries said they did so for the sake of convenience.

Following receipt of Diary 2 from each participant, I conducted an individual semi-structured, online interview with them, lasting between 45 and 60 minutes. The interview protocol included:

• an invitation to reflect on the experience of creating the diary entries;
• questions on differences experienced when writing from retrospective and contemporaneous perspectives;
• an invitation to focus on specific content from Diary 1 and Diary 2 entries;
• more generic questions about university policies and practices as well as the impact of the pandemic on their own research, writing for publication and career progression;
• an invitation to consider ways in which remote working and other shifts in higher education practices may have impacted existing gender equalities in the wider higher education sector.

Interviews were recorded and transcribed. The transcript documents were then returned to participants for verification, and they had the option of redacting content if they wished. In practice, very few redactions were made, and these were primarily related to names, places and job titles. The transcript verification process was a critical element of building research relationships with participants; this has been described as 'a process that starts before any data collection takes place and continues well beyond the conclusion of fieldwork' (Roberts, 2018, p 117). Participant information and consent forms had stated that diary entries and interview transcripts may be quoted, presented and published and that an 'illustrated digital archive' was a key output of the research, and transcript verification offered another layer of transparency in a situation where participants were sharing details of their personal and professional lives. In practice, while many participants told me that they found participating in the research cathartic, as the researcher, I became party to multiple, ongoing narratives – many challenging, some traumatic.

At the conclusion of this data-gathering process, I had accumulated a large volume of qualitative data in 75 documents: 50 diary entries and 25 interview transcripts. I was to find, as Latham (2003, p 2005) suggests, that in using DDIM, 'the parallel narratives of the diary and the diary–interview do not sum together to produce a single unified narrative … but an interrelated mosaic of interpretive snapshots and vignettes of a particular social space and social practices in the making'. The reference to social space and social practices 'in the making' has a particular resonance in relation to the extended period of crisis, upheaval and adjustment I was investigating. The interrelationship of the documents and their data would demand an analytical approach which acknowledged complexity. The use of illustration as an integral part of that approach was informed by MacLure's (2013, pp 174–5) argument for 'immersion in and entanglement with the minutiae of "the data" … a very different kind of engagement with data from the distanced contemplation of the table that is the arrested result of the process'.

Analysing data from the documents

I used a reflexive thematic analysis approach (Braun and Clarke, 2019), where themes are generated through fluid and contextual processes and around a central organising concept or idea (Braun et al, 2022). Successive phases of data gathering (diary, diary, interview) meant that analysing data from the documents was an incremental and, to an extent, cyclical process. As each of the Diary 1 documents arrived in my inbox, I read them through but did not begin actively developing initial themes until all 25 Diary 1 documents had been submitted. I then re-read and reflected on each one and coded for initial themes. I recorded and described, also noting the extent to which themes were shared across the cohort. I followed the same process for Diary 2 documents. By this stage, I had generated four overarching themes and facets associated with them (which I call sub-themes). I then added an analytic iteration, which was to re-read each participant's Diary 1 and Diary 2 documents in tandem. This enabled me to explore the trajectories of participants' experiences over time, but also to clarify or modify the themes identified. The process also served as preparation for the forthcoming interview, during which the participant and I revisited specific diary content. Analysis of verified interview transcripts followed the same process as that of Diary 1 and Diary 2. On completion of this stage of analysis, I had consolidated four overarching themes and 19 associated sub-themes (Table 13.1).

The central organising concept of the overarching theme 'Working from home' is the discourses and relationships of power which shaped participants' experiences of spaces of 'work' and 'home' and the relationships between them. Participants detailed how these had been reinforced or disrupted by the pandemic as the domestic/household space became a site of paid work. 'Working from home' sub-themes also include lockdown-specific phenomena, such as home-schooling and the role of digital technologies in facilitating online teaching and learning. Participants' articulations of the spatial and the temporal in diary entries and

Table 13.1: Themes and sub-themes

Overarching theme	Sub-themes
Working from home	Pivot: working from home
	Pivot: online
	Experiences of home-schooling
	Burden of care
	Hidden labour
	Benefits of tech
	Productivity and career progression
Dimensions of space and time	Changing spaces
	Therapeutic spaces
	Stretching time
	Pandemic temporalities
Changing working practices	What the university did
	The return
	Future flexibility
Well-being	Physical well-being
	Overwhelmed
	Mental health
	Depleted
	Alternatives

interview transcripts are encapsulated in the theme 'Dimensions of space and time', and this theme is underpinned by Massey's understanding of space as inherently temporal, 'a confluence and product of histories, relationships' (2005, p 9). The overarching themes 'Changing working practices' and 'Well-being' are less abstract. The former concerns participants' experiences of university strategies during the pandemic, including the 'return' to work and evolution of new working norms. The latter addresses short- and long-term effects on physical, mental and emotional well-being over this extended period.

The final stage of the document analysis process was the creation of individual participant datasets, from which I later selected extracts for the archive. Each participant dataset comprised the two diary entries and the interview transcript, enabling me to review individual narratives over time. I used a further reading of the datasets to review and strengthen themes and sub-themes.

Creating the archive

I co-created the project's illustrated digital archive with a professional web designer, Ben Robertson.[1] Our initial discussions focused on the purpose and desired 'look and feel' of the archive site. I wanted the design to reflect both the physicality of 'an archive' and the spatiality of the analytical framework. Ben and I decided on the concept of an exhibition space with four themed 'galleries' and a landing or home page featuring a floor-plan of the space. In the final version, each gallery page features a context piece outlining the central organising concept and referencing relevant literature. I also created a pen-and-ink illustration for each gallery page. Sub-theme links from the page take the viewer/reader to a set of selected and curated texts extracted from diary and transcript documents. Sub-theme pages also feature an illustration. I retitled the themes (or galleries) 'Work/Home', 'Space/Time', 'New/Normal?' and 'Well/Being?' to highlight blurred boundaries and exacerbated tensions present in the data. Visitors to the site can engage with the archive in any order or in any way – wandering, browsing, pausing, just as you might in an exhibition or gallery space.

To select texts from the documents, I went back to the 25 coded datasets and identified relevant extracts ranging from 75 to 275 words. I did not censor the number or length of selections too much at this stage. Having collated the extracts in theme and sub-theme order, I edited longer extracts down to make them more suitable for online viewing and reading. I gave each extract a short descriptive title, using only the participant's words or phrases. The next task was to order the extracts within each sub-theme section; in some cases, this was to establish a loose narrative flow, and in others, it was to juxtapose different perspectives on common experiences to convey the breadth and complexity of participant data.

Case study

To illustrate the process of working with the documents to select and curate content for the archive, I use the dataset of one participant, a mid-career academic who lived with her partner and two school-age children, as an example. I'll call her Anna. Anna submitted both of her diary entries in text format. In common with most participants, themes of Work/Home and Space/Time were dominant in Anna's Diary 1 document. While these continued in Diary 2 and the interview transcript, the themes of New/Normal? and Well/Being? became more visible as her university tested return to campus plans and the longer-term impact of the pandemic took its toll on her physical and emotional health. I selected a total of ten extracts from Anna's three documents for inclusion in the archive, and I quote from six in this section, in each case outlining my reason for selecting the extract. After each quote, I indicate the location within the archive, using the format: *Extract title*: Overarching theme – Sub-theme.

Anna's first extract is placed in the Work/Home gallery and concerns the pivot to working from home. In around a hundred words, she pithily summarises the challenges of the shift of paid labour into the home at the time of lockdown restrictions. The extract also prefigures challenges which would endure throughout the period. Anna had titled her Diary 1 entry 'Thoughts from a grumpy swan', and I use the same title for this extract:

> Finding an extra four or five hours a day on top and around the eight to ten hours of academic work was practically impossible. I had to get up early to start work early, then try to catch up in the evenings and weekends. I hadn't realised before how much my commute had functioned as me-time, as time to adjust and recalibrate from academic to mother. Working from home and all hours to blend home-school with academic work, the switching required is constant, immediate and exhausting. Like a swan, I was paddling furiously beneath the surface just to try to stay afloat. (*Thoughts from a grumpy swan*: Work/Home – The pivot: working from home)

The poignant simile of a furiously paddling swan is, I would discover, typical of a rich vein of visual imagery and references throughout many participants' documents. I have wondered whether, in a similar way to the cartoon style I use in the archive, the reliance on humour was not to make light of the situation but to make it more manageable?

Later in Diary 1, Anna, a parent of school-age children, explains why she, rather than her male partner, took on responsibility for home-schooling in March 2020. She reflects that it was more because she was an educator by profession rather than because of her gender, but notes that home-schooling became an additional responsibility alongside increased workload and caring duties. I selected the following extract for its clear articulation of guilt and tension experienced within the crowded space of work/home/schooling:

> I actually really enjoyed the home-schooling when I could focus and give it my full attention. I even learnt alongside the kids. But finding the time was tricky, and the guilt was almost unbearable – having to turn one of the kids away when they needed help because I had to be in a work call. (*Fronted adverbials rule*: Work/Home – Experiences of home-schooling)

Anna returns to the topic of home-schooling in Diary 1, but this time I included the extract, *Second shutdown*, in the Space/Time gallery. It exemplifies the diary method's capacity to capture an 'ever-changing present' (Elliott, 1997, para 2.4) and speaks to the complexity of the pandemic not only as an immediate and shocking experience but also as a lived experience over time – 'the crisis of the COVID-19 pandemic as fast, slow and ongoing' (Carruthers Thomas, 2024, abstract).

> It was better because they had online learning as well but they still needed constant support. They couldn't do it on their own ... I actually sent an email to my line manager, head of institute and the associate dean and said, 'I need an urgent meeting. I can't do everything I've got to do in these circumstances.' (*Second shutdown*: Space/Time – Pandemic temporalities)

Anna's workload challenges are evident throughout her dataset. Indeed, the issue of an increased and often impossible workload looms large in all participant data. Diary and interview documents across the cohort provide multiple reasons for this, depending on role and career stage. In Anna's case, she refers in Diary 1 to an increased burden of supporting students:

> Trying to do a lot of the additional pastoral work with PhD students fell on me, which I think is a gendered issue. Some male co-supervisors ... students won't go to them. They won't deal with it ... I also had to support funded students to access funding extensions and to calm their fears about the impact on their future careers. (*Students were isolated, scared and angry*: Work/Home – Hidden labour)

I selected this extract for inclusion in the 'Hidden labour' sub-theme to make the point that female academics' already disproportionate responsibility for pastoral care and 'academic housework' (Heijstra et al, 2017) seemed to be exacerbated by the pandemic.

Throughout data gathering, I had been struck and dismayed by the increasing volume of data related to well-being. Many participants wrote frankly about the ways in which lockdown, remote working, home-schooling, additional care responsibilities and workloads resulted in pain, ill health, anxiety and fatigue in the short and longer terms. It was important to me to include as many examples of those impacts as was feasible. In our interview, Anna and I had explored her diary entries on this theme and the following extract from the transcript is included in the Well/Being? gallery:

> I was walking from my study to the dining room and the kitchen, and that was it. And when doing the home-schooling, I would be not really moving for ten to twelve hours a day, which was not good. I had quite significant back issues and problems. So, physically it's not been good, and I'm struggling to get back to exercise. I think I need to go and see an osteopath and get a few things sorted out. Add in the perimenopause and it's great! (*Add in the perimenopause!* Well/Being? – Physical well-being)

Later in the same transcript extract, Anna mentions 'a bubbling seething resentment' as legacy of the COVID-19 period. This is linked back to her reflections in both Diary 1 and Diary 2 on not only the challenges to her own research productivity but also the exacerbation of long-standing structural and gender inequalities in the sector. I quote the following extract in full because it is an example of one participant's words describing effectively and affectively the core problem the research project seeks to address:

> I am so very tired. At the same time, I am aware that pausing isn't good for a research career. Two periods of maternity leave made me realise

that. I was lucky, I managed to keep going with research last year as the pandemic hit and also had papers already under review. I even managed to complete a new journal article earlier this year, which has been accepted for publication. But I know that having nowt in the pipeline now will mean that the COVID impact will show in my professional track record for the next couple of years at least. I won't have a gap in 2020 or 2021, but if I can't find the energy and time to start something soon, there won't be publications from 2022 onwards. The pressure of 'publish or perish' lurks in the background always. I have missed funding bid deadlines, again. I have missed deadlines to submit for professional recognition, again ... and it isn't over ... Another colleague is talking about how great it was not having to commute and how they could just sit down and get on with their own research and write things. Male and female colleagues, but colleagues without caring responsibilities. So, for them the pandemic was a real opportunity. ('*Nowt in the pipeline*': Work/Home – Productivity and career progression)

Conclusion

One of the biggest challenges I encountered when working with the documents to create the archive was what to leave out. This is not an uncommon dilemma in writing up research based on qualitative data. I have experienced it to an extent with every project. Was it more challenging in this project? Perhaps, in the context of research in and about a global health crisis. Probably, due to the frank and personal nature of the data gathered through diary entries and revisited in detail through interview. Certainly, because, in such circumstances, I did not want selection – or non-selection – for the archive to imply a hierarchy of worth. A robust set of overarching themes and sub-themes were, therefore, critical in guiding selection of data to meet my aim of representing a collective memory of COVID-19 which foregrounds female voices and experiences.

Another challenge was managing the sometimes difficult and traumatic nature of the data – see also Niziołek (Chapter 2) and Pagan (Chapter 5) – while living through the same social crisis myself. Many participants told me that they found participating in the research cathartic. Some, when asked in interview to reflect on events or statements they had written about in earlier diary entries, had no memory of those entries. In contrast, I continued to engage with their narratives through data analysis and then again in curation of the archive. Over time, I became aware of the significant expenditure of emotional labour the project required of me (also noted by Winter et al in Chapter 7), not least due to 'the sharing of traumatic accounts without being able to fix or repair their causes' (Mannay, 2018, p 92). I later addressed this issue in the research poem *Poetry in Emotion: Writing Up Emotional Labour* (Carruthers Thomas, 2023), and I myself found the process of writing this cathartic.

However, there are advantages to working with documents in this way. The archive records a set of lived experiences in an extraordinary global health crisis. It responds to our 'hyper-connected world affording new possibilities to re-imagine observation and the generation of alternative forms of research data' (Back and Puwar, 2012, p 7). It remains accessible to audiences beyond academia and, therefore, takes the findings out into a wider territory. The archive's design and structure create room for the detail and richness of the documents' content, articulated through and across themes and concepts. Selecting and curating content from individual documents also allows participants' words to interact, build on, reflect and extend each other. In doing so, they create a new 'virtual document' in which female academics reach for 'sweaty concepts, generated by trying to describe something that is difficult, that resists being fully comprehended in the present ... a description of not being accommodated by a world' (Ahmed, 2017, p 12).

Key considerations for using this method

- When asking participants to 'keep a diary', it's helpful to be specific about the overall topic and the timescale (over which period, submission dates and so on).

- A diary prompt sheet is useful if you have specific requests in terms of, for instance, media and length. It can also offer participants suggestions and options to try if they feel stuck. In general, try to offer as much flexibility as possible to ensure they have 'leeway to write about what [is] important to them and to structure as they [feel] appropriate' (Elliott, 1997, para 4.2).

- When preparing to interview participants after submission of their diaries, ensure you revisit the entries thoroughly beforehand, for three key reasons. First, it is respectful of the time and effort the participant has taken with your research. Second, it will help you to identify topics or experiences you want to explore in more depth. Third, as I found, often participants don't remember or recognise what they have written, especially if it concerned difficult experiences. Approach the latter gently and with care.

- Part of the joy of qualitative data is that it doesn't always 'fit' into neat themes and categories. I created the 'Cabinet of Curiosities' for any content that I wanted to include but which didn't obviously align with the four 'themed' galleries in the archive.

- Consider your own emotional health when researching challenging and traumatic subjects. How will you manage your responses to difficult content? A research journal, mentor or peer group are just some ways of mediating the emotional labour of research.

Note
[1] The archive can be found at: www.deardiaryresearch.co.uk.

References

Advance HE (2023) *Equality and Higher Education: Staff Statistical Report 2023*, Advance HE.

Ahmed, S. (2017) *Living a Feminist Life*, Duke University Press.

Back, L. and Puwar, N. (2012) 'A manifesto for live methods: provocations and capacities', *The Sociological Review*, 60(suppl 1): 6–17.

Braun, V. and Clarke, V. (2019) 'Reflecting on reflexive thematic analysis', *Qualitative Research in Sport, Exercise and Health*, 11(4): 589–97.

Braun, V., Clarke, V. and Hayfield, N. (2022) '"A starting point for your journey, not a map": Nikki Hayfield in conversation with Virginia Braun and Virginia Clarke about thematic analysis', *Qualitative Research in Psychology*, 19(2): 424–45.

Carrigan, M. (2017) 'What is graphic social science?', *The Sociological Review*, 31 July. Available from: https://thesociologicalreview.org/collections/graphic-soc ial-science/what-is-graphic-social-science

Carruthers Thomas, K. (2020) *Living and Working in Lockdown: What's Gender Got to Do with It? Research Report*, Birmingham City University. Available from: www. thinkthreeways.com/research/archive-projects/living-and-working-in-lockd own-whats-gender-got-to-do-with-it

Carruthers Thomas, K. (2022) *Dear Diary: Equality Implications for Female Academics of Changes to Working Practices in Lockdown and Beyond: Final Report*, Society for Research into Higher Education. Available from: https://srhe.ac.uk/wp-cont ent/uploads/2022/10/DEAR-DIARY-REVISED-FINAL-REPORT-OCTO BER-2022.pdf

Carruthers Thomas, K. (2023) *Poetry in Emotion: Writing Up Emotional Labour*, Research poem, first performed at the International Creative Research Methods Conference, Manchester, UK, 9 September.

Carruthers Thomas, K. (2024) 'Fast, slow, ongoing: female academics' experiences of time and change during COVID-19', *Area*, 56(1): art e12894. doi: 10.1111/ area.12894

Elliott, M.H. (1997) 'The use of diaries in sociological research on health experience', *Sociological Research Online*, 2(2): 38–48.

Heijstra, T.M., Steinthorsdóttir, F.S. and Einarsdóttir, T. (2017) 'Academic career making and the double-edged role of academic housework', *Gender and Education*, 29(6): 764–80.

Hochschild, A. and Machung, A. (1989) *The Second Shift: Working Families and the Revolution at Home*, Viking Penguin.

Kenten, C. (2010) 'Narrating oneself: reflections on the use of solicited diaries with diary interview', *Forum: Qualitative Social Research/Forum Qualitative Sozialforschung*, 11(2): art 16. Available from: http://nbn-resolving.de/ urn:nbn:de:0114-fqs1002160

Latham, A. (2003) 'Research, performance and doing human geography: some reflections on the diary-photograph, diary-interview method', *Environment and Planning A: Economy and Space*, 35(11): 1993–2017.

MacLure, M. (2013) 'Classification or wonder? Coding as an analytic practice in qualitative research', in R. Coleman and J. Ringrose (eds) *Deleuze and Research Methodologies*, Edinburgh University Press, pp 164–83.

Mannay, D. (2019) 'Revisualizing data: engagement, impact and multimodal dissemination', in L. Pauwels and D. Mannay (eds) *The SAGE Handbook of Visual Research Methods* (2nd edn), SAGE, pp 659–69.

Mannay, D. (2018) '"You just get on with it": negotiating the telling and silencing of trauma and its emotional impacts in interviews with marginalised mothers', in T. Loughran and D. Mannay (eds) *Emotion and the Researcher: Sites, Subjectivities, and Relationships* Emerald, pp 81–95.

Massey, D. (1993) 'Power-geometry and a progressive sense of place', in J. Bird, B. Curtis, T. Putnam, G. Robertson and L. Tuckner (eds) *Mapping the Futures: Local Culture, Global Chance*, Routledge, pp 59–69.

Massey, D. (2005) *For Space*, SAGE.

Massey, D. (2007) *World City*, Polity Press.

Parker, C., Scott, S. and Geddes, A. (2019) 'Snowball sampling', in P. Atkinson, et al (eds) *SAGE Research Methods Foundations*, SAGE.

Pebdani, R.N., Zeidan, A., Low, L. and Baillie, A. (2023) 'Pandemic productivity in academia: using ecological momentary assessment to explore the impact of COVID-19 on research productivity', *Higher Education Research and Development*, 42(4): 937–53.

Roberts, E. (2018) 'The "transient insider": identity and intimacy in home community research', in T. Loughran and D. Mannay (eds) *Emotion and the Researcher: Sites, Subjectivities, and Relationships*, Emerald, pp 113–25.

Schwartz, J.M. and Cook, T. (2002) 'Archives, records, and power: the making of modern memory', *Archival Science*, 2: 1–19.

Zimmerman, D.H. and Wieder, D.L. (1977) 'The diary: diary-interview method', *Urban Life*, 5(4): 479–98.

14

Conclusion

Helen Kara and Aimee Grant

Introduction

In this book, we have seen researchers using documents in national and international research, discipline-based and transdisciplinary research, and conventional and creative research, among other distinctions. The documents used were historical and current, digital and analogue, official and personal. Some researchers collected existing documents; others worked with participants to generate documents for use in research. And the researchers whose work is presented here come from a variety of disciplines, fields, backgrounds and professions.

Documents are evidently accessible and versatile sources of data, and data from documents can be analysed in a wide range of ways. In this volume alone, we have seen analytic techniques including thematic analysis, content analysis, discourse analysis, narrative analysis and collaborative analysis, among others. Theory, also, plays nicely with documents. Again, in this volume alone, we have seen researchers using documents with postcolonial theory, post-structural constructivism, feminist theory, re-enactment theory, transformative learning theory and others. Moreover, George Jennings has used documents to test his own theory of martial creation, and in Chapter 4 he sets out his 12-step method for use by other researchers.

You might think that using documents as data means you will spend all your time at your computer or in a library or archive. This is far from the truth. Working with documents can shed light on a wide range of places, both metaphorically and literally. In this book, we have gained insight into theatres, Victorian asylums, contemporary businesses, national borders, social and medical care settings, and academics' homes in lockdown, among others. Indeed, some of the places this work can take researchers to can be threatening or dangerous. In Chapter 6, José Ragas tells of being confronted by a senior police officer who was suspicious about his interest in the history of the police in Peru and their practices of identification. And in Chapter 10, Anna J. Davis describes having to cut short a trip to Armenia because of a conflict developing in the country.

There are caveats for researchers who may be considering working with documents. The documents you want are not always easy to get hold of, particularly – as Davis explains – when your research is interrupted by unpredictable events. Though, José Ragas suggests that 'the scarcity of documents … should be considered a critical piece of information in the analysis, not just an impediment to further exploration' (Chapter 6). In a similar vein, Rosemary

Golding (Chapter 3) and Victoria Pagan (Chapter 5) both recognise the potential importance of including silences and lacunae in analysis, as well as the explicit content of documents, to gain a fuller picture of what documents can tell us.

Ethics

Although the chapters reveal a great deal of divergence among contributors in their methodological and theoretical approaches, they also show a lot of commonality when it comes to ethics.

Research ethics committees (RECs) and institutional review boards (IRBs) don't always require ethical approval for research using documents (although this may be changing as, in our experience, social media analysis now often requires ethical approval). This is because RECs and IRBs have a role in protecting institutions from litigation and, therefore, are primarily concerned with any potential harm to humans from participating in research (Kara, 2018). Documents can't sue organisations, and their authors don't tend to, so RECs and IRBs rarely regard them as potential ethical hazards. Of course, this is in some ways an advantage of using documents in research, as there's no need to spend time completing a lengthy ethics application form and waiting for the committee's decision.

That said, in our view, there are a number of ethical issues to take into account when working with documents in research. To begin with, as Katarzyna Niziołek (Chapter 2), Abigail Winter et al (Chapter 7) and Kate Carruthers Thomas (Chapter 13) suggest, the contents of documents can be triggering, traumatising or retraumatising for readers or viewers. Abigail Winter and colleagues recognise the difficulties for researchers who find themselves needing to read documents which are 'full of emotion and vivid, sometimes horrific details' (Chapter 7). If this is – or might be – the case for you, make sure you identify and implement measures to guard yourself against being traumatised or retraumatised by the material you need to work with. Also, as Max Edward Perry articulates, doing research with documents can be laborious, requiring 'close, attentive, deep, contextualised and critical engagement' with the documents (Chapter 12). Again, this implies a need for good self-care practices, including taking regular breaks, reflecting on your emotional response as you work and seeking support from peers and your institution (Grant, 2022).

Furthermore, working with documents does not change the principles of good practice in research. So, as always, you need an ethically acceptable research question, a well-constructed research design, a systematic approach to analysis and so on. As both Perry (Chapter 12) and Ella Houston (Chapter 11) advise, reflexive work is useful. And you need to pay attention to other ethical issues, such as whether to seek consent from whoever generated the documents you intend to use. Sometimes this is relatively clear. For example, if you are a feminist researcher studying representations of gender in newspapers, we would argue that you do not need consent because newspapers are produced for public consumption. However, if you are a tourism researcher studying people's experiences of travel through their blogs, you may decide you do need to seek consent because most travel blogs, even if they are in the public domain, are intended for the writers' family and friends.

Also, you need to be as clear as possible about the status of your data. You can assess this through metadata – information about the documents you collect. This means, for each document, asking questions like: When was it created? By whom? For what purpose? On what is it based? How solid are those foundations? (Scott, 1990). The answers will help you decide how much confidence you can have in each document. You could even develop a scoring system as a useful shorthand or aide-mémoire.

Some argue that if you are using documents, there are no participants. At face value this is true, but there may be interested parties such as the person or people who created the document and the person or people for whom the document was created. Even if the document is historical, descendants may still have an interest in its use or reuse. For example, Golding (Chapter 3) includes an interesting discussion of the pros and cons of anonymising or naming deceased individuals when reporting on their presence in historical documents. Helen Abnett (Chapter 8) extends this by considering the pros and cons of anonymising or naming organisations in research with contemporary documents.

A further issue, identified by Davis (Chapter 10), is the challenge of using documents in different languages as data; Jennings (Chapter 4) touches on this too. Jennings also highlights the need for cultural humility when using documents in cross-cultural research. Furthermore, Winter et al (Chapter 7) and Pagan (Chapter 5) highlight the potential of documents to amplify voices that might otherwise go unheard. Pagan also points out that this can help to counteract the power of people who might prefer those voices to remain silenced.

Where next for research with documents?

There is a vast and ever-increasing number of documents in the world, and this resource is under-used by researchers. So, we decided to create this book to encourage researchers to do more research with documents and to inform them about some ways they can approach a document-based project.

This book has highlighted some of the practical and ethical reasons for using documents in research. It is far from exhaustive, not least because there is so much scope for using documents across disciplines and fields and with different theoretical and methodological approaches. In fact, an exhaustive book on documents would be an impossibility. However, this book does effectively demonstrate the potential and versatility of documents as a source of data in research.

We have seen that documents can reveal dimensions of human life that you might not expect to find in this context. These include sounds and silences, embodied experiences and relationships between countries. This shows that using documents in research is a powerful and flexible way to investigate a wide range of phenomena.

If you are considering using documents in research, some key questions to consider are:

1. How can I find or generate suitable documents to use as data in my research?
2. How can I use those documents ethically?
3. Which theoretical perspective(s) will be most appropriate for my research?
4. Which method(s) of analysis will be most useful in my research?
5. How many documents should I include in my sample in light of my planned analysis strategy?

Reading and reflecting on the chapters in this book will help you to find your own answers to these questions.

We are confident that using documents will become more popular with researchers in time. And we look forward to finding out how researchers use documents in the future.

References

Grant, A. (2022) *Doing Your Research Project with Documents: A Step-by-Step Guide to Take You from Start to Finish*, Policy Press.

Kara, H. (2018) *Research Ethics in the Real World: Euro-Western and Indigenous Perspectives*, Policy Press.

Scott, J. (1990) *A Matter of Record*, Wiley.

Bibliography

Abnett, H. (2024) 'Collaborator or quasi–grant maker? Revealing the dissonance in international development charities' partnership representations', *Development in Practice*, 34(5): 585–96.

Abnett, H., Bowles, J. and Mohan, J. (2023) 'The role of charitable funding in the provision of public services: the case of the English and Welsh National Health Service', *Policy & Politics*, 51(2): 362–84.

About, I., Brown, J. and Lonergan, G. (eds) (2013) *Identification and Registration Practices in Transnational Perspective: People, Papers and Practices*, Oxford University Press.

Acas (2013) 'Code of Practice 4: Settlement Agreements (under section 111A of the Employment Rights Act 1996)', *Acas*, 29 July. Available from: www.acas.org.uk/acas-code-of-practice-settlement-agreements

Addley, E. and Sabbagh, D. (2018) 'British #MeToo scandal puts non disclosure agreements in spotlight', *The Guardian*, 24 October. Available from: www.theguardian.com/world/2018/oct/24/british-metoo-scandal-puts-non-disclosure-agreements-in-spotlight

Advance HE (2023) *Equality and Higher Education: Staff Statistical Report 2023*, Advance HE.

Ahmed, S. (2017) *Living a Feminist Life*, Duke University Press.

Aidley, D. and Fearon, K. (2021) *Doing Accessible Social Research: A Practical Guide*, Policy Press.

Aiello, G. and Parry, K. (2020) *Visual Communication: Understanding Images in Media Culture*, SAGE.

Alexievich, S. (2016) *Chernobyl Prayer: A Chronicle of the Future*, Penguin Books.

Alexievich, S. (2018) *The Unwomanly Face of War*, Penguin Books.

Amoore, L. (2008) 'Foucault against the grain', *International Political Sociology*, 2(3): 274–6.

Amos, I. (2019) '"That's what they talk about when they talk about epiphanies": an invitation to engage with the process of developing found poetry to illuminate exceptional human experience', *Counselling and Psychotherapy Research*, 19(1): 16–24.

Antaki, C. (2008) 'Discourse analysis and conversation analysis', in P. Alasuutari, L. Bickman and J. Brannen (eds) *The SAGE Handbook of Social Research Methods*, SAGE, pp 431–46.

Arendt, H. (1998) *The Human Condition*, The University of Chicago Press.

Armitage, D. (2022) 'In defense of presentism', in D.M. McMahon (ed) *History and Human Flourishing*, Oxford University Press, pp 59–84.

Ashcraft, K.L. and Muhr, S.L. (2018) 'Coding military command as a promiscuous practice? Unsettling the gender binaries of leadership metaphors', *Human Relations*, 71(2): 206–28.

Bibliography

Ashley, F. (2020) 'Accounting for research fatigue in research ethics', *Bioethics*, 35(3): 270–6.

Atwood, B. (2021) *Underground: The Secret Lives of Videocassettes in Iran*, The MIT Press.

Bailey, P. (1996) 'Breaking the sound barrier: a historian listens to noise', *Body and Society*, 2(2): 49–66.

Barnes, C. (1992) *Disabling Imagery and the Media: An Exploration of the Principles for Media Representations of Disabled People*, The British Council of Organisations of Disabled People and Ryburn.

Barnes, T. (1997) 'Am I a man? Gender and the pass laws in urban colonial Zimbabwe, 1930–1980', *African Studies Review*, 40(1): 59–81.

Baumgartner, L.M. (2012) 'Mezirow's theory of transformative learning from 1975 to present', in E.W. Taylor and P. Cranton (eds) *The Handbook of Transformative Learning: Theory, Research, and Practice*, John Wiley & Sons, pp 99–115.

Bell, C. (2017) 'Is disability studies actually white disability studies?', in L. Davis (ed) *The Disability Studies Reader*, Routledge, pp 406–16.

Bennett, C.J. and Lyon, D. (eds) (2008) *Playing the Identity Card: Surveillance, Security and Identification in Global Perspective*, Routledge.

Berg, M. And Bowker, G. (1997) 'The multiple bodies of the medical record: toward a sociology of an artifact', *The Sociological Quarterly*, 38(3): 513–37.

Berger, P.L. (1990) *The Sacred Canopy: Elements of a Sociological Theory of Religion*, Knopf.

Bergström, G. and Boréus, K. (2017) 'Analysing text and discourse in the social sciences', in K. Boréus and G. Bergström (eds) *Analyzing Text and Discourse*, SAGE, pp 1–26.

Bhati, A. and Eikenberry, A.M. (2015) 'Faces of the needy: the portrayal of destitute children in the fundraising campaigns of NGOs in India', *International Journal of Nonprofit and Voluntary Sector Marketing*, 21(1): 31–42.

Bishop, C. (2006) 'The social turn: collaboration and its discontents', *Artforum*, 44(6): 178–83.

Bolt, D. (2014) 'An advertising aesthetic: real beauty and visual impairment', *The British Journal of Visual Impairment*, 32(1): 25–32.

Bolt, D. (2016) 'Negative to the extreme: the problematics of the RNIB's See the Need campaign', *Disability & Society*, 31(9): 1161–74.

Bolt, D. (2021) *Metanarratives of Disability: Culture, Assumed Authority, and the Normative Social Order*, Routledge.

Bolt, D. (2024) *Disability Duplicity and the Formative Cultural Identity Politics of Generation X*, Routledge.

Bowman, P. (2016) 'Making martial arts history matter', *International Journal of the History of Sport*, 33(9): 915–33.

Braddy, P.W., Sturm, R.E., Atwater, L., Taylor, S.N. and McKee, R.A. (2020) 'Gender bias still plagues the workplace: looking at derailment risk and performance with self–other ratings', *Group and Organization Management*, 45(3): 315–50.

Braun, V. and Clarke, V. (2006) 'Using thematic analysis in psychology', *Qualitative Research in Psychology*, 3(2): 77–101.

Braun, V. and Clarke, V. (2013) *Successful Qualitative Research: A Practical Guide for Beginners*, SAGE.

Braun, V. and Clarke, V. (2019) 'Reflecting on reflexive thematic analysis', *Qualitative Research in Sport, Exercise and Health*, 11(4): 589–97.

Braun, V. and Clarke, V. (2022) *Thematic Analysis: A Practical Guide*, SAGE.

Braun, V., Clarke, V. and Hayfield, N. (2022) '"A starting point for your journey, not a map": Nikki Hayfield in conversation with Virginia Braun and Virginia Clarke about thematic analysis', *Qualitative Research in Psychology*, 19(2): 424–45.

Breckenridge, K. (2008) 'The elusive panopticon: the HANIS project and the politics of standard in South Africa', in C.J. Bennett, and D. Lyon (eds) *Playing the Identity Card: Surveillance, Security and Identification in Global Perspective*, Routledge, pp 39–56.

Breeze, B. and Dean, J. (2012) 'Pictures of me: user views on their representation in homelessness fundraising appeals', *International Journal of Nonprofit and Voluntary Sector Marketing*, 17(2): 132–43.

Brinkmann, S. (2020) 'Unstructured and semi-structured interviewing', in P. Leavy (ed) *The Oxford Handbook of Qualitative Research*, Oxford University Press, pp 424–57.

British Educational Research Association (2024) *Ethical Guidelines for Educational Research* (5th edn), British Educational Research Association, Available from: www.bera.ac.uk/publication/ethical-guidelines-for-educational-research-fifth-edition-2024-online

Britt, M.A., Rouet, J.-F. and Durik, A. (2017) *Literacy Beyond Text Comprehension: A Theory of Purposeful Reading*, Routledge.

Brown, A., Bonneville, G. and Glaze, S. (2021) 'Nevertheless, they persisted: how women experience gender-based discrimination during postgraduate surgical training', *Journal of Surgical Education*, 78(1): 17–34.

Brown, A.D. (2004) 'Authoritative sensemaking in a public inquiry report', *Organization Studies*, 25(1), 95–112.

Brown, A.D., Ainsworth, S. and Grant, D. (2012) 'The rhetoric of institutional change', *Organization Studies*, 33(3), 297–321.

Cain, P., Chejor, P. and Porock, D. (2023) 'Chemical restraint as behavioural euthanasia: case studies from the Royal Commission into Aged Care Quality and Safety', *BMC Geriatrics*, 23(1): art 444. doi: 10.1186/s12877-023-04116-5

Candiotto, L. (2019) 'From philosophy of emotion to epistemology: some questions about the epistemic relevance of emotions', in L. Candiotto (ed) *The Value of Emotions for Knowledge*, Springer, pp 3–24.

Caplan, J. and Torpey, J. (eds) (2001) *Documenting Individual Identity: The Development of State Practices in the Modern World*, Princeton University Press.

Carrigan, M. (2017) 'What is graphic social science?', *The Sociological Review*, 31 July. Available from: https://thesociologicalreview.org/collections/graphic-social-science/what-is-graphic-social-science

Carruthers Thomas, K. (2020) *Living and Working in Lockdown: What's Gender Got to Do with It? Research Report*, Birmingham City University. Available from: www.thinkthreeways.com/research/archive-projects/living-and-working-in-lockdown-whats-gender-got-to-do-with-it

Carruthers Thomas, K. (2022a) *Dear Diary: Equality Implications for Female Academics of Changes to Working Practices in Lockdown and Beyond: Final Report*, Society for Research into Higher Education. Available from: https://srhe.ac.uk/wp-content/uploads/2022/10/DEAR-DIARY-REVISED-FINAL-REPORT-OCTOBER-2022.pdf

Carruthers Thomas, K. (2022b) 'Dear Diary Illustrated Digital Archive'. Available from: www.deardiaryresearch.co.uk

Carruthers Thomas, K. (2023) *Poetry in Emotion: Writing up Emotional Labour*, Research poem first performed at the International Creative Research Methods Conference, Manchester, UK, 9 September.

Carruthers Thomas, K. (2024) 'Fast, slow, ongoing: female academics' experiences of time and change during COVID-19', *Area*, 56(1): art e12894. doi: 10.1111/area.12894

Case Book A: Females. Certified patients admitted Aug 1885-Dec 1887 (1885–1907). Part of Holloway Sanatorium Hospital for the Insane (Wellcome Closed stores WMS 2 Shelfmark: MS 8159). Available from: https://wellcomelibrary.org/item/b19129932

Caswell, M. and Cifor, M. (2016) 'From human rights to feminist ethics: radical empathy in the archives', *Archivaria*, 81: 23–43.

Caswell, M. and Cifor, M. (2021) 'Revisiting a feminist ethics of care in archives', *Journal of Critical Library and Information Studies*, 3(2): 1–6.

Caswell, M., Migoni, A.A., Geraci, N. and Cifor, M. (2017) '"To be able to imagine otherwise": community archives and the importance of representation', *Archives and Records*, 38(1): 5–26.

Caswell, M., Cole, H. and Griffith, Z. (2018) 'Images, silences, and the archival record: an interview with Michelle Caswell', *disClosure: A Journal of Social Theory*, 27: 21–7.

Catala, A., Faucher, L. and Poirier, P. (2021) 'Autism, epistemic injustice, and epistemic disablement: a relational account of epistemic agency', *Synthese*, 199(3–4): 9013–39.

Chartered Institute of Personnel and Development (2021) 'Contracts of employment', *CIPD*. Available from: www.cipd.org/uk/knowledge/factsheets/terms-conditions-contracts-factsheet

Chen, J.C. and Roberts, R.W. (2010) 'Toward a more coherent understanding of the organization–society relationship: a theoretical consideration for social and environmental accounting research', *Journal of Business Ethics*, 97: 651–65.

Child, C. (2024) 'An overview of nonprofit sector theories', in E.M. Witesman and C.L. Child (eds) *Reimagining Nonprofits: Sector Theory in the Twenty-First Century*, Cambridge University Press, pp 17–40.

Coffey, A. (2014) 'Analysing documents', in U. Flick (ed) *The SAGE Handbook of Qualitative Data Analysis*, SAGE, pp 367–79.

Collingwood, R.G. (2018) *The Idea of History*, Lume Books.

Collins, H. and Pinch, T. (2014) *Dr. Golem: How to Think about Medicine*, Cambridge University Press.

Concert Programmes Database (nd). Available from: www.concertprogrammes. org.uk

Connerton, P. (2009) *How Societies Remember*, Cambridge University Press.

Connolly, A. (2019) 'The simple truth at the heart of the aged care royal commission', *ABC News*. Available from: www.abc.net/au/news/2019-11-03/aged-care-royal-commission-coverage-imbalance/11666490

Contreras Islas, D. and Jennings, G. (2023) 'A typology of martial art scholar-practitioners: types, transitions, and tensions in Capoeira', *Societies*, 13(10): art 214. doi: 10.18452/27543

Cordery, C. and McConville, D. (2023) 'Annual reporting in voluntary organisations: opportunities for content analysis research', in J. Dean and E. Hogg (eds) *Researching Voluntary Action: Innovations and Challenges*, Policy Press, pp 110–21.

Corti, L. (2018) 'Data collection in secondary analysis', in U. Flick (ed) *The SAGE Handbook of Qualitative Data Collection*, SAGE, pp 164–81.

Crichton Royal Institution Case Book vol. 1 (June 1839–May 1840) Part of Records of Crichton Royal Hospital, Dumfries and Galloway Archives DGH1/5/21/1/1. Available from: https://wellcomecollection.org/works/wpbpjymq

C.R.I. Scrapbook (1838–1938) Part of Records of Crichton Royal Hospital, Dumfries and Galloway Archives DGH1/6/17/1. Available from: https://wellcomecollection.org/works/qbqnpe4v

Crowson, S. (2021) 'VQGAN+CLIP(Updated)' *Colab*. Available from: https://colab.research.google.com/github/justinjohn0306/VQGAN-CLIP/blob/main/VQGAN%2BCLIP(Updated).ipynb

Croxford, R. (2019) 'UK universities face "gagging order" criticism', *BBC*, 17 April. Available from: www.bbc.co.uk/news/education-47936662

Crudelli, C. (2008) *The Way of the Warrior: Martial Arts and Fighting Skills from around the World*, Dorling Kindersley.

Cunliffe, A.L. (2002) 'Reflexive dialogical practice in management learning', *Management Learning*, 33(1): 35–61.

Cunliffe, A.L. (2003) 'Reflexive inquiry in organizational research: questions and possibilities', *Human Relations*, 56(8): 983–1003.

Cunliffe, A.L. (2004) 'On becoming a critically reflexive practitioner', *Journal of Management Education*, 28(4): 407–26.

Cunliffe, A.L. (2008) 'Orientations to social constructionism: relationally responsive social constructionism and its implications for knowledge and learning', *Management Learning*, 39(2): 123–39.

Cunliffe, A.L. (2018) 'Wayfaring: a scholarship of possibilities or let's not get drunk on abstraction', *M@n@gement*, 21(4): 1429–39.

Da Escóssia, F. (2021) *Invisíveis: Uma etnografia sobre brasileiros sem documento*, FGV Editora.

Dalglish, S.L., Khalid, H. and McMahon, S.A. (2020) 'Document analysis in health policy research: the READ approach', *Health Policy and Planning*, 35(10): 1424–31.

Daskalova, M. (2022) *Printing and Periodical Culture in the Nineteenth-Century Asylum*, unpublished PhD thesis, University of Strathclyde.

da Sousa Correa, D. (ed) (2020) *The Edinburgh Companion to Literature and Music: Edinburgh Companions to Literature and the Humanities*, Edinburgh University Press.

Dear, P. (2001) 'Science studies as epistemography', in J. Labinger and H. Collins (eds) *The One Culture? A Conversation about Science*, The University of Chicago Press, pp 128–41.

Decker, S. and McKinley, A. (2020) 'Archival ethnography', in R. Mir and A.-L. Fayard (eds) *The Routledge Companion to Anthropology and Business*, Routledge, pp 17–33.

Deleuze, G. (2008 [1963]) *Kant's Critical Philosophy: The Doctrine of the Faculties*, Continuum.

Deleuze, G. and Parnet, C. (1987) *Dialogues*, Columbia University Press.

Dhanani, A. (2019) 'Identity constructions in the annual reports of international development NGOs: preserving institutional interests?', *Critical Perspectives on Accounting*, 59: 1–31.

Dhanani, A. and Connolly, C. (2012) 'Discharging not for profit accountability: UK charities and public discourse', *Accounting, Auditing & Accountability Journal*, 25(7): 1140–69.

Dhanani, A. and Kennedy, D. (2023) 'Envisioning legitimacy: visual dimensions of NGO annual reports', *Accounting, Auditing & Accountability Journal*, 36(1): 348–77.

Dickson-Swift, V., James, E.L., Kippen, S. and Liamputtong, P. (2009) 'Researching sensitive topics: qualitative research as emotion work', *Qualitative Research*, 9(1): 61–79.

Di Placido, M. (2020) 'Blending martial arts and yoga for health: from the Last Samurai to the first Odaka Yoga warrior', *Frontiers in Sociology*: art 597845. doi: 10.3389/fsoc.2020.597845

Domańska, E. (2007) '"Zwrot per formatywny"' we współczesnej humanistyce', *Teksty Drugie*, 5: 48–61.

Dotson, K. (2011) 'Tracking epistemic violence, tracking practices of silencing', Hypatia, 26(2): 236–57.

Douglas, B. and Di Rosa, D. (2020) 'Ethnohistory and historical ethnography', in *Oxford Bibliographies*, Oxford University Press.

Dunning, C. (2022) *Nonprofit Neighborhoods: An Urban History of Inequality and the American State*, The University of Chicago Press.

Earl Rinehart, K. (2021) 'Abductive analysis in qualitative inquiry', *Qualitative Inquiry*, 27(2): 303–11.

Elliott, M.H. (1997) 'The use of diaries in sociological research on health experience', *Sociological Research Online*, 2(2): 38–48. doi: 10.5153/sro.3

Ellis, W. (1838) *A Treatise on the Nature, Symptoms, Causes, and Treatment of Insanity*, Samuel Holdsworth.

Equality and Human Rights Commission (2018) *Turning the Tables: Ending Sexual Harassment at Work*, Equality and Human Rights Commission. Available from: www.equalityhumanrights.com/turning-tables-ending-sexual-harassment-work

Erlmann, V. (2010) *Reason and Resonance: A History of Modern Aurality*, Zone.

Eurofound (2017) *6th European Working Conditions Survey: 2017 Update*, Publications Office of the European Union.

Eybers, O.O. (2023) 'Coloniality as appropriation of Indigenous ontologies: insights from South Africa and Ethiopia', *Journal of Black Studies*, 54(1): 45–61.

Fairclough, N. (2003) *Analysing Discourse: Textual Analysis for Social Research*, Routledge.

Ferdman, B. (2014) 'From content to context: the emergence of the performance curator', *Theater*, 44(2): 5–17.

Feyerabend, P. (1978) *Against Method*, Verso.

Fiorito, T. (2023) 'Beyond research as a dirty word? Searching for ethical and reflexive ways of doing research with and for migrant communities', *Migration Studies*, art mnad027, advance online publication. doi: 10.1093/migration/mnad027

Fong, A. (1982) *Fong's Wing Chun* (Vol 1), Fong's Wing Chun Federation Headquarters.

Foucault, M. (1967) *Madness and Civilization: A History of Insanity in the Age of Reason* (trans R. Howard), Tavistock.

Foucault, M. (2002 [1971]) *Archaeology of Knowledge* (2nd edn), Routledge.

Frantzis, B. (2003) *The Big Book of Tai Chi*, Thorsons.

Fraser, C. (2022) 'Cripple punk: the disabled young people smashing ableism', *Vice*, 18 July. Available from: www.vice.com/en/article/akevzj/what-is-cripple-punk

Fricker, M. (2007) *Epistemic Injustice: Power and the Ethics of Knowing*, Oxford University Press.

Fürsich, E. (2009) 'In defense of textual analysis: restoring a challenged method for journalism and media studies', *Journalism Studies*, 10(2): 238–52.

Fürsich, E. (2018) 'Textual analysis and communication', *Oxford Bibliographies*. Available from: www.oxfordbibliographies.com/display/document/obo-9780199756841/obo-9780199756841-

Galletta, A. (2013) *Mastering the Semi-Structured Interview and Beyond: From Research Design to Analysis and Publication*, New York University Press.

Gardner, B. (2019) 'Sir Philip Green scandal shows that the law on NDAs must change, Lord Hain says', *The Telegraph*, 8 February. Available from: www.telegraph.co.uk/news/2019/02/08/sir-philip-green-scandal-shows-law-ndas-must-change-lord-hain

Garrahan, M. (2017) 'Harvey Weinstein: how lawyers kept a lid on sexual harassment claims', *Financial Times*, 23 October. Available from: www.ft.com/content/1dc8a8ae-b7e0-11e7-8c12-5661783e5589

Garton Ash, T. (1997) *The File: A Personal History*, Vintage Books.

Gawande, A. (2018) 'Why doctors hate their computers', *New Yorker*, 5 November. Available from: www.newyorker.com/magazine/2018/11/12/why-doctors-hate-their-computers

Gee, G., Meng, B. and Loewenhagen, R. (2004) *Mastering Kung Fu: Featuring Shaolin Wing Chun*, Human Kinetics.

General Report of the Royal Hospitals of Bridewell and Bethlem, and of the House of Occupations: for the year ending 31st December, 1843 (1844), Part of Bridewell Royal Hospital, Bethlem Royal Hospital Archive BAR-03. Available at: https://wellcomecollection.org/works/xp259a42

Gilliland, A. and Caswell, M. (2016) 'Records and their imaginaries: imagining the impossible, making possible the imagined', *Archival Science*, 16: 53–75.

Gitelman, L. (2014) *Paper Knowledge: Toward a Media History of Documents*, Duke University Press.

Gold, D. (2008) 'The accidental archivist: embracing chance and confusion in historical scholarship', in G. Kirsch and L. Rohan (eds) *Beyond the Archives: Research as a Lived Process*, Southern Illinois University Press, pp 13–19.

Golding, R. (2021) *Music and Moral Management in the Nineteenth-Century English Lunatic Asylum*, Palgrave Macmillan.

Goodman, F. (2000) *Practical Handbook: Kung Fu*, Dorling Kindersley.

Gordillo, G. (2006) 'The crucible of citizenship: ID-paper fetishism in the Argentinean Chaco', *American Ethnologist*, 33(2): 162–76.

Gouk, P., Kennaway, J., Prins, J. and Thormahlen, W. (eds) (2018) *The Routledge Companion to Music, Mind, and Well-being*, Routledge.

Grant, A. (2018) 'Shock and offence online: the role of emotion in participant absent research', in T. Loughran and D. Mannay (eds) *Emotion and the Researcher: Sites, Subjectivities, and Relationships* (Studies in Qualitative Methodology, Vol 16), Emerald Publishing, pp 143–58.

Grant, A. (2019) *Doing Excellent Social Research with Documents: Practical Examples and Guidance for Qualitative Researchers*, Routledge.

Grant, A. (2022) *Doing Your Research Project with Documents: A Step-by-Step Guide to Take You from Start to Finish*, Policy Press.

Green, M. (2016) 'Neoliberalism and management scholarship: educational implications', *Philosophy of Management*, 15(1): 183–201.

Green, T.A. (2003) 'Sense in nonsense: the role of folk history in the martial arts', in T.A. Green and J. Svinth (eds) *Martial Arts in the Modern World*, Praeger, pp 1–12.

Griffith, A.I. and Smith, D.E. (eds) (2014) *Under New Public Management: Institutional Ethnographies of Changing Front-Line Work*, University of Toronto Press.

Gruber, H. (2024) 'Snyder and Habermas on the war in Ukraine: a critical discourse analysis of elite media discourse in Germany', *Critical Discourse Studies*, advance online publication. doi: 10.1080/17405904.2024.2331164

Gunn, S. and Faire, L. (eds) (2015) *Research Methods for History*, Routledge.

Gupta, A. (2024) 'Polysemy and the sociolinguistics of policy ideas: resilience, sustainability and wellbeing 2000–2020', *Journal of Computational Social Science*, 7: 331–60.

Gupta, A. (2025) *The Pragmatics of Governmental Discourse Resilience, Sustainability and Wellbeing*, Routledge.

Habermas, J. (1981) 'Modernity versus postmodernity', *New German Critique*, 22: 3–14.

Halbwachs, M. (1992) *On Collective Memory*, The University of Chicago Press.

Hall, R. (2020) *Mixing Methods in Social Research: Qualitative, Quantitative and Combined Methods*, SAGE.

Hall, P. (2021) 'Giving voice to a foxtrot from Auschwitz-Birkenau', *Music Theory Online*, 27(3). Available from: https://mtosmt.org/issues/mto.21.27.3/mto.21.27.3.hall.pdf

Hall, S. (1973) *Encoding and Decoding in the Television Discourse: Centre for Contemporary Cultural Studies*, University of Birmingham.

Haller, B. and Ralph, S. (2006) 'Are disability images in advertising becoming bold and daring? An analysis of prominent themes in US and UK campaigns', *Disability Studies Quarterly*, 26(3). doi: 10.18061/dsq.v26i3.716

Halliwell, P. (2019) 'The psychological & emotional effects of discrimination within the LGBTQ, transgender, & non-binary communities', *Thomas Jefferson Law Review*, 41(2): 222–37.

Haniffa, R. and Hudaib, M. (2007) 'Exploring the ethical identity of Islamic banks via communication in annual reports', *Journal of Business Ethics*, 76: 97–116.

Hansen, L. (2006) 'Security as practice: discourse analysis and the Bosnian war', Routledge.

Hansen, L. (2016) 'Discourse analysis, post-structuralism, and foreign policy', in S. Smith, A. Hadfield and T. Dunne (eds) *Foreign Policy: Theories, Actors, Cases* (3rd edn), Oxford University Press, pp 95–111.

Hansen, R.K. (2023) 'Applying a stakeholder management approach to ethics in charitable fundraising', *Journal of Philanthropy and Marketing*, 28(4): art e1731. doi: 10.1002/nvsm.1731

Haraway, D. (1988) 'Situated knowledges: the science question in feminism and the privilege of partial perspective', *Feminist Studies*, 14(3): 575–99.

Hardy, D. (2021) 'Using positionality and theory in historical research: a personal journey', *Journal of Cultural Research in Art Education*, 38: 78–94.

Healthcare Financial Management Association (2022) *Example NHS charity annual report and accounts 2021/22*, HFMA. Available from: www.hfma.org.uk/system/files/nhs-charitable-funds-example-ara-202122.pdf

Heckert, R., Boumans, J. and Vliegenthart, R. (2020) 'How to nail the multiple identities of an organization? A content analysis of projected identity', *Voluntas: International Journal of Voluntary and Nonprofit Organizations*, 31(1): 129–41.

Heijstra, T.M., Steinthorsdóttir, F.S. and Einarsdóttir, T. (2017) 'Academic career making and the double-edged role of academic housework', *Gender and Education*, 29(6): 764–80.

Hibbert, P., Sillince, J., Diefenbach, T. and Cunliffe, A. (2014) 'Relationally reflexive practice: a generative approach to theory development in qualitative research', *Organizational Research Methods*, 17(3): 278–98.

Hirsch, M. (2012) *The Generation of Postmemory: Writing and Visual Culture after the Holocaust*, Columbia University Press.

Ho, M.-H., Duffy, B. and Benjamin, L.M. (2023) 'Documents in a field of action: using documents to address research questions about nonprofit and voluntary organizations', *Voluntas: International Journal of Voluntary and Nonprofit Organizations*, 34(1): 133–9.

Hoad, C. (2022) '"Images and words": textual analysis and its uses for metal music studies', in A. Bennett (ed) *The Bloomsbury Handbook of Popular Music and Youth Culture*, Bloomsbury, pp 151–71.

Hochschild, A. (2016) *Strangers in Their Own Land: Anger and Mourning on the American Right*, The New Press.

Hochschild, A. and Machung, A. (1989) *The Second Shift: Working Families and the Revolution at Home*, Viking Penguin.

Hopf, T. (1998) 'Constructivism in international relations theory', *International Security*, 23(1): 171–200.

Hopf, T. (2012) *Reconstructing the Cold War: The Early Years, 1945–1958*, Oxford University Press.

Houston, E. (2017) *The Representation of Disabled Women in Anglo American Advertising: Examining How Cultural Disability Tropes Impact on the Subjective Wellbeing of Disabled Women*, PhD thesis, Lancaster University.

Houston, E. and Haller, B. (2022) 'Introduction. Advertising and diversity: the framing of disability in promotional spaces', *Journal of Literary & Cultural Disability Studies*, 16(4): 361–8.

Howarth, D. (1998) 'Discourse theory and political analysis', in E. Scarbrough and E. Tanenbaum (eds) *Research Strategies in the Social Sciences*, Oxford University Press, pp 268–93.

Hsieh, H.-F. and Shannon, S.E. (2005) 'Three approaches to qualitative content analysis', *Qualitative Health Research*, 15(9): 1277–88.

Hunt, J. (1981) 'Settling accounts with the parasite people', in Disability Challenge, Union of the PhICally Impaired Against Segregation, pp 37–50.

Hunter, W. and Brill, R. (2016) '"Documents, please": advances in social protection and birth certification in the developing world', *World Politics*, 68(2): 191–228.

IAEA (International Atomic Energy Agency) (2006) *Basic Infrastructure for a Nuclear Power Project* (IAEA-TECDOC-1513), IAEA. Available from: www-pub.iaea.org/MTCD/Publications/PDF/TE_1513_web.pdf

IAEA (International Atomic Energy Agency) (2019) *IAEA Annual Report 2019*, IAEA.

Instytut Pamięci Narodowej (2005) 'Informacja o ustaleniach końcowych śledztwa S 28/02/Zi w sprawie pozbawienia życia 79 osób – mieszkańców powiatu Bielsk Podlaski w tym 30 osób tzw. furmanów w lesie koło Puchał Starych, dokonanych w okresie od dnia 29 stycznia 1946r. do dnia 2 lutego 1946', *Instytut Pamięci Narodowej*, 30 June. Available from: https://ipn.gov.pl/pl/dla-mediow/komunik aty/9989,Informacja-o-ustaleniach-koncowych-sledztwa-S-2802Zi-w-sprawie-pozbawienia-zycia.html

Ipsos MORI (2017) *The National Student Survey Good Practice Guide*, Ipsos MORI. Available from: www.hefce.ac.uk/media/HEFCE,2014/Content/Learn ing,and,teaching/NSS/Allegati ons/NSS-2018-Good-Practice-Guide.pdf

Istvandity, L. (2021) 'How does music heritage get lost? Examining cultural heritage loss in community and authorised music archives', *International Journal of Heritage Studies*, 27(4): 331–43.

Jackson, D.L. (2018) '"Me Too": epistemic injustice and the struggle for recognition', *Feminist Philosophy Quarterly*, 4(4): 1–19.

Jennings, G. (2019) 'Bruce Lee and the invention of Jeet Kune Do: the theory of martial creation', *Martial Arts Studies*, 8: 60–72.

Jennings, G. (2022) '"Filthy lefties!": the humorous stigmatization of left-handers in historical European martial arts', *STAPS*, 136(2): 17–36.

Johnson, J. (1995) *Listening in Paris: A Cultural History*, University of California Press.

Johnson, K.B., Neuss, M.J. and Detmer, D.E. (2021) 'Electronic health records and clinician burnout: a story of three eras', *Journal of the American Medical Informatics Association*, 28(5): 967–73.

Jones, S. (2004) *The Intelligent Warrior: Command Personal Power with Martial Arts Strategies*, Thorsons.

Kamla, R. and Roberts, C. (2010) 'The global and the local: Arabian Gulf States and imagery in annual reports', *Accounting, Auditing & Accountability Journal*, 23(4): 449–81.

Kant, I. (2015 [1781]) *The Critique of Pure Reason*, Philosophical Library/ Open Road.

Kara, H. (2018) *Research Ethics in the Real World: Euro-Western and Indigenous Perspectives*, Policy Press.

Kara, H. (2020) *Creative Research Methods: A Practical Guide* (2nd edn), Policy Press.

Kara, H. and Khoo, S-M. (2022) 'Conclusion', in H. Kara and S.-M. Khoo (eds) *Qualitative and Digital Research in Times of Crisis: Methods, Reflexivity, and Ethics*, Policy Press, pp 247–52.

Kara, H., Mannay, D. and Roy, A. (2024) *The Handbook of Creative Data Analysis*, Policy Press.

Karatsareas, P. (2022) 'Semi-structured interviews', in R. Kircher and L. Zipp (eds) *Research Methods in Language Attitudes*, Cambridge University Press, pp 99–113.

Keltner, D. (2017) 'Sex, power, and the systems that enable men like Harvey Weinstein', *Harvard Business Review*, 13 October. Available from: https://hbr.org/2017/10/sex-power-and-the-systems-that-enable-men-like-harvey-weinstein

Kenten, C. (2010) 'Narrating oneself: reflections on the use of solicited diaries with diary interview', *Forum: Qualitative Social Research/ Forum Qualitative Sozialforschung*, 11(2): art 16. Available from: http://nbn-resolving.de/urn:nbn:de:0114-fqs1002160

Kernsprecht, K. (1997) *On Single Combat* (2nd edn), Wu Shu Verlag Kenrsprecht.

King, M. (2015) 'Working with/in the archives', in S. Gunn and L. Faire (eds) *Research Methods for History*, Routledge, pp 15–30.

Kinouani, G. (2020) 'Silencing, power and racial trauma in groups', *Group Analysis*, 53(2): 145–61.

Kitchin, R. (2000) 'The researched opinions on research: disabled people and disability research', *Disability & Society*, 15(1): 25–47.

Kovala, U. (2002) 'Cultural studies and cultural text analysis', *CLCWeb: Comparative Literature and Culture*, 4(4): 1–7.

Kukkonen, T. and Cooper, A. (2019) 'An arts-based knowledge translation (ABKT) planning framework for researchers', *Evidence & Policy*, 15(2): 293–31.

Lakoff, G. and Johnson, M. (2003) *Metaphors We Live By*, The University of Chicago Press.

Latham, A. (2003) 'Research, performance and doing human geography: some reflections on the diary-photograph, diary-interview method', *Environment and Planning A: Economy and Space*, 35(11), 1993–2017.

Latour, B. (1999) *Pandora's Hope: Essays on the Reality of Science Studies*, Harvard University Press.

Law, J. (2004) *After Method: Mess in Social Science Research*, Routledge.

Leavy, P. (2009) *Method Meets Art: Arts-Based Research Practice*, The Guilford Press.

Leavy, P. (2015) *Methods Meets Art: Arts-Based Research Practice* (2nd edn), The Guildford Press.

Leavy, P. (2017) *Research Design: Quantitative, Qualitative, Mixed Methods, Arts-Based, and Community-Based Participatory Research Approaches*, The Guilford Press.

Le Roy Ladurie, E. (1966) *Les paysans de Languedoc*, Bibliothèque Génerale de l'École des Hautes Études.

Levy, B. and Emmery, L. (2021) 'Archival research in music: new materials, methods, and arguments', *Music Theory Online*, 27(3). Available from: https://mtosmt.org/issues/mto.21.27.3/mto.21.27.3.levyemmery.pdf

Lewis, P. (1998) *Myths and Legends of the Martial Arts*, Prion.

Leyshon, A., Matless, D. and Revill, G. (eds) (1998) *The Place of Music*, Routledge.

Lindsay, C. (2003) 'From the shadows: users as designers, producers, marketers, distributors, and technical support', in N. Oudshoorn and T. Pinch (eds) *How Users Matter: The Co-Construction of Users and Technology*, The MIT Press, pp 29–50.

Liu, H. (2022) 'How we learn whiteness: disciplining and resisting management knowledge', *Management Learning*, 53(5): 776–96.

Loebner, J. (2022) 'Crip theory and creative briefs: interpreting disability in the creative process', *Journal of Literary & Cultural Disability Studies*, 16(4): 369–86.

Longmore, P. (2016) *Telethons: Spectacle, Disability, and the Business of Charity*, Oxford University Press.

Lorge, P. (2016) 'Practising martial arts versus studying martial arts', *International Journal of the History of Sport*, 33(9): 904–14.

Luken, P.C. and Vaughan, S. (eds) (2021) *The Palgrave Handbook of Institutional Ethnography*, Palgrave Macmillan.

Lund, R.W.B. and Nilsen, A.C.E. (eds) (2020) *Institutional Ethnography in the Nordic Region*, Routledge.

Lund, S. (2001) 'Bequeathing and quest: processing personal identification papers in bureaucratic spaces (Cuzco, Peru)', *Social Anthropology*, 9(1): 3–24.

Lyon, D. (2009) *Identifying Citizens: ID Cards as Surveillance*, Polity Press.

Malterud, K., Siersma, V.D. and Guassora, A.D. (2016) 'Sample size in qualitative interview studies: guided by information power', *Qualitative Health Research*, 26(13): 1753–60.

Mannay, D. (2018) '"You just get on with it': negotiating the telling and silencing of trauma and its emotional impacts in interviews with marginalised mothers', in T. Loughran and D. Mannay (eds) *Emotion and the Researcher: Sites, Subjectivities, and Relationships* Emerald, pp 81–95.

Mannay, D. (2019) 'Revisualizing data: engagement, impact and multimodal dissemination', in L. Pauwels and D. Mannay (eds) *The SAGE Handbook of Visual Research Methods* (2nd edn), SAGE, pp 659–69.

Margetts, H. and Dorobantu, C. (2023) 'Computational social science for public policy', in E. Bertoni, M. Fontana, L. Gabrielli, S. Signorelli and M. Vespe (eds) *Handbook of Computational Social Science for Policy* (1st edn), Springer Nature, pp 3–18.

Markula, P. and Silk, M. (2011) *Qualitative Research for Physical Culture*, Palgrave Macmillan.

Marx, G.T. (2002) 'What's new about the "new surveillance"? Classifying for change and continuity', *Surveillance & Society*, 1: 9–29.

Massey, D. (1993) 'Power-geometry and a progressive sense of place', in J. Bird, B. Curtis, T. Putnam, G. Robertson and L. Tuckner (eds) *Mapping the Futures: Local Culture, Global Chance*, Routledge, pp 59–69.

Massey, D. (2005) *For Space*, SAGE.

Massey, D. (2007) *World City*, Polity Press.

Mattingly, C. (2019) 'Defrosting concepts, destabilizing doxa: critical phenomenology and the perplexing particular', *Anthropological Theory*, 19(4): 415–39.

McCredie, B., Docherty, P., Easton, S. and Uylangco, K. (2016) 'The channels of monetary policy triggered by central bank actions and statements in the Australian equity market', *International Review of Financial Analysis*, 46: 46–61.

McKee, A. (2003) *Textual Analysis: A Beginner's Guide*, SAGE.

McLuhan, M. (2001 [1964]) *Understanding Media: The Extensions of Man*, Routledge.

Meekosha, H. and Shuttleworth, R. (2009) 'What's so "critical" about critical disability studies?', *Australian Journal of Human Rights*, 15(1): 47–75.

Mehmood, T. (2008) 'India's new ID card: fuzzy logics, double meanings and ethnic ambiguities', in C.J. Bennett and D. Lyon (eds) *Playing the Identity Card: Surveillance, Security and Identification in Global Perspective*, Routledge, pp 112–27.

Mezirow, J. (1990) *Fostering Critical Reflection in Adulthood: A Guide to Transformative and Emancipatory Learning*, Jossey-Bass.

Mezirow, J. (2003) 'Transformative learning as discourse', *Journal of Transformative Education*, 1(1): 58–63.

Mezirow, J. (2009) 'Transformative learning theory', in J. Mezirow and E.W. Taylor (eds) *Transformative Learning in Practice: Insights from Community, Workplace, and Higher Education*, John Wiley & Sons, pp 18–31.

Mignolo, W.D. and Walsh, C.E. (2018) *On Decoloniality: Concepts, Analytics, Praxis*, Duke University Press.

Miller, E. (2021) *Creative Arts-Based Research in Aged Care: Photovoice, Photography and Poetry in Action*, Routledge.

Miller, E. (2024) 'The Black Saturday bushfire disaster: found poetry for arts-based knowledge translation in disaster risk and climate change communication', *Arts & Health*, advance online publication. doi: 10.1080/17533015.2024.2310861

Mills, C.-W. (1959) *The Sociological Imagination*, Oxford University Press.

Mol, A. (2002) *The Body Multiple: Ontology In Medical Practice*, Duke University Press.

Moran, J. (2018) *First You Write a Sentence: The Elements of Reading, Writing…and Life*, Penguin.

Morgan, H. (2022) 'Conducting a qualitative document analysis', *The Qualitative Report*, 27(1): 64–77.

Morris, A. (2015) *A Practical Introduction to In-Depth Interviewing*, SAGE.

Murray, Ó.M. (2018) 'Feel the fear and killjoy anyway: being a challenging feminist presence in precarious academia', in Y. Taylor and K. Lahad (eds) *Feeling Academic in the Neoliberal University: Feminist Flights, Fights and Failures*, Palgrave Macmillan, pp 163–89.

Murray, Ó.M. (2019) *Doing Feminist Text-Focused Institutional Ethnography in UK Universities*, PhD thesis, University of Edinburgh. Available from: http://hdl.handle.net/1842/35719

Murray, Ó.M. (2020a) 'Beyond confession: doing holistic reflexivity and accountability', in *Doing Feminisms in the Academy: Identity, Institutional Pedagogy and Critical Classrooms in India and the UK*, Zubaan Books, pp 222–32.

Murray, Ó.M. (2020b) 'Text, process, discourse: doing feminist text analysis in institutional ethnography', *International Journal of Social Research Methodology*, 25(1): 45–57.

Murray, Ó.M. (2025) *University Audit Cultures and Feminist Praxis: An Institutional Ethnography*, Bristol University Press.

Muzanenhamo, P. (2022) 'Black scholarship: autoethnographies and epistemic (in)justice', *Discourses on Culture*, 18(1): 79–87.

Nemer, D. (2022) *Technology of the Oppressed: Inequity and the Digital Mundane in Favelas of Brazil*, The MIT Press.

Nordstrom (2014) Print advertisement featuring Jillian Mercado. Available from: https://models.com/work/nordstrom-summer-sale

Oudshoorn, N. and Pinch, T. (eds) (2003) *How Users Matter: The Co-Construction of Users and Technology*, The MIT Press.

Oxford English Dictionary (2023) 'Presentism', *Oxford English Dictionary*. Available from: www.oed.com/dictionary/presentism_n?tab=meaning_and_use (Accessed 3 May 2024).

Pagan, V. (2019) 'Being and becoming a "good" qualitative researcher? Liminality and the risk of limbo', *Qualitative Research in Organizations and Management: An International Journal*, 14(1): 75–90.

Pagan, V. (2021) 'The murder of knowledge and the ghosts that remain: non-disclosure agreements and their effects', *Culture and Organization*, 27(4): 302–17.

Pagan, V. (2022) 'Fantasy to (evade) order: vicarious schadenfreude', *Ephemera: Theory & Politics in Organization*, 22(1): 173–88.

Pagan, V. (2023) '21st century bridling: non-disclosure agreements in cases of organizational misconduct', *Human Relations*, 76(11): 1827–51.

Pardo-Figueroa, C. (2000) 'Los gitanos y el proyecto de control migratorio de 1952', *Boletín del Instituto Riva-Agüero*, 27: 309–55.

Patrick, L.D. (2016) 'Found poetry: creating space for imaginative arts-based literacy research writing', *Literacy Research: Theory, Method, and Practice*, 65(1): 384–403.

Peacock, V., Bruun, M.K., Dungey, C.E. and Shapiro, M. (2023) 'Surveillance', in H. Nieber (ed) *The Open Encyclopedia of Anthropology*. Available from: www.anthroencyclopedia.com

Pebdani, R.N., Zeidan, A., Low, L. and Baillie, A. (2023) 'Pandemic productivity in academia: using ecological momentary assessment to explore the impact of COVID-19 on research productivity', *Higher Education Research and Development*, 42(4): 937–53.

Perceval, J. (1838) *A Narrative of the Treatment Experienced by a Gentleman, during a state of Mental Derangement; Designed to Explain the Causes and the Nature of Insanity*, Effingham Wilson.

Pernot, L. (2021) *The Subtle Subtext: Hidden Meanings in Literature and Life* (trans W.E. Higgins), Penn State University Press.

Phillips, R., Freeman, R.E. and Wicks, A.C. (2003) 'What stakeholder theory is not', *Business Ethics Quarterly*, 13(4): 479–502.

Piazza, P. (2004) *Histoire de la carte nationale d'identité*, Odile Jacob.

Picker, J. (2003) *Victorian Soundscapes*, Oxford University Press.

Pina-Cabral, J. (2014) 'World: an anthropological examination (part 1)', *Journal of Ethnographic Theory*, 4(1): 49–73.

Pinch, T. and Bijker, W. (1984) 'The social construction of facts and artefacts: or how the sociology of science and the sociology of technology might benefit each other', *Social Studies of Science*, 14 (3): 399–441.

Pollner, M. (1991) 'Left of ethnomethodology: the rise and decline of radical reflexivity', *American Sociological Review*, 56(3): 370–80.

Porter, R. (1985) 'The patient's view: doing medical history from below', *Theory and Society*, 14: 175–98.

Potter, J. (2002) 'Two kinds of natural', *Discourse Studies*, 4(4): 539–42.

Prasad, V. (2018) 'If anyone is listening #MeToo: breaking the culture of silence around sexual abuse through regulating non-disclosure agreements and secret settlements', *Boston College Law Review*, 59(7): 2507–49.

Price, C. (2022) 'Experiments in methodology: sensory and poetic threads of inquiry, resistance, and transformation', *Qualitative Inquiry*, 28(1): 94–107.

Pring, J. (2016) 'DPAC will use Paralympics to highlight austerity impact in week of action', *Disability News Service*, 11 August. Available from: www.disability newsservice.com/dpac-will-use-paralympics-to-highlight-austerity-impact-in-week-of-action

Prior, L. (2003) *Using Documents in Social Research*, SAGE.

Prior, L. (2008) 'Repositioning documents in social research', *Sociology*, 42(5): 821–36.

Professional Record Standards Body (2017) *Outpatient Letter Standard Example Letters*, Professional Record Standards Body. Available from: https://theprsb.org/wp-content/uploads/2018/02/Outpatient-Letter-Examples.pdf

Prymaka-Oniszk, A. (2016) *Bieżeństwo 1915. Zapomniani uchodźcy*, Wydawnictwo Czarne.

Pullen, A., Harding, N. and Phillips, M. (2017) 'Introduction: feminist and queer politics in critical management studies', in A. Pullen, N. Harding and M. Phillips (eds) *Feminists and Queer Theorists Debate the Future of Critical Management Studies* (Dialogues in Critical Management Studies, Vol 3), Emerald, pp 1–11.

Ragas, J. (2015) *Documenting Hierarchies: State Building, Identification, and Citizenship in Modern Peru*, PhD thesis, Department of History, University of California, Davis.

Ragas, J. (2020a) 'Forgotten faces, missing bodies: understanding techno-invisible populations and political violence in Peru', in A. Sims Bartel and D. Castillo (eds) *The Scholar as Human: Research and Teaching for Public Impact*, Cornell University Press, pp 93–107.

Ragas, J. (2020b) 'The official making of undocumented citizens in Peru, 1880–1930', in B. Fallaw and D. Nugent (eds) *State Formation in the Liberal Era. Capitalisms and Claims of Citizenship in Mexico and Peru*, University of Arizona Press, pp 107–26.

Ragas, J. (2021) 'Internal passports, forgery, and subversive practices in early Republican Peru', *Journal of Social History*, 55(1): 27–45.

Raj, A., Johns, N.E. and Jose, R. (2020) 'Gender parity at work and its association with workplace sexual harassment', *Workplace Health and Safety*, 68(6): 279–92.

Rapley, T. and Rees, G. (2018) 'Collecting documents as data', in U. Flick (ed) *The SAGE Handbook of Qualitative Data Collection*, SAGE, pp 378–91.

Recreation and Printing Scrapbook (1842–1947) Part of Records of Crichton Royal Hospital, Dumfries and Galloway Archives DGH1/6/17/2. Available from: https://wellcomecollection.org/works/vruyy366

Register of Entertainments (1889–1896) Brookwood Asylum archives, Surrey History Centre 3043/1/11/2/2.

Reich, R. (2018) *Just Giving: Why Philanthropy Is Failing Democracy and How It Can Do Better*, Princeton University Press.

Reissner, S.C. (2019) '"We are this hybrid": members' search for organizational identity in an institutionalized public–private partnership', *Public Administration*, 97(1): 48–63.

Riccucci, N.M. (2010) *Public Administration: Traditions of Inquiry and Philosophies of Knowledge*, Georgetown University Press.

Roberts, E. (2018) 'The "transient insider": identity and intimacy in home community research', in T. Loughran and D. Mannay (eds) *Emotion and the Researcher: Sites, Subjectivities, and Relationships*, Emerald, pp 113–25.

Roe, A.J. (2023) *Legendary Masters of the Martial Arts: Unraveling Fact from Fiction*, YMAA.

Rosenfeld, S. (2011) 'On being heard: a case for paying attention to the historical ear', *American Historical Review*, 116(2): 316–34

Rotem, N. (2024) 'Historical ethnography: key characteristics and the journey before, during, and after the archival field', *Forum: Qualitative Social Research*, 25(2). doi: 10.17169/fqs-25.2.4106

Royal Commission into Aged Care Quality and Safety (2019) *Interim Report: Neglect* (3 vols), Commonwealth of Australia. Available from: www.royalcommission. gov.au/aged-care/interim-report

Ruggiano, N. and Perry, T.E. (2019) 'Conducting secondary analysis of qualitative data: should we, can we, and how?', *Qualitative Social Work*, 18(1): 81–97.

Santamaría, D.R.L. (2023) 'From epistemic injustice to epistemicide: a comparative analysis of the two concepts', *Electronic Notebooks of Philosophy of Law*, 48: 314–45.

Schmidt, A. and Schultz, C. (2024) 'Researcher as curator: making room for the politics of emotion in leisure research', *Leisure Studies*, 43(3): 511–21.

Schneider, R. (2011) *Performing Remains: Art and War in Times of Theatrical Reenactment*, Routledge.

Schwartz, J.M. and Cook, T. (2002) 'Archives, records, and power: the making of modern memory', *Archival Science*, 2: 1–19.

Scott, J. (1990) *A Matter of Record: Documentary Sources in Social Research*, Polity Press.

Scrapbook of Entertainments (1866–1940) West Riding Pauper Lunatic Asylum archives, West Yorkshire Archive Service, Wakefield C85/1382.

Scull, A. (1993) *The Most Solitary of Afflictions: Madness and Society in Britain, 1700–1900*, Yale University Press.

Sellar, T. (2014) 'The cure', *Theater*, 44(2): 1–3.

Shakespeare, T. (2014) *Disability Rights and Wrongs Revisited* (2nd edn), Routledge.

Shankar, K., Hakken, D. and Østerlun, C. (2016) 'Rethinking documents', in U. Felt, R. Fouché, C.A. Miller and L. Smith-Doerr (eds) *The Handbook of Science and Technology Studies*, The MIT Press, pp 59–86.

Shapin, S. and Schaffer, S. (1985) *Leviathan and the Air-Pump: Hobbes, Boyle, and the Experimental Life*, Princeton University Press.

Shek-Noble, L. (2022) 'Supercrip in motion: a critical visual analysis of promotional materials for the Tokyo 2020 Paralympic Games', *Journal of Literary & Cultural Disability Studies*, 16(4): 405–22.

Shilling, C. (2008) *Changing Bodies: Habit, Crisis, Creativity*, SAGE.

Shook, J. (2023) *Pragmatism*, The MIT Press.

Shuttleworth, R. and Kasnitz, D. (2006) 'The cultural context of disability', in G. Albrecht (ed) *Encyclopedia of Disability* (Vol 1), SAGE, pp 330–6.

Sikorska-Miszczuk, M. and Zapałowski, A. (2011) 'The suitcase', *PAJ: A Journal of Performance and Art*, 33(1): 93–117.

Silverio, S.A., Sheen, K.S., Bramante, A., Knighting, K., Koops, T.U., Montgomery, E. et al (2022) 'Sensitive, challenging, and difficult topics: experiences and practical considerations for qualitative researchers', *International Journal of Qualitative Methods*, 21: 1–16.

Singh, S. (2021) 'Queer hair semiotics: analysis of the select LGBTIQ documentaries', *dialog*, 1(38): 30–48.

Smith, A.E., Hassan, S., Hatmaker, D.M., DeHart-Davis, L. and Humphrey, N. (2021) 'Gender, race, and experiences of workplace incivility in public organizations', *Review of Public Personnel Administration*, 41(4): 674–99.

Smith, B. (2016) 'Narrative analysis in sport and exercise: how can it be done?', in B. Smith and A.C. Sparkes (eds) *Routledge Handbook of Qualitative Research in Sport and Exercise*, Routledge, pp 260–73.

Smith, B. and Sparkes, A.C. (2008) 'Narrative and its potential contribution to disability studies', *Disability & Society*, 23(1): 17–28.

Smith, B. and Sparkes, A.C. (2009) 'Narrative inquiry in sport and exercise psychology: what can it mean, and why might we do it?', *Psychology of Sport and Exercise*, 10(1): 1–11.

Smith, D.E. (1987) *The Everyday World as Problematic: A Feminist Sociology*, University of Toronto Press.

Smith, D.E. (1990a) *Texts, Facts, and Femininity: Exploring the Relations of Ruling*, Routledge.

Smith, D.E. (1990b) *The Conceptual Practices of Power: A Feminist Sociology of Knowledge*, University of Toronto Press.

Smith, D.E. (1999) *Writing the Social: Critique, Theory, and Investigations*, University of Toronto Press.

Smith, D.E. (2005) *Institutional Ethnography: A Sociology for People*, AltaMira Press.

Smith, D.E. (ed) (2006) *Institutional Ethnography as Practice*, Rowman & Littlefield.

Smith, D.E. and Turner, S.M. (eds) (2014) *Incorporating Texts into Institutional Ethnographies*, University of Toronto Press.

Smith, D.E. and Griffith, A.I. (2022) *Simply Institutional Ethnography: Creating a Sociology for People*, University of Toronto Press.

Smith, G.W. (2014) 'Policing the gay community: an inquiry into textually-mediated social relations', in D.E. Smith and S.M. Turner (eds) *Incorporating Texts into Institutional Ethnographies*, University of Toronto Press, pp 17–40.

Smith, K.M. (2020) 'Facing history for the future of nursing', *Journal of Clinical Nursing*, 29(9–10): 1429–31.

Smith, K.M. (2021) 'No medical justification: segregation and civil rights in Alabama's psychiatric hospitals, 1952–1972', *Journal of Southern History*, 87(4): 645–72.

Smith, L. (2020) *Private Madhouses in England, 1640–1815: Commercialised Care for the Insane*, Palgrave Macmillan.

Smith, M. (2004) *Hearing History: A Reader*, University of Georgia Press.

Smith, M. (2007) *Sensing the Past: Seeing, Hearing, Smelling, Tasting, and Touching in History*, University of California Press.

Smith, M. (2024) 'Asylum history from the bottom up', *Psychology Today*, 19 May. Available from: www.psychologytoday.com/gb/blog/a-short-history-of-mental-health/202405/asylum-history-from-the-bottom-up

Snyder, S.L. and Mitchell, D.T. (2006) *Cultural Locations of Disability*, The University of Chicago Press.

Speak Out Revolution (2023) 'Global Insights Dashboard', *Speak Out Revolution*. Available from: www.speakoutrevolution.co.uk/dashboard

Spivak, G.C. (1988) 'Can the subaltern speak?', in C. Nelson and L. Grossberg (eds) *Marxism and the Interpretation of Culture*, Macmillan, pp 271–313.

Stanley, L. (2017) 'How to analyse a document in detail', *Whites Writing Whiteness*. Available from: www.whiteswritingwhiteness.ed.ac.uk/how-to/how-to-analyse-a-document-in-detail

Stanley, L. and Wise, S. (2008) 'Feminist methodology matters!', in D. Richardson and V. Robinson (eds) *Gender and Women's Studies*, Palgrave Macmillan, pp 221–43. Available from: www.research.ed.ac.uk/en/publications/feminist-methodology-matters

Stokel-Walker, C. (2019) 'UK universities issue 11K non-disclosure agreements in five years', *Times Higher Education*, 11 April. Available from: www.timeshighereducation.com/news/uk-universities-issue-11k-non-disclosure-agreements-five-years

Syal, R. (2019) 'I was told of hundreds of grievance cases against Philip Green, says peer', *The Guardian*, 23 May. Available from: www.theguardian.com/business/2019/may/23/philip-green-peter-hain-says-told-of-hundreds-of-grievance-cases-peer

Szumiec-Zielińska, E. (2016) *Żywe torpedy 1939*, Wydawnictwo Demart.

Tarrant, A. and Hughes, K. (2022) 'Qualitative data re-use and secondary analysis: researching in and about a crisis', in H. Kara and S.-M. Khoo (eds) *Qualitative and Digital Research in Times of Crisis: Methods, Reflexivity, and Ethics*, Policy Press, pp 156–71.

Taylor, D. (2003) *The Archive and the Repertoire: Performing Cultural Memory in the Americas*, Duke University Press.

Teo, S. (2021) *Chinese Martial Arts Film and the Philosophy of Action*, Routledge.

Thapar-Björkert, S., Samelius, L. and Sanghera, G.S. (2016) 'Exploring symbolic violence in the everyday: misrecognition, condescension, consent and complicity', *Feminist Review*, 112(1): 144–62.

The Law Society (2019) 'Practice note: non-disclosure agreements and confidentiality clauses in an employment law context', *The Law Society*, 12 December. Available from: www.lawsociety.org.uk/topics/employment/non-disclosure-agreements-and-confidentiality-clauses-in-an-employment-law-context

Thomas, C. (1999) *Female Forms: Experiencing and Understanding Disability*, Open University Press.

Thomas, S. (2001) 'Reimaging inquiry, envisioning form', in L. Neilsen, A.L. Cole and J.G. Knowles (eds) *The Art of Writing Inquiry*, Backalong Books, pp 273–82.

Thompson, E.P. (1993) *Customs in Common: Studies in Traditional Popular Culture*, The New Press.

Thompson, J. (2022) 'A guide to abductive thematic analysis', *The Qualitative Report*, 27(5): 1410–21.

Thomson, T.J., Miller, E., Holland-Batt, S., Seevinck, J. and Regi, S. (2024) 'Visibility and invisibility in the aged care sector: visual representation in Australian news from 2018-2021', *Media International Australia*, 190(1): 146–64.

Timmermans, S. and Berg, M. (2003) *The Gold Standard: The Challenge of Evidence-Based Medicine and Standardization in Health Care*, Temple University Press.

Toepler, S. and Abramson, A. (2021) 'Government/foundation relations: a conceptual framework and evidence from the U.S.' federal government's partnership efforts', *Voluntas: International Journal of Voluntary and Nonprofit Organizations*, 32(2): 220–33.

Trades Union Congress (2016) *Still Just a Bit of Banter? Sexual Harassment in the Workplace in 2016*, Trades Union Congress. Available from: www.tuc.org.uk/research-analysis/reports/still-just-bit-banter

Tsai, W.S. (2012) 'Political issues in advertising polysemy: the case of gay window advertising', *Consumptions Markets & Culture*, 15(1): 41–62.

Tse, M. and Ip, C. (1998) *Wing Chun: Traditional Chinese Kung Fu for Self-Defence and Health*, Piatkus.

Turner, B. (1987) *Medical Power and Social Knowledge*, SAGE.

UK Parliament (2020) 'Committees', *UK Parliament*. Available from: www.parliament.uk/business/committees

Under the Dome, The Quarterly Magazine of Bethlem Royal Hospital (1892–1930), Bethlem Royal Hospital Archive UTD-01 to UTD-09.

Vega-Bendezú, K. (2013) 'Relación entre el Estado y las poblaciones vulnerables a través del acceso a los documentos de documentación e identificación', *Nombre*, 1(1): 38–78.

Vila-Henninger, L., Dupuy, C., Van Ingelgom, V., Caprioli, M., Teuber, F., Pennetreau, D. et al (2022) 'Abductive coding: theory building and qualitative (re) analysis', *Sociological Methods and Research*, 53(2): 968–1001.

Volume of Programmes (1879–1899) Bethlem Royal Hospital Archive BEN-01.

Walton, Q.L., Kennedy, P.P., Oyewuwo, O.B. and Allen, P. (2022) '"This person is safe": an exemplar of conducting individual interviews in qualitative research with Black women', *International Journal of Qualitative Methods*, 21(1): 1–14.

Waltz, M. (2012) 'Images and narratives of autism within charity discourses', *Disability & Society*, 27(2): 219–33.

Weztler, S. (2014) 'Myths of the martial arts', *JOMEC Journal*, 5: 1–12.

White, J.D. (1999) *Taking Language Seriously: The Narrative Foundations of Public Administration Research*, Georgetown University Press.

Women and Equalities Committee (2018a) 'Non-disclosure agreements: committee to examine wider issues', *UK Parliament*, 13 November. Available from: www.parliament.uk/business/committees/committees-a-z/commons-select/women-and-equalities-committee/news-parliament-2017/nda-launch-17-19

Women and Equalities Committee (2018b) 'Sexual harassment in the workplace inquiry', *UK Parliament,* 25 July. Available from: https://publications.parliament.uk/pa/cm201719/cmselect/cmwomeq/725/72502.htm

Women and Equalities Committee (nd) 'The use of non-disclosure agreements in discrimination cases inquiry | Publications', *UK Parliament.* Available from: https://committees.parliament.uk/work/6022/the-use-of-nondisclosure-agreements-in-discrimination-cases-inquiry/publications

Wong, A. (2020) 'Introduction', in A. Wong (ed) *Disability Visibility: First-Person Stories from the Twenty-First Century*, Vintage Books, pp xv–3.

Wong, K.-K. (1996) *The Complete Book of Tai Chi Chuan*, Vermillion.

Yates-Doerr, E. and Labuski, C. (eds) (2023) *The Ethnographic Case* (2nd edn), Mattering Press.

Ybema, S., Yanow, D., Wels, H. and Kamsteeg, F.H. (2009) 'Studying everyday organizational life', in S. Ybema, D. Yanow, H. Wels and F.H. Kamsteeg (eds) *Organizational Ethnography: Studying the Complexities of Everyday Life*, SAGE, pp 1–20.

Yin, R.K. (2018) *Case Study Research and Applications: Design and Methods* (6th edn), SAGE.

Zelazny, F. (2012) *The Evolution of India's UID Program: Lessons Learned and Implications for Other Developing Countries* (CGD Policy paper 008), Center for Global Development.

Ziewitz M. (2024) 'On STS and valuation', in: A.K. Krüger, T. Peetz and H. Schäfer (eds) *The Routledge International Handbook of Valuation and Society*, Routledge, pp 43–53.

Zimmerman, D.H. and Wieder, D.L. (1977) 'The diary: diary-interview method', *Urban Life*, 5(4): 479–98.

Index

References to figures appear in *italic* type; those in **bold** type refer to tables. References to endnotes show the page number, note number and chapter number (141n4 (ch10)).

Index

Index

Index